The Rankins of Montana

ALSO BY KATHERINE H. ADAMS
and from McFarland

*Claiming Her Place in Congress: Women
from American Political Families as Legislators* (2019)

BY KATHERINE H. ADAMS
and MICHAEL L. KEENE

Paper Dolls: Fragile Figures, Enduring Symbols (2017)

Women, Art and the New Deal (2016)

*Winifred Black/Annie Laurie
and the Making of Modern Nonfiction* (2015)

Women of the American Circus, 1880–1940 (2012)

*After the Vote Was Won:
The Later Achievements of Fifteen Suffragists* (2010)

BY KATHERINE H. ADAMS, MICHAEL L. KEENE
and JENNIFER C. KOELLA

*Seeing the American Woman, 1880–1920:
The Social Impact of the Visual Media Explosion* (2012)

The Rankins of Montana
*Risk Takers, History Makers,
American Dreamers*

KATHERINE H. ADAMS

McFarland & Company, Inc., Publishers
Jefferson, North Carolina

LIBRARY OF CONGRESS CATALOGUING-IN-PUBLICATION DATA

Names: Adams, Katherine H., 1954– author.
Title: The Rankins of Montana : risk takers, history makers, American dreamers / Katherine H. Adams.
Description: Jefferson, North Carolina : McFarland & Company, Inc., Publishers, 2021 | Includes bibliographical references and index.
Identifiers: LCCN 2021030655 | ISBN 9781476685304 (paperback : acid free paper) ∞
ISBN 9781476643809 (ebook)
Subjects: LCSH: Rankin family. | Rankin, John, 1841-1904—Family. | Rankin, Wellington Duncan, 1884-1966. | Rankin, Jeannette, 1880-1973. | McKinnon, Edna Rankin, 1893-1978. | McGregor, Harriet Rankin, 1883-1879, | Politicians—Montana—Biography. | Lawyers—Montana—Biography. | Political activists—Montana—Biography. | Montana—Biography. | BISAC: HISTORY / United States / State & Local / West (AK, CA, CO, HI, ID, MT, NV, UT, WY)
Classification: LCC F731.R23 A33 2021 | DDC 978.6/0320922—dc23
LC record available at https://lccn.loc.gov/2021030655

BRITISH LIBRARY CATALOGUING DATA ARE AVAILABLE

ISBN (print) 978-1-4766-8530-4
ISBN (ebook) 978-1-4766-4380-9

© 2021 Katherine H. Adams. All rights reserved

No part of this book may be reproduced or transmitted in any form or by any means, electronic or mechanical, including photocopying or recording, or by any information storage and retrieval system, without permission in writing from the publisher.

Front cover: Olive Rankin with her children and grandchildren. On the back row, from left to right: Harriet, Mary, Wellington, Edna, Dorothy McKinnon Brown in Edna's arms, Grace, Jeannette; 2nd row, both in white blouses: Mary Elizabeth Sedman, Virginia Sedman; 3rd row: Janet Kinney and Olive; 4th row: John Kinney, Thomas E. Kinney (in lap), Kenneth Bragg; in front, Mary Jane Bragg (Schlesinger Library, Radcliffe Institute, Harvard University); background photograph of western Montana (Shutterstock / Tom Reichner)

Printed in the United States of America

*McFarland & Company, Inc., Publishers
Box 611, Jefferson, North Carolina 28640
www.mcfarlandpub.com*

For Mandy, Chapel and Easton

Acknowledgments

I would like to thank my chair, Hillary Eklund, for her kindness and support as well as my dean, Maria Calzada. With their help, I obtained a sabbatical in the spring of 2020, which enabled me to finish this project. I also used funds from my Hutchinson Professorship to travel to research sites and purchase images.

As always when I write, I want to thank the fine librarians of Loyola University, especially Jessica Perry, our interlibrary loan officer. I also received so much help from librarians in Helena at the Montana Historical Society Research Center, including Rich Aarstad, Laura Tretter, Jeff Malcomson, and April Sparks; in Missoula at the Maureen and Mike Mansfield Library of the University of Montana, including Mark Fritch and Donna McCrea; in Boston at the Schlesinger Library, including Hayley Mercer; and in Washington, D.C., at the American Red Cross, including Susan Watson and Jean Shulman.

I also had the opportunity to visit Grant Creek, outside of Missoula, and see where the Rankins lived, where I was fortunate to be guided by Lynn Thee.

For the excellent images included here, I am indebted to the Photoshop skills and generosity of Willie Wax. I would also like to thank Heidi Braden for help with processing these images.

I am always so pleased to be working with the fine editors at McFarland. I feel fortunate to publish with this press.

Table of Contents

Acknowledgments	vi
Introduction	1
ONE. The Myth and Reality of the Risky West: Olive Pickering and John Rankin	3
TWO. Victorian Social Classes and the End of the Wild West	25
THREE. The Risk of Illness and What Religion Could Do	40
FOUR. Progressivism and American Politics	55
FIVE. Pacifism and American Wars, Changing and Deepening Views	83
SIX. Twentieth-Century Stages of Acceptance: The Educated Woman	108
SEVEN. The Campaign for Birth Control, a Pact with the Devil	128
EIGHT. The Risks and Judgments of the Postwar World	146
Conclusion	172
Chapter Notes	175
Bibliography	197
Index	215

Introduction

"One person—in any cause or place—can make a difference in his part of the world."[1]

John Rankin, from a Scottish family, left eastern Canada in 1869 for the adventure of gold mining. Olive Pickering, from an English family, left New Hampshire in 1878 to become a teacher on the frontier and to seek a husband in the west: after the Civil War her older sisters remained at home, having not married, but she imagined a more exciting future for herself. After making the voyage west, John moved from the lure of gold mining to ranching and then to a building career in the new western town of Missoula; Olive taught for a year in a one-room school there and then married John and had seven children.[2] Though much of the literature of the west concerns men as miners, ranchers, and cowboys, both women and men, like Olive and John, took the risk of coming into this dangerous space, far from the eastern seaboard. This couple provides a window into difficult treks to the west as well as sheriffs with absolute power on the edge of the law, the hardships faced by miners and ranchers, the few career choices available to women and to men, the realities of childbearing and child raising, the constant presence of illness, and the desire for eastern social status in brand new crossroad towns.[3]

In a second generation of this family in Montana, John and Olive's children moved into other forms of ambition and risk as they sought their own careers. These children included a highly competitive brother, Wellington, who became one of the biggest landowners in the country and a power in the Progressive and Republican parties, as well as sisters Jeannette, Harriet, Mary, Grace, and Edna, who included the first woman in a national legislature, one who opposed two world wars; a birth control activist who traveled the nation and world; an early dean of women developing co-educational university spaces; and a director of a World War II lodging facility for soldiers in London. As these children embarked on careers not available to their parents, they made difficult decisions, beginning with whether to avoid marriage and children so that they could concentrate on their chosen work. These siblings' stories concern independence, education, activism, the boundaries created by gender, religious choices and especially the lure of Christian Science, and the changing meaning of the west. The Rankin children experienced both national adulation and condemnation for the risks undertaken as they participated in and shaped American history.

Risk is certainly an important topic in contemporary research and life. Today people are confronted with risks generated by illness, financial markets, natural disasters like hurricanes and fires, privacy leaks, and war. Certainly in 2020, with the coronavirus, risk shaped American life. Given the array of threatening possibilities, it is not surprising that risk is now studied in medicine, economics, criminal justice, and many other fields. Much of this theory and data, as well as news coverage, focuses on risk as a negative, something dangerous or hazardous, to avoid, contain, deny, or fix. Insurance policies factor in risks of accident and death; the National Weather Service tracks tornadoes and hurricanes to warn us of danger and predict future storms; environmental groups test air and water to investigate the threats to our being alive. While Americans enjoy viewing the dangers encountered by race car drivers or extreme skiers or those stranded on television's desert islands—types of "edgework," to use researcher Stephen Lyng's term—the majority will seek safety.[4] Some researchers argue that women especially tend to "self-regulate, reduce risks, avoid unhealthy activities, be responsible and take appropriate precautions," but others recognize that the types of risks that women do take, as they leave home, enter inhospitable careers, and have children, may be less credited as hazardous than riding motorcycles without helmets or jumping from planes.[5]

Certainly there are dangers, like those created by viruses, that we should seek to avoid—and that we may feel are worse than anything that came before. Though analysis of risky behavior, as undertaken by women and by men, generally focuses on contemporary society and on disease or storms, Americans have always encountered frightening dangers, and both women and men have always chosen meaningful risk as they sought to make their way and realize their ambitions, choices for which they might pay a high price. This constant of American life operated in different manners on the frontier, during the Progressive and Victorian eras, during two world wars, and after World War II—as Americans formed and re-formed the nation. In these key eras, what was considered risky contrasted with what was construed as traditional or safe, for both genders.

In the story of the Rankins of two generations, we can read the shifting parameters of meaningful engagements and lives worth living. From the far frontier of Montana to frontiers of politics, education, religion, and capitalism, the Rankins offer a complex story of the gendered risk and ambition that transformed a nation.

ONE

The Myth and Reality of the Risky West

Olive Pickering and John Rankin

From the forming of the first settlements, the highest purpose for white pioneers involved frontier dangers. The risk was certainly real—fierce winters without protection, attacks by Native Americans, the constant toil of ranch and farm, all far from eastern family.[1] The ever moving, challenging frontier immediately engaged historians and reporters along with its new residents. In both reality and legend, the west varied by decade and by gender, as did the risks chosen, glorified, and endured.

The power of the frontier, the special mission of inhabiting and depicting it, served as a key part of American consciousness long before cowboy movies and Marlboro ads. To describe a providential onward movement, newspaper editor John O'Sullivan coined the term "manifest destiny" in 1845, as the mission "to overspread the continent allotted by Providence for the free development of our yearly multiplying millions."[2] At a meeting of the American Historical Association in Chicago in 1893, Frederick Jackson Turner spoke of "the significance of the frontier in American history" as he claimed that American identity stemmed from "an area of free land, its continuous recession, and the advance of American settlement westward."[3] In his analysis, the civilized had repeatedly overwhelmed the primitive: the farmer lauded by Thomas Jefferson had dominated fertile spaces beyond eastern cities; dense forests had become fertile farms and industrious towns; the white man was controlling the savage—and purposeful, adventurous risk was building a nation.[4] Beyond an actual space, as Richard Slotkin noted in *Fatal Environment*, the frontier was by the time of Turner's speech "the longest-lived of American myths," a "deeply encoded set of metaphors" of a virtuous republic, a seal of approval for the often violent building of an empire.[5]

Throughout the nineteenth century, both treaty negotiation and war extended this powerful vision of destiny. The purchase of Louisiana in 1803 created a huge propeller for this story, as it doubled the nation's land mass. Later treaties also expanded American territory in the southwest and west. Until the Oregon Treaty, land west of the Continental Divide had been disputed between England and the United States. The British finally agreed in early 1846 to divide the region along the 49th parallel, the current border in the west between the United States and Canada. The 1848 Treaty of Guadalupe Hidalgo, forced upon the Mexican government, created the Mexican Cession, ceding Alta California and Santa Fe de Nuevo México to the United States. Mexico also acknowledged the loss of what became the state of Texas and accepted the Rio Grande as its northern border. Also expanding the territory for settlement by white Americans was Indian removal, first of Native Americans from ancestral homelands in the eastern United States to a designated Indian Territory in modern Oklahoma and then of other tribal groups in the west, like the Salish of Montana, forced to less desirable land far north of their home.

This vision—of the American's need for land in the expanding west—involved a particularly male construction of virile risk. In his 1893 address, Frederick Jackson Turner claimed that this faraway space had the power to transform the eastern male: "The wilderness masters the colonist.... It takes him from the railroad car and puts him in the birch canoe. It strips off the garments of civilization and arrays him in the hunting shirt and the moccasin ... he shouts the war cry and takes the scalp in orthodox Indian fashion."[6] In the 1890s, Teddy Roosevelt described the purpose of "the strenuous life" in western spaces as forming the "kind of American man of whom America can be really proud," the kind that could build a world and dominate it.[7] In the frontier west, there were in fact many more men than women: in nineteenth-century Montana, the ratio was ten to one.[8] But images of what men achieved as nation builders elided even the limited presence of women. As Annette Kolodny noted in *The Lay of the Land*, it was men—as cowboys, soldiers, ranchers, miners, and desperadoes—that received credit for "taming" the west.[9] Only recently have scholars begun to evaluate the contributions of western women, attempting to create "a vision of past cultures as multilayered composites of women's and men's experiences, rich in complexity and conflict."[10]

The primarily male western incursion, in image and in reality, occurred in several waves in Montana and the Missoula Valley. The first Euro-Americans to enter the valley were members of the Lewis and Clark Expedition, who explored the Clark Fork River, downstream from present-day Missoula, on their way back from the west coast: the land in Montana east of the Continental Divide was part of the Louisiana Purchase in 1803, what Lewis and Clark came west to see. English-Canadian explorer David Thompson visited in 1811, mapping the valley and surrounding peaks. In the decades following these expeditions, American, British, and French explorers operated a fur trade along with Native Americans throughout this region.

Into this western space of adventure, exploration, and trading next came settlements of Catholic priests. In 1841, responding to requests from Iroquois and Salish afflicted with smallpox and cholera, Father Pierre-Jean De Smet ventured from St. Louis to the Missoula Valley, bringing with him what were probably the first wagons and oxen to enter the area. Jesuit missionaries followed and settled there, on the banks of the Clark Fork River, though they did not remain long due to the hostile response of other local tribes: Pend d'Oreille, Nez Percés, and Blackfeet. Leaving this contested area, De Smet's group established St. Mary's Mission in present-day Stevensville, to the south of Missoula. They next created St. Ignatius Mission, to the north, where they received government subsidies for educating Indian children, the intention being to remove them from tribal traditions and engage them, often forcefully, in white society.[11]

Beyond a few missionaries, larger amounts of white and especially male citizens came to Montana with the gold rush, a mad spate of activity that occurred after the big strikes in California. In the early 1850s, Granville and James Stuart found gold at a spot they excitedly named Goldcreek, in southwest Montana. When they wrote a letter to their brother to join them, the news sparked a rush to the area. Then in July of 1862, a prospector named John White made a strike along Grasshopper Creek, a tributary of the Beaverhead River to the south of Goldcreek. Miners built a small town named Bannack and staked out the entire length of the creek, where mines soon produced five million dollars' worth of gold ($90 million today). In 1863, two prospecting parties left Bannack to search for gold to the east, near the Yellowstone River in Crow territory, the tribe forcing these prospectors to leave. These men later found gold at Alder Gulch, near Virginia City, while others successfully prospected at Last Chance Gulch. This site quickly boomed into the town of Helena, a source of nineteen million dollars' worth of ore ($221 million today).[12]

With profits beginning and ending at these mines at great speed, prospectors who stayed in the region went on to other occupations—in areas that had been the domain of Native Americans. This increased settlement in towns and on farms spurred the desire to remove local tribes from the best Montana lands. White settlers coming into the Bitterroot Valley, south of present-day Missoula, prompted the Hell Gate Treaty of 1855. When Salish tribal leaders met with Isaac Stevens, governor of the Washington territory, of which Montana was still a part, they accepted an offer of $120,000 in annuities annually for twenty years in exchange for heading to less desirable lands to the north. No strict enforcement of the requirement to move occurred for fifteen years, however, so the Salish assumed that they could remain permanently in smaller sections of the Bitterroot. But the Garfield Agreement of 1872 contained an executive order for the Salish people to head north to the Flathead Reservation, a dictate that they fought though they finally moved by 1889.[13]

With land becoming available, the new town of Missoula grew in an area that had been heavily traversed by tribes voyaging to the east in search of bison. The town was founded in 1860 as Hellgate Trading Post, the name indicating the fear of ambush as various tribes traversed the area. By 1866, the settlement moved east and took the name of Missoula Mills, later shortened to Missoula, from a Salish name for the Clark Fork River. This post provided supplies to settlers traveling west, with some of them remaining in the area as it became a safer space for families.

The town of Missoula, which would house the Rankin family, only predated the arrival of John Rankin and Olive Pickering by little more than a decade. In January 1901, for an article concerning a thirtieth wedding anniversary party, the reporter commented that the party goers, including John and Olive, had been together in the "wild and wooly pioneer days."[14] The risky American west, and indeed different gendered versions of it, had caused both Rankins to make the trip as young people, from Canada and New Hampshire, in 1869 and 1878.

John Rankin

The history of both John and Olive involved the assumption of risk taken by generations of emigrants who left Europe for the New World. John Rankin was born, around 1839, on a farm between Ekfrid and New London, in eastern Canada, near Lake Erie.[15] His parents Hugh, called Big Hugh, and Jeannette (Jannet), a name often spelled differently in census records, came with their families from Scotland as children. Their son, John Rankin, who left Canada first for Illinois and then for Montana, grew up hearing heroic stories of the adversities overcome and the bravery exhibited by his family of New-World explorers.

At the beginning of the nineteenth century, newspaper advertisements, guidebooks, and paid agents urged people to leave Scotland and come to Canada. Hugh Rankin, born in 1804, came from a family of farmers in the Highlands. Until the late seventeenth century, Scots did not cross the Atlantic as commonly as the English, primarily just criminals and political prisoners forced to flee. But in the nineteenth century, 1.8 million Scots headed to non–European destinations, a total that would have constituted

38 percent of the Scottish population at the 1911 census. Of this group, 21 percent went to Canada, first to Nova Scotia and later to the eastern townships of lower Canada. Enclosures of common lands and a change from farming to sheep rearing, a transformation carried out by aristocratic landowners, led to this long-term emigration trend.[16] Some landlords relied on public funds to pay for their tenants' removal, a form of coercion euphemistically labeled as "assisted passage." This large, often desperate emigrant group, searching for the farmland no longer available in the Highlands, included Hugh Rankin's parents. Coming to eastern Canada at around the same time was Jeannette Stewart, ten years younger, her family from the lowlands of Scotland. Emigration from that area was much less common, generally of groups in less arduous circumstances, families that sought to attain larger tracts of land while maintaining traditions from home.

These immigrants built up Gaelic-speaking enclaves in the eastern townships of Quebec, the St. Andrew's Society providing funds to help new arrivals as did Masonic lodges.[17] Though Canada encouraged this trend, local citizens often ridiculed and shunned the new arrivals, who spoke a foreign language and worshipped separately from their neighbors. Coastal artist Frederick Cozzens described an oft repeated, prejudicial judgment: of Scots as "a canting, covenanting, oat-eating, money-gripping tribe."[18] The majority lived on small tracts of land and barely managed to eke out a living. Up to a third returned home, and others, like Hugh Rankin's sons, emigrated again, moving beyond eastern Canada as young adults.[19]

In the early 1830s, after Big Hugh Rankin and Jeannette Stewart married, they engaged together in the risks encountered by not-completely-welcome farm owners. The couple settled on "a tract of wild land" outside of New London.[20] There in a challenging farm space Big Hugh and Jeannette had twelve children in eighteen years, eight sons and four daughters, John the sixth child and the fourth son. With a farm needing their labor, these children rarely went to school: John attended for only short parts of three years.

John's sisters married and either stayed in the area or left well into adulthood with their husbands. His sister Annie Agnes, for example, lived in nearby Ekfrid with her husband and then moved with him to Houghton, Michigan, where he found work in the copper mines. Angus, the second son, joined them and also became a miner. Copper mining in the Upper Peninsula had boomed, and from 1845 to 1887 the Michigan Copper Company was the nation's leading producer. When Horace Greeley said "Go West, young man" in 1865, he was directing the easterner not to the far west but to mines in Houghton. Later, after visiting the area, Greeley wrote that his lasting impression was not of prosperity but of "clouds of mosquitoes and gnats," and dreary, dangerous work: with just chisel and hammer, poorly paid men cut billions of tons of copper to be hauled out of the dark and dangerous tunneling.²¹

John and his younger brother Duncan, growing up on the family farm where their parents had twelve children to support, knew they had to find their own way as adults. Indeed, of all of these sons, only the two youngest, Alexander and Hugh, stayed to work this land and would be there in 1877 when Big Hugh died. John and Duncan felt the pull of gold fever, of movement well beyond eastern Canada, the choice of far-flung emigration moving from grandparents and parents to these sons as they sought another frontier, a "volatile environment in which human life was precariously cast," one that might engender a better life.²²

John Rankin as a young man in the west, ca. 1875 (Archives & Special Collections, Mansfield Library, University of Montana).

The oldest of the Rankin children, Donald Hugh Rankin, called D.H., provided the first destination for his younger brothers after they left the farm. D.H. moved as a young man to Shelby, Michigan, near the eastern shore of Lake Michigan, where he worked as a carpenter and then built a kiln, making charcoal from beach and maple wood, for use in factories that produced industrial metals. Taking on increasing financial risk, D.H. opened a second, larger kiln site, near Mears, ten miles to the north of Shelby, at these two facilities producing 90,000 bushels of charcoal a month by 1885, with 125 employees, including two of his brothers for a short time.²³ At the kilns John and Duncan learned construction skills as well as how to turn lumber into profit, which John later did on his own land in Montana. Then, when John was thirty and Duncan twenty-four, they traveled on to find their future, their own means of sustenance and success, by heading to Montana.

When these brothers struck out for the far west, way beyond Michigan, what drew them was gold-bearing lodes near Helena, news of which had been filtering slowly, and indeed too slowly, to Canada and Michigan. In 1866 and 1867, before the brothers left home, Canadian newspapers and newsletters featured stories of overcoming Indians and extracting riches, with emphasis on the true manifest destiny, of Canadians, in lending a moral tone to the effort. As the *Gazette of Montreal* claimed, manifest destiny had become a "miserably bad argument for crime which passes current among the more villainous portion of the people of the neighboring Union," and superior Canadian explorers and miners could help stem that tide while bringing riches to worthy Canadian families.[24]

In Michigan the brothers encountered further newspaper evidence of the "unusual production of gold" in Montana. One article in February 1868, for example, concerning a strike worth twenty million dollars, claimed that this triumph was just the beginning. A poem printed along with the news articles spoke of a bridge of Montana gold found near Helena, readily available for breaking off into ribbons that a young man could lay at his beloved's feet.[25]

With construction tools and money from their work for D.H., John and Duncan undertook the 2000-mile trip to Helena. These brothers joined the half a million emigrants heading west from 1840 to 1870.[26] Any route was grueling and expensive, and the brothers' exact choices are not known. John's children Wellington and Jeannette repeated details that focused on their father overcoming adversity, on his gumption and strength, on his ability to assume risk as a pioneer and thrive.

As nineteenth-century surveyor Ferdinand Hayden wrote, "Montana has always been far-off in miles, in time, and facilities for getting there ... it is almost an outside world."[27] Overland travelers ventured by wagon or horseback on the Bozeman Trail, a dangerous trek through Sioux country. Rail travel was possible but expensive, on the just completed Union Pacific-Central Pacific line. The most popular means of travel was on the Missouri River, a route chosen by Lewis and Clark, fur traders, and gold miners. Fort Benton, which began as a small trading post on the banks of the upper Missouri, became a busy way station for boats, overland travelers, and freight wagons. In 1860, the first steamboat, the *Chippewa*, arrived there.

Although the brothers' means of travel in 1869 was not recorded, John and Duncan certainly didn't have money for a train trip. Wellington's biographer Volney Steele assumes that they made their way from Michigan to St. Louis, 480 miles to the south, by horseback and wagon to board a steamboat for the 1500-mile trip to Fort Benton.[28] But both Wellington and Jeannette believed that the brothers traveled from St. Louis on a more risky and slow flatboat. On either vessel, without the significant funds needed to travel as customers, they would have worked to pay their way, poling and pulling on a flatboat or cutting wood on a steamboat.

As this story of overcoming risk continued, the boat that the brothers traveled on ground to a halt on Cow Island, many miles from Fort Benton, a place where low water often stranded vessels, and the brothers continued on to the fort over land. Wellington speculated that either his well-prepared and strong father had brought oxen with him from Michigan or that the brothers purchased a team at Fort Benton with which to start south, securing money for this final segment of the trip by hauling cargo from the fort to the mines. These two thus made their way to Helena, the site of well-publicized gold strikes.

As the brothers traveled, they moved through risky sites of conflict between white settlers and Native Americans, tensions having escalated with the Indian removal effort. In the summer of 1869, just a few miles from Fort Benton, a group of Crows attacked a small wagon train and killed two white men. In retribution, citizens at Fort Benton killed a Blood as well as a Piegan who was the brother of an important leader, Mountain Chief, and not involved in the wagon attack. Then by October, with several tribes involved, forty-six white people were killed and at least a thousand horses stolen, with attack and counterattack continuing to occur.[29] As John Rankin described the trip west to his children, his stories concerned attacks by marauding Indians, the strenuous work of steering a flatboat, and the rough overland journey with oxen, his emphasis on two brothers who prevailed on their own.

Though Helena still had its mining moniker of Last Chance Gulch when the brothers arrived in the fall of 1869, the gold had been gone for some time. A mining fortune not possible, John Rankin attempted to make a living with his carpentry skills. A devastating fire in February had gutted the Gulch, but John found when he arrived that most of the small town had already been rebuilt. As Wellington mentioned to an interviewer, his father had to again change his plans and press onward to find work.

With limited success at prospecting and at building, the brothers ventured on to Cedar Creek, two hundred miles to the northwest of Helena, and began mining in the mountains where there had been additional gold strikes. They then prospected in the Bitterroot Mountains, where gold had been found in 1865. Not striking it rich quick, John and Duncan, called the "Canada boys," went on to Unionville, south of Helena, where they secured jobs running a stamp mill, crushing ore that others had dug.[30]

Given their difficulties with gold mining and the hard work of a mill, the brothers parted, with Wellington later saying that Duncan was the less industrious of the two, uninterested in the daily grind of carpentry or a mill.[31] When an interviewer asked Wellington if his father was an adventurer, he replied that instead "he was a young man interested in, in getting ahead"; Wellington continued by saying that "Father was a worker" and

Duncan less so. A noisy, big fellow capable of getting into trouble, Duncan talked "too damn much.... I never liked him." His father came to Montana "just to make his way," Wellington continued, but Duncan sought immediate riches, as many men did in the decades of gold rush, and he left the frustrations of Montana and ventured on to California.[32] Though Wellington said that his father had big fists and fought when he had to, both Wellington and Jeannette claimed that their father never chose violence and ultimately achieved prosperity, not by the quick strike or the quick fight, but by decades of hard work.

When John had enough of everything about mining, he went on to the new town of Missoula. In a growing frontier town, John took on the risk of large building projects, at the edge of his knowledge and experience, and moved into several other businesses at once—a frontier entrepreneur. As a history of the state maintains, John Rankin was "closely connected with the growth and development of this city," beginning as soon as he arrived there.[33] Studying engineering at night and adding to his tools as he could, John secured contracts to build bridges in the Bitterroot Valley and in town, some of the first in the area, including the 250–foot Blockhouse Bridge, five miles to the south.[34] As bridges brought safer approaches and the population grew, John also began constructing the first stone buildings, including in 1872 the town's first church, for Presbyterians, Episcopalians, and Methodists to worship in.

With the money gained from these construction projects, John began purchasing land from which he could harvest lumber, as his brother D.H. did to make charcoal. In 1877, he bought a small ranch and saw mill on Grant Creek, to the northwest of Missoula, and soon began buying more land from which to harvest lumber. The Montreal-born Captain Richard Grant, who fought for Great Britain in the War of 1812 and worked in the fur trade, had built a home on the creek in 1858 when he retired. Subsequent owners developed the small mill. When John Rankin purchased the property, a newspaper article from Helena indicated that local residents were glad to see such a "live man" take over the property, with plans to amass a large supply of lumber from which to manufacture shingles, sashes, and doors. Rankin also added a planing mill, producing specially dressed lumber, moving forward to meet community needs as "an agreeable and accommodating business man."[35]

John's status as a prominent citizen and builder also involved him in the removal of Native Americans as Missoula sought to expand and defend its surroundings. Fort Fizzle was the name ultimately given to a temporary military barricade, erected by the U.S. Army in July 1877, its purpose to intercept the Nez Perce as their hunting took them from Idaho into Montana, where white settlers did not want them to go. Captain Charles

Rawn received orders to "compel the Indians to surrender their arms and ammunition, and to dispute their passage, by force of arms, into Bitterroot Valley."[36] On July 25, Rawn employed both soldiers and local residents like John Rankin to build a wooden barricade of logs and earth, two miles below where the tribal group camped, to stop their movement forward. On July 28, the Nez Perce climbed ridges to the north of the area and bypassed the barricade, leaving its defenders in the rear. The makeshift fort thus acquired the Fort Fizzle appellation, an embarrassment to the town and to John Rankin.[37] Though he was not proud of his involvement, it led to a large contract: in 1877, John served as primary contractor for a military post, Fort Missoula, for which he supplied 175,000 feet of board.[38] In a territory of boom and bust, with an expansion into building and lumber as well as cattle ranching on his land, John succeeded through determination and hard work, in the mold of the early western entrepreneur.

Olive Pickering

John and Duncan, as well as D.H., left home for various locales of the west, for the adventure, but also to make a living, seeking a better life by each man's definition, just as their grandparents did as they came to Canada from Scotland and their parents did in starting a farm in New London.

Sisters as well as brothers had various reasons for making the voyage west. They might travel along with parents or other relatives. They might help to enact choices made by the husband, as when Annie Agnes moved to the Upper Peninsula of Michigan so that her husband could work in the mines. The desire to "Go West, young woman" could also involve a chance for employment, especially for the single woman.[39] The image of the frontier woman has often centered on the long-suffering, frightened wife, enduring endless childbirth on a lonely farm, but research has led to a more complex if contradictory picture "of western Anglo women who were both brave and timid, resourceful and dependent, aggressive and retiring," with many reasons possible for their western venture.[40] Historian Glenda Riley has written that "myths of the West and of women snarl and interweave until it is almost impossible to speak in rational terms regarding frontier women…. If there is a truth about frontierswomen, it is that they were not any one thing."[41] This complexity certainly describes the motives and actions of Olive Pickering, who was influenced by stories of western Edens, by the adventures of a wild-west sheriff, and by eastern realities after the Civil War.

Olive Pickering grew up on a farm, in a more economically established family than John Rankin's and in a more settled area. She was born in 1854 in Newington, New Hampshire, a member of a family with ancestors from England and Ireland. Her family had a long history in the state. In the late seventeenth century, her ancestor John Pickering became a leader in Portsmouth, one of a small select group of men who "served as deputies in the General Court and associates on the county court, gained election to town offices, received large grants in the distribution of community property, owned the local grain mills, and controlled much of Portsmouth's overseas trade." When Pickering served as House Speaker in the 1690s, King William III awarded him with a grant-in-land, marked only in latitudes with the longitude statement of "as far west as you can go." William used these grants, in a colony dominated by the fishing industry, to encourage further development through farming as well as to award loyal officials and subjects after New Hampshire became a separate province in 1680.⁴²

Both sides of Olive's family, of English and Irish ancestry, had other members who became prominent citizens of the state. Another John Pickering served as president of New Hampshire in 1789. From her mother's side, Nathaniel S. Berry settled in Bristol and became governor during the Civil War. Olive's grandfather, Isaiah Berry, and father, William Berry, fought in the War of 1812. Isaiah served for many years in the New Hampshire legislature.⁴³

This long political history in the state ceded land to the family but did not ease the difficulties of farming on the small tracts that eventually came to individual heirs. In the household in 1860, seven miles outside of Portsmouth, Olive's parents John S. Pickering and Mary J. Berry Pickering engaged in the hard work of New England farm life, with a small amount of arable land and with railroads bringing wheat and other products from the middle west, lessening the price that eastern farmers could get for their crops.⁴⁴ According to census and cemetery records, this couple had eleven children between 1838 and 1861, with a first unnamed child and two sons named John dying as infants, Anne dying at age five, and two sons, Charles and William, dying as teenagers. These children had little education, attending school only during winter days when they were not required to help on the farm.

While men like John and Duncan Rankin might be motivated by newspaper articles about gold mines and triumph over Indians, other genres, like autobiographies and short stories, lured women like Olive Pickering to the west. Mary Austin Holley wrote about a land of milk and honey in Texas, a place she had visited from her home in Connecticut but never lived. In *Life in Prairie Land*, Eliza Farnham, who became a matron of the women's ward at Sing Sing Prison, created a strong contrast as she lauded the abundant land of central Illinois, where she lived before taking that job. Poet Alice Cary's popular short story collection *Clovernook* and

Olive Rankin and her three sisters in New Hampshire. Clockwise from the back row are Philena, Mandana, Mary, and Olive, ca. 1870–1873 (Schlesinger Library, Radcliffe Institute, Harvard University).

Caroline Soule's *Little Alice; Or, the Pet of the Settlement* concerned leaving the industrialized north and slavery-tainted south for a purer existence in the west. Some writers included realistic passages: Margaret Fuller, in *Summer on the Lakes*, depicted the Rock River country of Illinois as an Edenic space, but she also described men out hunting and fishing while women endured "a comfortless and laborious indoor life"; Caroline Kirkland, in *A New Home—Who'll Follow?*, set on the Michigan frontier, warned readers of bad weather, inadequate shelter, and an isolated life alone with children ("a long, solitary, wordless day"). But Kirkland's description of the new home also involved a sentimental rendering of the virtuous, resplendent frontier, as did other popular works.[45]

For Olive Pickering, these visions of an Edenic rural space had great appeal; years later she suggested these books for her own daughters.[46] But she also felt the lure of adventure and freedom. In 1878, her uncle Billy Berry returned to the east and regaled the family with his tall tales. In 1849, that most tempting year for western adventure, her mother's brother, Charles William (Billy) Berry, then twenty-two, had left New Hampshire as an adventurer and hopeful miner, traveling to San Francisco via the Isthmus of Panama. Billy succeeded at placer mining in stream beds above Coloma, California, near where James W. Marshall found gold at Sutter's Mill. From 1851 to 1861, Billy continued mining in surrounding areas and, when that income dried up, began driving freight wagons throughout the northwest.

On one of these trips, as Billy's retelling of wild-western risk would have it, an Indian's arrow passed through his beard as he sat by a fire at night. Another adventure story concerned a trip to Idaho where his brother was living, two vigilantes overwhelming local lawmen. After Billy was robbed of a thousand dollars, he rounded up a posse and chased the robbers. When the local sheriff took over his captives, Billy stormed the jail, overpowered the guards, and took the robbers "into custody." The accused were found dead the next morning, "hanging by the neck" in a barn. After this raid, Billy and his brother took over as sheriffs in this dangerous gold-mining area, the story told back east casting them as the toughest of marauders and heroes.

Billy's adventures next took him to Alder Gulch, Montana, where he worked as a miner and a trapper. He arrived in Missoula County in 1869, the same year that John Rankin came west, and soon took over the positions of postmaster, notary public, road supervisor, and coroner. He was elected as sheriff at a time when the county took up most of western Montana. In this position, he secured a place as town fixture, as someone who had been there almost since the beginning, dealing with "saloon brawls, stagecoach robberies, vigilante raids, and shootings."[47]

Olive considered a move west not just because of Edenic dreams or tall tales of vigilante justice, but because of post-war eastern realities. The Civil War created a "marriage squeeze" for women, with the deaths of 620,000 mostly young men. Between 1800 and 1900, women generally married for the first time between the ages of twenty and twenty-two, but those who reached this age during or after the war missed out on this traditional expectation. In the 1860s, many women found themselves living well into adulthood in their parents' home without a long-term means of support, and they married older widowers or someone not entirely appropriate, perhaps well below their socioeconomic status.[48]

When Olive Pickering took the risk of heading west in 1878, at age twenty-four, she had seen the choices made and not made by her sisters. In the census of 1870, the year that Olive turned sixteen, living in the home were three daughters at and past traditional marriage age: Mandana, 31; Philena, 27; and Mary, 21. These older daughters ultimately married, but under different circumstances than would have occurred in earlier decades. As historical records reveal, Mandana, who turned twenty-one in 1860, married at age forty in 1879; her husband was George B. Foss, forty-three, a blacksmith from Portsmouth whose wife had died in 1875, leaving him with two daughters. Philena, who turned twenty-one in 1865, married Andrew Hanson, a farmer, in 1886, when she was forty-two and he was sixty-one, his second marriage. Mary Pickering, who turned twenty-one in 1870, married Benjamin Pinkham in 1876 when she was twenty-seven and he was thirty-two.

After the Civil War, with many eastern young women not marrying, Olive began looking for another path. She had taught part-time at the local school but, with other unmarried women seeking that work, she had little hope of a permanent position. She was ready for something new, seeking adventure along with a means of earning a living and perhaps finding a husband in an area where men far outnumbered women as was certainly not the case in New Hampshire.

Olive Pickering Rankin as a young woman in New Hampshire, ca. 1870–1873 (Schlesinger Library, Radcliffe Institute, Harvard University).

One. The Myth and Reality of the Risky West

As Wellington later recalled, Billy's wife Annie had died in 1867 and left him with two young children, one of them just four months old. When he came back east in 1878, leaving them in Montana, he was seeking family help. The first Missoula teacher had married, and he wanted Olive to take her place while also helping him out at home. When she chose to accompany him, she did so for an array of reasons, romantic and adventurous and extremely practical.

Olive's parents allowed her to make this frightening, risky choice only after her sister Mandana, thirty-eight, agreed to accompany her. In relative luxury for the time, the three took the Union Pacific train to Corinne, Utah—there were no trains running in Montana in 1878. They then traveled 460 miles to the north by mule stage, via Virginia City, a treacherous seven-day journey, in much more primitive accommodations. On one downward slope, slippery with pine needles, the driver tied a large log against the back wheels to act as a brake. Olive later recalled the difference in how the two sisters viewed this moment: "I laughed and Mannie prayed." On the trail, the specter of Indian attack created a "climate of rumor and alarmism," and the passengers were instructed to get down on the floor of the stage as it traveled through Indian country.[49]

After the long journey ended, Mandana chose to return to her fiancé and her parents' home; she married George Foss the next year. Olive later told her children that her sister felt they should both leave since the west wasn't safe: "This is no place to raise children, out in Montana," Mandana had told her. As Wellington claimed in an interview about his aunt's strong reaction to the dangerous west, "My mother always laughed about it."[50] Though Mandana went straight home, Olive did not return for seventeen years and then only for a short visit with family and friends.

Women that came to the west needing employment, as Olive did, found work as schoolteachers, cooks, laundresses, tailors, maids, and prostitutes. Teaching represented "a higher social class than the other choices, deemed appropriate for young women like Olive from eastern farms, an extension of their natural concern for children that would soon lead to marriage and motherhood."[51] Between 1847 and 1858, more than 600 teachers traveled to the frontier to work in schools that they helped to form, some of them having received special training for this challenging environment. Catharine Beecher, who opened schools for girls in the east, turned her attention next to training westward-bound teachers, her challenging goal being "to unite American women in an effort to provide a Christian education for 2,000,000 children in our country."[52] She thought of each teacher's commitment as temporary, as she described it: "The great purpose of a woman's life—the happy superintendence of a family—is accomplished all the better and easier by preliminary teaching in school."[53] Of her group that went west, two thirds remained there, but generally not as teachers.[54] While hundreds of women secured special instruction, others, like Olive, journeyed west with little preparation for the frontier school. Olive told her own children that she was young and well dressed, well connected through her uncle, but she had to learn the algebra that she taught the older students.[55]

On the frontier, new teachers might encounter in one room pupils from grades one to eight, with the younger seated in the front and older in the back, girls on one side and boys on the other. The curriculum generally included reading, spelling, penmanship, arithmetic, and history, with ten to fifteen minute sessions dedicated to each grade level. A school year might last twelve weeks, from Thanksgiving to early spring, a period when children were less needed in the fields; they might also attend a short summer session.

As she began a teaching career in Montana, Olive followed in the footsteps of other hard-working women educators in the state. Eliza Mott in Carson Valley, Montana, taught in her own kitchen beginning in 1852, with two copies of the *McGuffey Reader,* its moralistic stories a staple of nineteenth-century education for proper citizenship.[56] Mott supplemented her instruction with everything that she could find for students to read, including inscriptions on tombstones in the local cemetery. In 1863, Lucia Darling, at age twenty-seven, traveled with her uncle, Chief Justice Sidney Edgerton, to Bannack. Expected to locate an appropriate space for a schoolroom, she finally decided on her uncle's living room: the winter weather made it impossible to outfit any other site. In the spring, she moved the school into a cabin, furnished with makeshift chairs and desks.[57]

In 1878, Olive Pickering, living with her uncle, taught eleven students of all ages in a single room cabin. The older students helped with teaching the younger; each student came to the front of the room to read or recite; slate and chalk pieces enabled all students to do math and handwriting exercises, and they also displayed their work on the school blackboard, a rough plank coated with black paint. And Olive had an additional audience, members of the Salish tribe who came to the fence outside to listen through open windows as she read to students, her focus on morality. Using the *McGuffey's Reader*, she read, for example, a story about three boys at a boarding school, to whom each mother sent a cake: the first two hoarded theirs and became ill; the third gave slices to his friends and to a blind man, thereby setting a good example while enjoying a fit portion of dessert. After reading ethical lessons such as this one, at the end of the school day, Olive waved goodbye to her students both inside the classroom and outside.[58]

As was true for many women, Olive taught only for a short time, just while she remained single. Within a year of coming to Missoula, in August

1879, she married John Rankin. Though he wanted to marry her as soon as they met, at a town meeting, she insisted on completing her year's contract first. At the time of their marriage, she was twenty-six and he was forty. In a simpler time in a small town, there was nothing in the newspaper about the ceremony. Right after they married, Olive moved to John's undeveloped land on Grant Creek. Standards varied across the country, but married women were generally not allowed to work as teachers. Certainly John's ranching concerns took precedence, and Olive's short teaching career ended.

Moving to the Ranch

Both John and Olive had left eastern homes to find something more. His path of adventure included a long river trip and the lure of gold and then his development of entrepreneurial businesses on the frontier. Olive's own adventure involved a risky western trip with her uncle and a quick teaching career before she took on a rural ranch life, childbirth, and child care. In *Parallel Lives: Five Victorian Marriages*, Phyllis Rose claims that "marriage, whether we see it a psychological relationship or a political one, has determined the story of all our lives more than we have generally acknowledged," and this marriage certainly determined the lives of both of these Montana pioneers, though more so for Olive whose place of residence, occupation, physical health, and mental health changed with this choice.[59]

Jeannette Rankin's biographers James J. Lopach and Jean A. Luckowski referred to the Grant Creek property as a "gentleman's ranch" in a "mountain meadow," but the reality, especially for Olive, was more stark and complex.[60] Even today, this land is down a rutted road, isolated from town. It still contains the small visible footprint of where the Rankin home stood.[61] On the ranch, Olive dealt with the extremes of climate in Montana, from as high as 90 in the summer to as low as minus 20 with vast snow falls in winter. Hail could be big enough to kill chickens and ruin crops. There was little other precipitation besides the snow, with Grant Creek, which fluctuated in depth with the seasons, desperately needed to provide water for the stock, mill, and home. In this isolated space, Olive had few neighbors: the distance between ranches was too great for casual visiting or for immediate assistance in emergencies.[62]

Olive gave birth at home like the majority of women throughout the nineteenth century. But unlike women in towns, she had few neighbors and no relatives to provide help. With Mary E. Keset, who helped with cooking for the mill hands, as the only woman to turn to and a husband often in

The Rankin house on Grant Creek, a picture taken in the 1940s. The rooms on the back were added after the Rankins moved to Missoula in 1885 (Kenneth D. Swan Photographs; MSS 345, Archives & Special Collections, Mansfield Library, University of Montana).

Formal group portrait of the Rankin family in Missoula, 1888. From left to right: Wellington, Harriet, John, Olive, Jeannette, and Philena. The girls wear identical dresses, each with a different collar, with Wellington in Scottish garb (Schlesinger Library, Radcliffe Institute, Harvard University).

Group portrait with studio backdrop of four Rankin family siblings as children, 1891–1892. Seated clockwise: Wellington (top), Harriet, Grace (infant) and Mary (Schlesinger Library, Radcliffe Institute, Harvard University).

Formal portrait of Jeannette (front, left), Philena (front, right), and Harriet (rear, seated on prop wall), 1889–1890. The photographer, Frank M. Ingalls, had a studio in Missoula from 1890 to 1912 (Schlesinger Library, Radcliffe Institute, Harvard University).

Missoula working on construction projects, Olive gave birth to four children in four years: Jeannette in June 1880, ten months after her marriage, followed by Philena in 1882, Harriet in 1883, and Wellington in 1884. As Helen Bonner, who knew both Jeannette and Wellington from childhood, said in an interview, these older siblings seemed to the younger ones, born later and in town, almost like another generation.[63]

In any location and certainly in such isolation, giving birth to large numbers of children in rapid succession was hard physically and mentally. Women on the frontier had little other choice: their ineffective birth control methods included prolonged suckling, the rhythm method, withdrawal, and hot water douching.[64] Through much of the nineteenth century, women bore an average of more than seven live children and had additional pregnancies resulting in miscarriages and stillbirths. In this era, repeated pregnancy and childbirth, occurring year after year, was filled with dangers. Most women on farms or ranches lacked pre-natal care and professional assistance with delivery, and the death of infants was all too common: during the last quarter of the nineteenth century in the United States, one in ten infants died before age one.[65] Additionally, one mother died for each 154 living births, a figure that by 1980 would be one for each 10,000. In her description of what a pioneer woman faced as she gave birth for the fourth time, Elizabeth H. Emerson described the realities known by so many: "Between oceans of pain, there stretched continents of fear; fear of death and a dread of suffering beyond bearing. She knew. After a woman had been through it three times, nobody need tell her, 'It may not be as bad as the last time.' It was always worse."[66]

On the ranch, Olive dealt with a child's birth each year along with the exhaustion of breast feeding and the daily requirements of child care. Additionally, she did the other substantial work of women on ranches. Wives made candles and soap; they churned butter and dried fruit; they tended domestic gardens; they sewed clothes for children; they washed clothes using washtubs and clotheslines. Women also had nursing duties, employing a variety of nostrums and remedies to treat children and ranch laborers. Beyond taking on all of these tasks, Olive helped to cook for ranch and mill hands and marketed the ranch's apples and the eggs from chickens in her care, with no training for this complex world well beyond New Hampshire and the classroom.[67]

This story of young people, from immigrant families, who headed west to establish a new life reveals many of the complexities of American frontier history as well as the constant need for adaptation, a repeated coming-of-age process. Two brothers left the family farm in Canada to find their own way, with gold as a stirring possibility. John and Duncan's story concerns one man changing his plans to the more conventional and the other continuing on to the uncertainty of California and perhaps a fortune to be made on the next frontier. John Rankin turned himself into an entrepreneur, not just establishing a farm like his father in Canada or a kiln like his brother in Michigan, but instead a western combination needed to succeed, including ranching, milling, and construction. And his whirlwind of activity would determine the story of Olive, who had various reasons for heading west, involving work opportunities and family needs as well as youthful adventure, and whose life would soon be conscribed by childbirth and a ranch.

Women and men came to the west propelled by various myths and dreams, by an attraction to risk and the requirement of repeatedly embracing it to succeed. Though the deeds and bravery of women have been less lauded, both women and men dealt with hardship and stretched their skills to make a living and create new homes. These complex stories involve individuals like Olive Pickering Rankin and John Rankin as well as the nineteenth-century formation of a country.

Two

Victorian Social Classes and the End of the Wild West

John Rankin came to Montana with his brother to involve himself in the glories of mining, for adventure and opportunity not found on a farm outside of New London, Canada, or at his brother D.H.'s kiln in Shelby, Michigan. Olive Pickering left a farm outside of Portsmouth, New Hampshire, with her sister, buoyed by her uncle's stories, with teaching in the west offering a chance at independence—and perhaps of finding a special young man. These two left home for an unknown future, their siblings remaining with them for only a short time. In their movement to the west, gender provided a key element of their experience, as it also would as they next moved into a growing Victorian city space.

When in Chicago in 1893 Frederick Jackson Turner spoke of "the significance of the frontier in American history," he recognized the power of a myth as well as the fact that the reality had receded, that many spaces in the west were changing into towns and small cities. Eleven million Americans moved from rural to urban areas between 1870 and 1900, and some of that movement involved the making of an urban west.[1] In 1885, Olive and John left the ranch and moved to Missoula where they took a lead in constructing social classes as well as buildings and bridges. While a life in town might seem to involve much less risk than crossing the country, establishing a ranch, and having children there, the highly scripted Victorian town created different challenges and involved different adaptations that ultimately took a toll on Olive and John and their children.

The Making of the Western Urban Space

American Victorianism is associated with heavily populated, established cities, such as Boston, New York, Philadelphia, Baltimore, and

Charleston. In eastern enclaves, the upper class of the Gilded Age, like the Four Hundred of New York, mimicked high society of the former mother country in their dress, manners, and homes. The "best" houses in Victorian America were elaborate, combining architectural styles and enhanced by turrets, gables, false fronts, and false chimneys. Ornamentation of lawns featured elaborate flower beds and exotic plants placed to accentuate architectural features of the home. Reports of upper-class visits and soirées in these enclaves, involving elaborate rituals, appeared in social columns prominent in city newspapers from 1880 onward. In this town life, the roles especially of upper-class men and women became increasingly separate, with women in the decorated home and men out at the office or factory.

This eastern city upper class began to influence the west, even in small, new towns: "The West adopted the foibles and flaws of Victorian America along with its finer attributes." In the west more than in the east, class structure involved occupations instead of ancestry. The upper level consisted of mercantile, financial, and other professionals; stockmen and ranchers; and contractors, all of which described John Rankin. Peace officers like Billy Berry had too much contact with the lower elements of society to reach the highest levels of this social structure. The privilege of acceptance could be indicated by dining in the best of Victorian homes, mingling at social events, attaining membership in the same clubs, and intermarrying, all within newly established codes. And this status included personal favoritism, as a natural and warranted benefit, with government contracts and largesse allowing members of the chosen group "to secure or preserve material advantages."[2] As historian Mark Wahlgren Summers noted about this "Era of Good Stealings," politicians and their associates in industry, in the west as well as the east, skillfully employed social connections as they wielded "padded expenses, lucrative contracts, outright embezzlements, and illegal bond issues"—and made their fortunes.[3]

Just as men reinvented themselves as Gilded Age industrialists on the frontier, women also "inherited an ideology that arose in the East" and developed it to fit new circumstances.[4] Creating the Victorian social space could be a challenging endeavor. Louisa Smith Clappe, known as Dame Shirley, described attempts of residents in a California mining town to establish social ritual "in a place where there were no newspapers, no churches, lectures, concerts, or theaters; no fresh books, no shopping, calling nor gossiping little tea-drinkings; no parties, no balls, no picnics, no tableaux, no charades … no promenades, no rides nor drives … no nothing." Young couples, she continued, were operating without the help of mothers or grandmothers, "left to fashion a new social order," without much in the way of guidance.[5] Mary Hallock Foote described women in high society in Boise, Idaho, who "had ridiculous social pretentions and showed bad taste in their attempts to imitate what they conceived to be the latest Eastern fashions." They used the popular *Godey's Lady's Book* as their social Bible, Foote noted, and created extreme imitations of everything eastern and au courant for the upper class.[6] Women in western towns, especially with husbands who sought power, became involved in intricate Victorian social laws, with the right clothes needed for each engagement. Etiquette manuals like *Manners; or, Happy Homes and Good Society All the Year Round*, by Sarah Josepha Hale, long-time editor of *Godey's Lady's Book*, helped to script appropriate dress for each day's occasions: a morning dress for home, a plain dress for the street, something more ornate, with a bustle, for visiting, and gowns for evening wear.[7]

The creation of a social code also involved expectations for children. A popular etiquette book noted that "boys are expected to have more or less of the bear in their natures but girls are born and bred to modest and lady-like behavior, and a saucy, pert, and selfish girl is simply beyond endurance. A girl who is disrespectful to her mother or to her superior, can never acquire the charm of manner which throws all beauty, style, fine dressing and diamonds into shadow." Sewing was considered a necessity for girls, as indicative of "a kind and unselfish heart." Daughters also needed to learn to cook, clean, and nurse the ill as well as to adorn themselves appropriately for all occasions.[8]

The Rankins in Town

In 1885, with four children from ages one to four, the Rankins moved into all of the Victorian realities of a growing town. Missoula had a population, mostly male, of 400 in 1870, dwindling to 347 in 1880 but then building to 3,426 to 1890 and to 4,366 by 1900.[9] Various developments spurred slow but steady growth. Fort Missoula had been established in 1877, the construction done by John Rankin and other contractors to protect arriving settlers from local tribes. Growth continued with the arrival of the Northern Pacific Railway in 1883, with sawmills like John's furnishing timber for the tracks. The town was chartered the same year. Further growth occurred after Congressional approval of statehood for Montana in 1889. Then in 1893, Missoula became the site of the state's first university after civic leaders went to Helena to lobby for this location over another applicant, Great Falls. Opening with a president and four faculty members, primarily as a preparatory school, the university adopted a first optimistic slogan, "It Shall Prosper."[10]

Even with a university and population growth, in the first years of the Rankins' residency and for the next decades, Missoula was still a small town without cement or brick sidewalks, with streetcars pulled by mules and roads like trails. There were a few stone buildings, many of them built by John Rankin, standing alongside rickety wooden structures.[11] Building with the population was a small local elite, all coming from elsewhere, creating a highly gendered social structure, a life in which civic leaders and their families mimicked and exaggerated what had been developed in the east.

Established families, which in Missoula meant by a decade or less, sought to display their status for other residents, as in New York or Boston. In 1885, John Rankin bought land near the small downtown, by the river, and built a home at 134 Madison Street, a site that indicated the family's rising economic and social status, a Missoula version of a mansion on New York's Fifth Avenue. Shaped like a Maltese cross, the large stone house featured a Burmese-style cupula with a glassed-in walk around it, secured to the mansard roof. It was the first in town with hot and cold running water, central hot-air heating, and a bathroom with a zinc tub. Like other expensive homes of the era, the Rankin house was heavily decorated, with machine-made wallpapers, wainscoting, carpets and parquet floors, elaborate window dressings, and dark, rich color harmonies.[12]

The large hall where visitors entered contained a piano, placed to immediately impress the family's guests. Off this hall were two parlors in

The Rankin home in Missoula, 134 Madison Street, 1890 (Schlesinger Library, Radcliffe Institute, Harvard University).

the front, one for family and another larger one, "chilly, orderly, slightly musty," for social occasions. This formal parlor featured center tables; étagères with prized possessions such as small pieces of china; chairs for men and women, large ones with high backs and arms for men and smaller ones without arms for women to accommodate their skirts—all creating a "romantic, excessively ornamented and over-decorated" Victorian space. Such a parlor provided the site of formal social visits as well as "marriages, wakes, clergymen's calls, holy day and holiday celebrations."[13] A large formal dining room completed the front part of the house, with a long table and heavy sideboard displaying china, silver, and table linens. The downstairs also had a kitchen and large pantry. Upstairs were the bedrooms, with Wellington in a separate space and the girls sharing two rooms. The outside featured two small porches in front and a long side porch, later screened in for summer sleeping. Lilac bushes, Lombard poplars, elm trees, pines, apple trees, and a Virginia creeper filled the carefully landscaped Victorian lawn, the outside as well as the inside intended to create an autocratic impression.[14]

Urban Realities for John

With his family well situated in Missoula, John Rankin moved into a fuller version of Victorian business and politics to create the income needed to drive an upper-class city life. Though city bosses and the industries that they protected are generally regarded as an eastern phenomenon of the Gilded Age, a new capitalistic network thrived on a smaller scale in the west, engaging John as a prominent Missoulian.[15]

On the ranch, in this time of growth, John Rankin expanded his planing mill, which was often seen to "loom up like a light house in the fog," to create the products required for his own projects and for other builders.[16] Additionally, beginning in 1897, when his property swelled to 2000 acres with land purchased from the Northern Pacific Railway, he began advertising that ranchers with insufficient land for their cattle could keep their stock on his land for a fee, and he rented out small parcels, of ten to thirty acres, to farmers seeking access to land by the creek. Given all of this activity at Grant Creek, local newspapers noted when John Rankin came to the home on Madison Street for a "visit" with his family.[17]

In town, John continued work on his own construction projects as well as city contracts. In 1883, he put up a "commodious double residence" near Rattlesnake on Mount Jumbo, one that would "vastly improve" the east side of town.[18] In 1884, he built a large residence near downtown for Fred Kennett, president of the Western Montana Bank, and then began work on his own home. In 1891, he erected what he labeled as the Rankin Block, on East Front Street, a three-story brick building that housed shops and offices and a hotel of sixty-five rooms, the entire structure described in the newspaper as a "credit to the town." In local newspapers, John constantly advertised his hotel, the Rankin House, where Chef R.J. Kitching also did catering.[19] These ads, like one on Christmas Eve in 1897 in the *Missoulian*, claimed that the restaurant was "conducted on the European plan" with "no questionable characters allowed on the premise." Given the involvement of Kitching, the ads stated further, "nearly everyone visiting Missoula" patronized the restaurant, which offered "a good, solid and substantial meal, with the best of service for 25 cents."[20] In 1897, John Rankin sold the hotel and restaurant but maintained other retail businesses on his block; he also owned twenty houses and office structures for which he served as landlord.

As Rankin built his construction, ranching, retail, and mill businesses, he moved into leadership positions in Missoula, contributing to the town becoming a small city while increasing his influence and profits, in true Gilded Age style. In October 1878, he ran for county commissioner as a

Front Street, Missoula, looking west. In the foreground are the Missoula Steam Laundry and Rankin Hotel. A horse-drawn coach with a Rankin Hotel sign waits in front of the hotel building, ca. 1904–1906 (Morton Elrod Photographs, MSS 486, Archives & Special Collections, Mansfield Library, University of Montana).

Bicycle riders on Front Street, then a dirt road, in Missoula. The building on the left is the Rankin Hotel, ca. 1904–1906 (William A. Hoblitzell, MSS 489, Archives & Special Collections, Mansfield Library, University of Montana).

Republican, a position he held for one four-year term. In February 1890, when Missoula established a new board of trade, he began serving as one of its directors. On the board's agricultural committee, he worked on settling disputes about grazing and water rights, issues that often pitted farmers against ranchers and that mattered to him. He also created policies regarding the railroads and the shipping of local products, making decisions that helped his own businesses. He was asked in 1891 to serve as a candidate for mayor, an article about the election labeling him as "at once a prominent and public-spirited business man and a heavy taxpayer." But he was not interested in a fulltime administrative job, which would take him away from his business projects. In the fall of 1894, he again ran successfully for the county commission, not a fulltime position but a powerful one, which enabled him to become the county's purchasing agent.[21] From this position, he extended his ability to secure contracts for public buildings, bridges, and roads and to sell his lumber to other city and county builders. Using his connections in county government, John Rankin also became a bondsman in legal cases, another source of income.

John's mill day books and records from the Rankin Block, both in his handwriting, reveal the hard work in which he engaged year after year to succeed in a changing city environment. In May 1889, for example, he provided the lumber and workmen for the Higgins Block, the Schilling Block, and the Gibson Hospital. He also recorded the rents at seventeen commercial and home rental properties, including the building that housed the Missoula Water Company, while keeping records of wages paid to employees in town and at the mill. His handwriting in the Rankin Block register additionally shows that he rented sixty hotel rooms for a month or a few days, with charges also for phone calls and dining. At the same time, for the ranch, John dealt with the planting, reaping, and selling of wheat, rye, and hay while also growing potatoes and apples for sale and tending his cattle. He had his account books set up, predated through February 1906, all empty past his death in May 1904.[22]

All of this involvement as a rancher, farmer, landlord, builder, and politician became John Rankin's life, making him a visitor to his home, a busy Gilded Age businessman. Certainly he was successful but also increasingly owned by his choices, paying a personal price for the grinding level of involvement and risk that he took on daily. He described this form of Victorian self-entrapment to Jessie Rankin Wilson, his brother D.H.'s daughter, in 1893: "It seems to me that I have too many irons in the fire. I am swamped with work all the time and I have not time to call my life my own. There is no one that I can leave in charge to take care of anything. I get nearly wild some times."[23]

Urban Realities for Olive and Her Children

While John Rankin lived a frenetic business life, another full city existence occurred within the grand house on Madison Street, with Olive in charge of, and engulfed by, this site of "gendered Victorian expectations."[24]

Olive's town life involved childbirth and young children, with more help than on the ranch but still the constant work, worry, and risk that the home involved. The first-born group from the ranch was followed by three miscarriages. Olive then had three additional daughters: Mary, born in 1888; Grace, in 1890; and Edna, in 1893.[25] She had thus been pregnant ten times in thirteen years, when she was age twenty-seven to forty. In more comfortable conditions in town, certainly, Olive continued to deal with her growing family, as their primary and often only caregiver, coping with everyday issues as well as disaster.

Within this space Olive saw not just to the maintenance of children but to their education and membership in the new city upper-class. Both Olive and John wanted their children to go to school for the full year, as they had been unable to do as children, and proceed on to college, the first in the family, an ambitious goal at a time when only 6.4 percent of Americans graduated from high school and 1.9 percent from college.[26] Certainly the family's moving into town when Jeannette was five had to do not just with business and social life but with education: there would be no school on Grant Creek until 1897 when more residents and John's gift of the land led to a small school, now located at the Historical Museum at Fort Missoula. In an application for a job years later, Edna said that "a thorough and comprehensive education seemed to be one of the normal expectations of all of my family," and indeed it was.[27] While Olive and John had a lower-school education, all of their children went to college and secured additional training with which to launch careers. Grace and Mary ultimately decided on more traditional lives than their siblings, involving stable homes and husbands and children, but all the Rankin siblings used their education in their activism and careers.

While the children attended school in town, they learned Victorian social codes and gender roles from Olive at home. As the oldest child and the only boy, Jeannette and Wellington were considered the responsible two, but with different expectations made of each of them. As historian Cathy Luchetti has written, the "usual fate of an oldest daughter" was to become "secondary mother."[28] As the oldest girl, Jeannette had the responsibility, year after year, to help her mother with the younger ones. Wellington remembered her reading to them from the Bible in the evenings, her responsibilities expanding over time. She made her sisters' clothes from the age of thirteen, having started with dolls' clothes. She also took over much of the housekeeping. Wellington, called "The Boy" by his father, leaned to wrestle and box, and he was expected as a teen to take over managing household budgets and to help with repairs on the large home.[29] From the frontier onward, an oldest son mattered to a family, as the one who took over financial responsibility for the land and for the younger children at the father's death. "In the taciturn, Victorian sense," fathers were "often gruff, no nonsense men so old-fashioned they would never dream of calling a youth by his first name." Outdoorsman Jack O'Connor wrote about a similar childhood relationship with his father: "Simply to call a boy of my age by his first name seemed to him to be an obscene and exhibitionist show of sentimentality. Generally he simply called me 'boy.' In the years I knew him I can recall only a couple of tentative hugs and a few pats on the head. He seldom talked to me and never talked idly."[30] While John Rankin was proud of his son and sought the best of education for him, he was not remonstrative and his business and political life meant that he was not generally present, and thus Wellington lived much more in the sphere of his mother and sisters, with a particular role set for him there.

Besides raising the children and seeing to various forms of their education, Olive, as the upper-class Victorian wife in town, had entertaining and socializing as a part-time job, with the requirement of doing everything right, again and again. As Edna's biographer claimed, the Rankin children grew up in "a society seeking the refinements of civilization," the attempt to pattern life in the west by eastern rituals involving considerable labor from their mother.[31] In February 1901, as the newspaper reported, Olive was receiving at the residence on Tuesday and did her own required visiting tours on other days. That same month she hosted large receptions at home each week, the parlor filled with her husband's business associates and their wives. Her large dinner parties also mattered for John's success. At these formally scripted gatherings, Olive was responsible for a menu of several courses, with the best of linens, a highly decorated table, and additional delicacies on the sideboard. She also guided the conversation at the table, meant to be light and lively, not centered on money or religion.[32]

With one of the largest houses in town, the Rankins also took in boarders involved in John's activities, and they became an additional responsibility for Olive. In 1897, circus strong man S.J. McMillan came to town to perform at the Missoula Fair and then left his wife at the Rankin house. McMillan said he would send for her, but he didn't, and she stayed with the family for six weeks, "in a predicament," with no money to contribute to the household.[33]

Beyond so much social activity of the parents, and especially Olive, this fashionable whirl engaged the children as well. Unlike members of most Missoula families, the Rankin children secured social mention of seemingly every small achievement and involvement at school and at church. When Wellington was twelve, for example, in December 1896, he secured newspaper notice for singing in the Christmas pageant at the Presbyterian church.[34] In May 1897, he did a recitation at a school assembly, on curing a cold, another noteworthy moment of a leading small-town family.

At the same event, Harriet took part in an instrumental trio and read an essay on the American flag.[35] In August 1897, again reported in the newspaper as other race results were not, Wellington won a quarter-mile race representing his high school. At the June 1898 commencement exercises, when he graduated from high school at age fourteen, an article on the front page noted that "with great feeling he sang 'The Burial of Montrose,' from the lavish funeral held for a romantic hero of the English Restoration."[36]

Through the years, not just school and church but social engagements of the Rankin children were deemed worthy of report on the society page, the spotlight on fancy clothes and presents and stellar decorum. A definite society tone came into these accounts, even concerning the youngest of party goers: a fête that Jeannette attended as one of the ten-year-old guests was described as an "exceedingly recherché affair."[37] These events could feature special games and activities, well scripted to pass the time of the social elite. A large group of girls donned their summer dresses in July 1903 for a forest-guessing party, attended by Mary Rankin, for which the hosts wrote out questions about forest animals and plants, with correct answers tallied as the party progressed: "a great deal of fun as well mental effort" was augmented by "very delicate and delicious refreshments." In March 1902, Harriet and Jeannette went to Bonner with a friend for a masquerade party featuring costumes from history. In January and February of 1902, Harriet hosted and sang at progressive dinners, convening at several of the best houses.[38] With young adulthood came not just invitations to parties but membership in social organizations. The Quanoozeh Club, a secretly constituted organization of eleven young women, their number chosen in the fall of 1901 to repeat the number of men on the university's football team, picked Harriet as one of its members. At a New Year's Day reception in one member's "palatial home," a hostess "presided over the punch bowl in a graceful manner" and "the daintiest of refreshments were served."[39]

College graduation, and the details of college work, also brought special attention to the Rankin children. At the University of Montana, Wellington's successes were carefully noted. The local paper reported that he played on the basketball team in 1903 and secured a patent for a new style of slot machine, "which was a noted success." Some notices seem to forecast his future as a brilliant courtroom attorney. In November of 1902, he participated in a mock trial held by the Hawthorne Literary Society in front of a room full of spectators, successfully defending a man accused of abusing a horse. In December 1902, newspapers noted that Wellington had joined the debating committee of the oratorical society, making plans for the university to participate in intercollegiate debates. As one of four men chosen through preliminary contests, the others not discussed in the article, he debated whether the United States should continue to adhere to the

Monroe Doctrine and its concept of isolationism, which later would be of great importance to Jeannette. As the newspaper further reported, at graduation, Wellington read the class will, in which he bequeathed to younger students his art of bluffing, labeled as his stellar trait, and to the whole faculty the pleasure they would feel at the departure of this argumentative and cocky student.[40]

A City Life Altered

From 1885 forward, as Olive ran the house in town, tended the children, and engaged her family in a well-publicized social life, all of this etiquette, hard work, and responsibility began to change her. She was no longer the young woman who had crossed the country with her uncle, defied her sister about

Wellington Rankin in his cap and gown, graduating from the University of Montana, 1903 (Photographer W.D. Ball, Schlesinger Library, Radcliffe Institute, Harvard University).

returning east, taught eight grades, and established a household on a ranch and in town. Though she stayed connected with local schools and teachers, she began to withdraw, and ultimately she barely left the house. Wellington thought of her as isolated, even frightened: increasingly, he told an interviewer, people had to "come to her"; she became "shy at mingling with people"; she "never went any place herself much."[41] Certainly she was not the only woman on a frontier ranch and in a frontier town who became overwhelmed with housekeeping and social requirements and child care. Popular author Marion Harland noted that "I have seen so many women of brains wear out and die in harness, trying to do their self-imposed duty": and Olive, with so much to cope with, certainly seemed to wear out.[42]

With years of constant work, exhaustion also began to overtake John. At age sixty-three, after years in which his many careers separated him from his family and divided his attention, John began to divest himself of some of his businesses. In the fall of 1903, he stopped taking on new construction

Two. Victorian Social Classes and the End of the Wild West 37

projects in town and closed the saw mill. Then in April 1904, he rented his ranch lands and moved back to Missoula to the house on Madison Street.[43]

At that point John had only another month to live. On Wednesday, May 4, 1904, his death notice in the newspaper said that he had died the night before at home, with Jeannette and Olive by his side to nurse him. His illness—tick fever, now referred to as Rocky Mountain Spotted Fever—started while he was at Grant Creek a week earlier. It began with flulike symptoms and a dark red rash. When left untreated, as this disease certainly was at the time in Missoula, it can damage blood vessels throughout the body and can be fatal. Death can occur within eight days of the onset of symptoms, as it did in John's case.[44]

For John Rankin's funeral, the local newspaper called the procession "a mile long," with a hundred carriages involved. Concerning his death, the *Missoulian* declared that "another old pioneer has crossed the river," an "esteemed citizen." This man "of sterling worth and integrity" had an estate estimated at $150,000, 4.5 million dollars today. He left funds for the education of all the children, with Wellington responsible for his accounts and with a maintenance provided for the house and for Olive.[45]

The death of the father and an increasingly limited role for his widow changed what an oldest daughter and sole son could do and would need to do. After she graduated from the new state university in Missoula in 1902, Jeannette taught for less than a year at the school on her family's land at

Jeannette Rankin in the science lab at the University of Montana, writing in a tablet, 1901 (Morton J. Elrod, Archives & Special Collections, Mansfield Library, University of Montana).

Grant Creek, a respectable choice for an unmarried woman, but a taxing job that she did not enjoy. She next took a teaching job in Whitehall, 150 miles away near Butte, but came back to Missoula after her father's death to care for her sisters, Mary, then age 16; Grace, 14; and Edna, 11. As the mother became more withdrawn and "laissez faire," Jeannette felt forced to turn into a strict older sister—not a role she wanted. "She was the decision maker," Edna recalled, and her sisters found her "irritable and domineering" as well as "restless and unhappy."[46] Jeannette also worked at a dressmaker's shop and took a correspondence course in furniture design, seeking a long-term alternative to marriage, child care, or teaching. In her journal, during her senior year in college, she had urged herself to obtain something more: "Go! Go! Go! It makes no difference where, just so you go! go! go! Remember, at the first opportunity, go!," but, as the oldest daughter, she found that going difficult to achieve.[47]

Wellington was at Harvard when their father died. He just came home to attend the funeral and arrange for management of the family's properties. He was expected not to return to Montana to care for his sisters but instead to continue his studies and prepare for a career in law and politics. That he attained sole administration of the family estate seemed unfair to Jeannette, who was expected to remain in the home but not to control family finances.[48]

On the frontier, the prosperous family might

Jeannette Rankin, graduation portrait, University of Montana, 1902 (photographer Robert Morrison, Schlesinger Library, Radcliffe Institute, Harvard University).

enter into the veneer of city life, the building of a social class, redefining themselves, adapting quickly, as they helped to form a new western reality. In the western town, after voyaging across the country and attempting to succeed at gold mining, John Rankin became more and more immersed in a hectic and varied business career until he reached his sixties, taking on the risky enterprises of the Gilded Age landlord, ranch owner, builder, and politician. At the same time, Olive went from Grant Creek to a city home, dealing with birth and child rearing while forging an eastern social life with its required rules and publicity. In the last decades of the nineteenth century, Victorian codes held sway in western towns just as they did in New York and Boston, specifying patterns of home and work life. Inhabiting a Victorian space, for which a farm in New Hampshire and a ranch at Grant Creek provided little preparation, had a definite cost for Olive, just as a successful business life did for her husband. Victorian social conventions, not just imprinted on Fifth Avenue in New York City but on Madison Street in Missoula, shaped the lives of Olive and John and provided their children with a code against which to rebel.

THREE

The Risk of Illness and What Religion Could Do

In an era of building cities, of setting up a social whirl, Americans moved from the frontier and ranch into the complex spaces of Victorian life. While families like the Rankins took on a veneer of security in town, the reality involved not just constant work and social requirements but constant illness and accidents. Americans, especially in the west, coped with disease without adequate medical treatment. Physical ailments often went untreated, and so did the mental toil taken by hard work and danger. As they coped with the hazards involved in staying alive, many Americans, including the Rankins, relied on the ministrations of mothers but also turned to Spiritualism, Christian Science, and other metaphysical faiths. This history of illness and responses to it has been given less attention than the building of ranches and cities, but it is a key element of the nation's, and the Rankins', response to the physical and mental risk that was all too prevalent in their lives.

Medical Treatment in the West

Part of the story of the nineteenth and early twentieth centuries, less studied than the frontier or Victorianism, was the constant presence of death. In the Civil War, 620,000 American soldiers died; 6,642 in the Spanish-American and Philippine-American Wars; 116,516 in World War I.[1] Stark realities of death shadowed families beyond involvement in war. The total number of deaths per thousand people in 1900 was 17.2, versus 9.6 in 1950.[2] In the west, one fifth of those who came to the gold rush died within the first six months of cholera, scurvy, and tuberculosis, with murder and suicide also common. Through subsequent decades, pneumonia, tuberculosis, and gastrointestinal infections attacked westerners of all ages. Childhood diseases also came west along with families: diphtheria, whooping cough, measles, and scarlet fever. In 1900, 30 percent of all deaths were of children less than five years old. The incidence of illness decreased as mining communities turned into towns, but accidents and death still stalked the west.[3]

In addition to other common causes, Americans died from the flu in 1918 in terrifying numbers. By that fall, cities were gripped with fear: school was canceled; theaters and churches had been shuttered. In that October alone 195,000 Americans died, the deadliest month in American history. During the fifteen months that this pandemic lasted, 500 million people fell sick worldwide, and between 3 and 5 percent of the world's population died, including more than 675,000 Americans, among them 45,000 soldiers.[4] In Montana, with treatment of infection centered on tick fever and a youthful population susceptible to the flu, "influenza's swath was broad, swift, and devastating": more than 5000 white Montanans died.[5] Throughout the west, the flu also devastated Native Americans who had inadequate health care and whose statistics were never collected.

At the turn of the twentieth century in Missoula and other western towns, areas assailed by so many ailments, medical services were not much better than on rural ranches. In 1810, the United States had only 100 graduates of medical schools, many of which were little more than diploma mills. In 1852, the new American Medical Association set standards that would at first be aspirational: the association sought for doctors to have at least a sixteen-week course of instruction that included anatomy, chemistry, midwifery, and surgery. The Johns Hopkins University School of Medicine, which opened in 1893, became the first medical school in America of a "genuine university-type."[6] Most doctors had much less training than Johns Hopkins offered. The lack of education caused especially the far west to be "fertile for quackery to flourish."[7] As Robert F. Karolevitz wrote concerning this medical care, "There was a time in America's Old West when becoming a doctor required little more than the inclination."[8] Montana passed a Medical Practices Act in 1889 to insure that doctors had proper credentials, but this act did not immediately lead to the presence of well-educated professionals.

In doctors' offices and hospitals, health care was virtually unregulated. The few hospitals provided minimal therapeutic care. Even though physicians generally had the best of intentions, they could do little to treat most illnesses.[9] Physicians employed dangerous medical procedures from earlier centuries, such as bloodletting and powerful purgatives. For cholera, the accepted remedy of calomel increased bowel action but was not curative; for diphtheria, there was only burning lime. That scurvy could be cured with vitamin C was not generally known.[10] Many doctors questioned germ theory and sanitation requirements, and so they might not even wash their hands as they offered their "cures." With little confidence in what might be gained from physicians, Americans often relied on nostrums from traveling medicine shows or newspaper ads, which might contain opium, morphine, and cocaine or little more than alcohol.[11]

As in many towns, the hospitals where doctors worked in Missoula lacked basic equipment and qualified personnel. In 1873, Mother Caron, Superior General of the Sisters of Providence, traveled to Missoula with other nuns to start a hospital and a school, beginning with five hundred dollars raised from begging tours. St. Patrick's, known locally as the sisters' hospital, began with a small frame building containing two examining rooms and a small ward.[12] In 1889, a new three-story hospital increased patient capacity, but the facility engaged just a few doctors, with minimal training.

Women, Like Olive Rankin, to Tend the Sick

In a period in which doctors and hospitals could offer few cures, daily health and critical care often fell to mothers. From the time that the Rankins moved to Missoula, Olive coped with illness almost every day, with little professional assistance: tending ill children involved her effort much more than John's. Like other women on ranches and in town, she processed herbs for medicines, relying on household booklets to help her deal with jaundice, thrush, mumps, measles, scarlet fever, whooping cough, and chicken pox.[13] When scarlet fever, a leading cause of death in children in the early twentieth century, with a 25 percent morbidity rate, hit Grace, Mary, and Edna, the city health officer quarantined the house on Madison Street. Olive, and not John, remained inside to tend their daughters, waiting to see whether the children would be strong enough to survive since no treatment was available. All she had to help them was herbal remedies that might ease the pain from the red rash.[14]

And during these many years of child rearing, the worst of untreated illness occurred: Philena died in November 1890, of an apparent ruptured appendix, at age nine. In cities, beginning in 1886, the death rate from appendicitis had begun to fall. But while successful diagnosis and treatment occurred in Boston and New York, in small towns like Missoula treatment still involved laxatives—a serious, sometimes fatal, mistake. Without adequate treatment, Philena, as newspaper articles reported, developed peritonitis, inflammation of the lining of the abdomen, and was ill for some time before she died, suffering from severe pain, fever, and weight loss. On December 3, 1890, the *Missoula Weekly Gazette* reported the largest procession in the city ever for the burial of a child, a demonstration of the esteem granted to her family. Her death devastated her mother.[15]

Three. The Risk of Illness and What Religion Could Do

Formal portrait of the Rankin Family. From left to right in the back row: John, Jeannette, Harriet, Wellington, and Olive. From left to right in the front row,: Mary, Edna and Grace. A portrait in the frame is of Philena, who had died of appendicitis in 1890, the picture allowing her to thus remain, at least in the portrait, as a member of the family, ca. 1897 (Montana Historical Society Research Center, Archives).

Along with illness, Olive contended with the risk from accidents occurring in a rough western town. In 1884, leaders at a political meeting fired an old cannon with ammunition lodged in a gunny sack. When John came around the corner, this wad knocked him unconscious, and he remained so for ten days. The accident permanently altered his hearing as well as the vision in his right eye, with Olive there to tend him as he recuperated.[16] In 1895, Wellington, at age eleven, lay unconscious for many hours after he was struck by lengths of cordwood thrown down from a wagon. When he awoke, he had what the newspaper labeled as "brain fever," a general diagnosis of the era that didn't relate to any form of treatment. Wellington did not recognize family members for some days, and he had to learn to walk and talk again. In the *Missoulian*, notices concerning his condition claimed that Olive stayed by his side while he was "still delirious much of the time."[17]

Illnesses and accidents also afflicted men at work, with little help available beyond their wives' ministrations. In September 1883, John Rankin "severely lacerated" all the fingers of his left hand while operating the planer.[18] In April 1885, a young worker, J.M. Betts, became "entangled in the machinery" of the mill. He broke the bones of his left arm, and his thigh bone protruded through his flesh. Even though doctors came out from town to give assistance, accompanied by Olive who provided nursing care, Betts died the next morning.[19]

When John Rankin became ill in 1904, the family dealt with another ailment with no hope of cure. In 1900, the tick fever that John Rankin died from, common in the Bitterroot Valley, had a mortality rate of 80 to 90 percent. It would be years before scientists recognized that this disease, also known as black measles, had the tick as its carrier but a bacterium as its source. Physicians tried all manner of poultices on John Rankin while his wife and eldest daughter nursed him, all to no avail.[20]

Metaphysical Faith and the Failure of Medicine

After John Rankin died within a week of contracting tick fever, Wellington became the next victim of illness when he returned to school: he found himself dealing with another poorly treated ailment of the time, crippling depression, and needing help.[21] During what he later described as a nervous breakdown, he felt extreme anxiety and fear, suffered from chest pains and labored breathing, and found himself unable to function. For Wellington, it had been difficult to be at Harvard even before his father died. He was a westerner, an outsider. Into the twentieth century, as noted in *Harvard Observed*, there remained the image of the "nineteenth-century type of leisure-type gentleman," the snobbish, eastern society effete known for torturing studious grinds and other forms of outsiders. The *Harvard Alumni Bulletin* depicted him, fondly, in a first-person narrative: "I am a snob. The rule here is snub or get snubbed. The old bromide about 'When in Rome' is good dope. Lonesome? I would be, though, if I insisted on acting like a human being."[22]

From his first year in Cambridge, Wellington found solace and healing through the ministrations of his roommate. Ellis Sedman, from Virginia City, Montana, was four years older than Wellington, the brother of the man that Harriet married. His closeness to Wellington stemmed from similarities that involved more than a home state. Ellis' father, Oscar Sedman, was an immigrant, miner, and landowner, like John Rankin. Oscar died of tick fever, but at a much younger age than John Rankin, at forty-three, when he was serving as a state legislator in Helena.[23] His fourth child, Ellis, was born a few months after he died.

After beginning college at the University of Montana where he was a Grizzly football star, Ellis went to Harvard and a dorm room shared with Wellington. After graduation, influenced by Mary Baker Eddy, Ellis remained in Boston, as a Christian Science practitioner and lecturer. In the 1940s, he moved to Los Angeles to continue serving as a practitioner and as a church administrator, at that city's First Church of Christ, Scientist.

When Wellington became ill, Jeannette embraced the opportunity to leave home and go nurse him, extending the traditional role of helpful sister and daughter, but in an exciting new venue, away from home. Accompanied by her friend Jimmie Rittenour, she turned this helping visit into several months. Jimmie and Jeannette went with Wellington to Theodore Roosevelt's inaugural ball in March 1905, their tickets arranged by Montana congressman Joseph Dixon, who had known John Rankin. Speaking with politicians at this event as well as seeing how various classes lived and worked in urban settings extended Jeannette's education, this experience ending when she had to return home to help with raising the two youngest girls.

While this visit proved a positive hiatus for Jeannette, ministrations of a kindly and well-meaning sister would not be enough to enable Wellington to heal. Though doctors had few tools with which to cope with physical ailments, treatment of mental illness was less advanced. "Madness," "lunacy," and "insanity" were accepted medical usage for extreme cases in the early 1900s, with depression being something a man should power through—certainly to avoid the diagnosis of hysteria common for women. Generally, mental institutions offered not treatment but segregation of inmates from society. Journalist Nellie Bly documented a threatening atmosphere when she entered Blackwell Island Insane Asylum in New York in 1887. Female patients told her that they had been beaten by guards, tied up, and held down in bathtubs of cold water, all to reduce their rebellious tendencies.[24]

In Boston as elsewhere, very little real help was available. The Boston Lunatic Hospital had been established as a municipal agency in 1839 and renamed the Boston Insane Hospital in 1897. This institution became responsible for all the state's mentally ill in 1904. The "cures" offered there included injections of malaria and arsenic delivered along with "a good dose of moral condemnation."[25] Though Wellington certainly did not choose to enter this hospital, he also rejected the new talk therapy. In Boston, psychiatrists felt the all-powerful influence of Freud, who had published *The Interpretation of Dreams* in 1899 and *The Psychopathology of Everyday Life* in 1901. Freud's methods led to a newly popular and slow form of cure: "the best way to relieve your symptoms was to unearth the hidden psychic conflicts generating your pathological behavior." In this regimen, the emphasis on dreams could overwhelm concern for everything else: "If you refused to talk about your dreams—if, instead, you wanted to talk about what could be done to prevent you from committing suicide if your depression took hold again—the psychoanalyst would interpret this desire to switch topics as 'resistance' that needed to be worked through."[26]

With little other effective help, Ellis offered Wellington a discipline of prayer and faith, a means of coping with Harvard and with his father's death. Instead of turning to the Presbyterian church of his childhood or to the healthcare industry, Wellington found solace in metaphysical faith, and especially Christian Science.

The metaphysical approach to healing began in Spiritualism, which reached its peak growth in membership from the 1850s to 1900. By 1897, this faith had more than eight million adherents in the United States and Europe, mostly drawn from the middle and upper classes. Spiritualism flourished for a half century without canonical texts or formal organization, recruiting followers through periodicals, camp meetings, and the missionary activities of accomplished mediums. Focused on eternal connections, this positive religion provided an antidote to the hellfire and damnation expounded upon from Protestant pulpits, and, during and after the Civil War and through the losses of World War I, it was a means of coping with so much death.

Spiritualism is based on the belief that spirits of the dead exist, they seek to communicate with the living, and they are capable of providing knowledge about ethical issues, the nature of God, and the true sources of illness and despair. This religion may have begun in 1848 with the Fox sisters, Kate, then twelve, and Margaret, fifteen, in Hydesville, New York. The family became frightened by unexplained sounds like knocking or moving furniture. Thirty years later, Margaret told the actual story of these mysterious "rappings" that ultimately gained attention not just from her family but from the nation: "When we went to bed at night, we used to tie an apple to a string and move the string up and down, causing the apple to bump on the floor, or we would drop the apple on the floor, making a strange noise every time it would rebound. Mother listened to this for a time. She would not understand it and did not suspect us as being capable of a trick because we were so young."[27] For family and neighbors, the sisters claimed to be communicating with spirits, and they quickly developed a code, by which raps could signify yes or no, in response to a question, or could indicate letters of the alphabet. With an older sister taking charge of their careers, Kate and Margaret enjoyed success as mediums for many years, staging séances for hundreds of people in which they delivered detailed "messages" from the dead.[28]

As more mediums began to seek followers, some maintained that their communications with the all-knowing dead allowed them to forecast and combat illness, this claim's attraction stemming from the questionable efficacy of the era's doctors and hospitals. Victoria Woodhull and her sister Tennessee (Tennie) Claflin, who went on to become infamous stock brokers, suffragists, and politicians, spent their childhoods involved in the worst of such manipulations. Buck Claflin, a "one-eyed snake oil salesman," marketed his beautiful daughters as mediums, able to cure ailments by speaking with ghosts. After her older sister left, Tennie spent long days in small towns across the Midwest selling hands-on spiritual cures along with Miss Tennessee's Magnetio Life Elixir. In a more dangerous iteration of this health scam, in Ottawa, Illinois, Buck set up an infirmary in an old hotel, claiming to cure cancers and other serious diseases through Tennie's sessions with the dead.[29]

Such mediums gained adherents in Boston in the decades before Wellington's arrival at Harvard. Helen and Gertrude Berry presented themselves as professional mediums, manipulating physical objects as proof of the presence of the dead. In a darkened room filled with their customers, they magically drained glasses, rang bells in each corner, and played floating autophones while out of wooden cabinets arose men in black, children who represented dead infants from the clients' families, and Asian dancers. After these spectacular healing sessions, the sisters' manager, George Albro, sold expensive sheets supposedly filled with electrical currents, with the power to cure any lingering illness. In Boston, believers in the Berrys and other spiritualists built the First Spiritual Temple on the corner of Exeter and Newbury Streets, a huge and imposing structure, one of the few churches of the spiritualist faith.[30]

Even Harvard skeptics found some Boston mediums credible. Psychologist and philosopher William James thoroughly investigated medium Leonora Piper, who had come from New Hampshire to Boston, and deemed her credible. After meeting with her, James concluded that Piper knew facts about family histories that she could only have discovered by supernatural means, as he wrote: "I am persuaded of the medium's honesty, and of the genuineness of her trance; and although at first disposed to think that the 'hits' she made were either lucky coincidences, or the result of knowledge on her part of who the sitter was and of his or her family affairs, I now believe her to be in possession of a power as yet unexplained."[31] Through the Metaphysical Club at Harvard, Wellington and Ellis learned about various judgments of these mediums and then went to visit the Spiritual Temple. While they concluded that many healers were frauds, they experienced the appeal of a personal, nurturing connection with the eternal, a bond and a chance for healing that medical professionals didn't seem to offer, and indeed had not offered their fathers, Wellington's sister Philena, or Wellington himself.

The Appeal of Christian Science

Wellington and Ellis ultimately rejected the faith of these spiritualists, but, like hundreds of thousands of Americans, beginning in Boston, they achieved a close association with divine power through Christian Science.[32] Mary Baker Eddy began establishing this religion first by separating her faith from Spiritualism although her beliefs and practices belonged to the same metaphysical movement. Like Leonora Piper and Olive Rankin, Eddy was born on a farm in New Hampshire, into a family of Protestant Congregationalists. From childhood she endured ill health, complaining of chronic indigestion, spinal inflammation, and fainting spells. Eddy also suffered the ill effects of four deaths in the 1840s, of her brother and her mother, of her first husband and a later suitor, with ailments like her husband's yellow fever beyond the scope of medical care.

In 1862, Eddy became a patient of Phineas Quimby, a spiritualist healer from Maine. Originally, Eddy credited Quimby's hypnotic treatments with easing her mental and physical conditions. But, after falling on ice soon after his death and healing herself with help from the Bible, she began to establish her own ministry and to offer her own healing services while asserting the difference between her religion and Quimby's. Chapter Four of Eddy's *Science and Health* from 1875, titled "Christian Science versus Spiritualism," recognized that both faiths stressed the impact of the eternal on the daily and mundane. But, she continued, her version of the metaphysical did not involve direct intercession by the dead.[33] Instead, Eddy argued that the living person could access the spiritual realm without endeavoring to commune with any individual. Her theology maintained that the immortal is the only reality and entirely good, and that the material world, with its evil, sickness, and death, is an illusion. She viewed disease as a mental error rather than a physical disorder, a misalignment with the universe. The "sick" should thus be treated not by medicine, but by prayer that corrects the mistaken beliefs responsible for the illusion of ill health. This connection to the eternal could be fostered by believers—without the sanction of doctors or hospitals. Christian Science healing is thus "not curative … on its own premises, but rather preventative of ill health, accident and misfortune, since it claims to lead to a state of consciousness where these things do not exist. What heals is the realization that there is nothing really to heal." Wellness, in this faith, "isn't so much something we access or acquire, as something we uncover."[34]

Three. The Risk of Illness and What Religion Could Do

In this faith, the role of the practitioner might be viewed as friend, helper, or persuader. As one practitioner described it, the relationship with the patient moves from getting together to read scripture and *Science and Health* to "taking away the sins of worldliness and opening the portals of spiritual life."[35] Training for practitioners first occurred at Eddy's Massachusetts Metaphysical College, which closed in 1889. A Board of Education then took over its mission and began offering a three-week course that, along with monitored practice, led to a practitioner's official listing with the church. A key to Christian Science's appeal at the time was the favorable success rate of these practitioners in comparison with physicians and hospitals.[36]

Eddy and twenty-six followers received a state charter in 1879 to found the Church of Christ, Scientist, in Boston, the large structure finally completed in 1894, as the Mother Church. By the end of 1886 Christian Science teaching institutes had sprung up around the country, and it was the nation's fastest growing religion. In 1906, the federal religious census recorded 85,717 Christian Scientists; thirty years later, the number was 268,915. In 1890 there were seven Christian Science churches in the United States, a figure that rose to 1,104 by 1910.[37]

The more conservative of the Protestant clergy, faced with this quick growth, viewed "Eddyism" as a cult, just as dangerous as the most deceptive forms of Spiritualism. Many Protestant sermons claimed that it was not scientific and certainly not Christian.[38] Religious leaders labeled the decision of this flawed woman to form a religion as the worst sort of hubris. They were not the only ones with a strong response. Even though he was interested in mental healing, Mark Twain labeled Eddy, in a book about Christian Science, as "grasping, sordid, penurious, famishing for everything she sees—money, power, glory."

What Twain saw as a weakness of this faith, an indication that Christian Science was truly not Christian, served as an attraction for many adherents. He maintained that Eddy "has delivered to them a religion which has revolutionized their lives, banished the glooms that shadowed them, and filled them and flooded them with sunshine and gladness and peace; a religion which has no hell." Though Twain denigrated this faith as a false promise, even in his criticism he noted the appeal of a positive connection to the eternal.[39]

Christian Science and its approach to healing drew in Wellington after the death of his father. Though Spiritualism seemed outlandish to him, Ellis offered something simple, involving practitioners like himself, westerners as well as easterners, with more power to help others than medical institutions had, an extension of individual codes that Wellington knew from Montana. Their speaking together about loss and sadness, along with reading from *Science and Health,* began as a natural extension of the closeness of roommates. With Ellis, Wellington established a habit that remained with him throughout his life, of meeting with healers, discussing all that mattered to him, and learning about the true sources of physical and emotional pain and how to move away from them.

In 1905 Wellington received his BA from Harvard. He then went abroad for a year to study philosophy and literature at Oxford and travel to other sites in Europe. In England, Christian Science had become a "society craze," attracting wide-ranging comment in the popular press as a controversial new choice.[40] Wellington easily found healers to meet with there, and he had the funds to pay them. Then he went back to Harvard to study law, enriching Ellis' healing methodology with what he had learned from practitioners abroad.

After he returned to Montana, Wellington did not become a churchgoer; Helena did not have a Christian Science church until 1917. But even after there were churches and reading rooms in Missoula and Helena, he rarely went there or consulted local healers; he may have felt that this public involvement would be negative for his legal and political career in the state. Instead he gave regularly to the national church organization as well as directly to Ellis Sedman and other practitioners. He spoke frequently, for example, with Maria Soubier of Chicago, who wrote for the *Christian Science Sentinel* and gave radio addresses about God's "abundant provision" that combined with "right thinking" could eliminate pain.[41] Wellington also turned to practitioner Paul Stark Seeley, of Portland, Oregon, a leading figure in the church for more than half a century, who had gone to law school with him. Through the years with these practitioners, with whom he regularly communicated in letters and on the telephone, Wellington prayed for his law business and ranches, for his sisters, and for his own mental and physical health. He increasingly recognized, through personal injury cases, how overwhelming loss could be, damaging the lives of his clients even if they succeeded in court. "Right thinking" helped him deal with their pain as well as his own.

A Family's Response to Christian Science

When Wellington returned from Harvard, his religious commitment impressed his mother who had dealt with the loss of her husband and daughter and had begun to withdraw. She joined the Christian Science church in Missoula and frequented its reading room, and she met with practitioners in her own home. Unlike Wellington, his mother preferred to speak with local church leaders from her own social group, especially

Three. The Risk of Illness and What Religion Could Do   51

Ruth Greenough, who created a home Bible for family reading sold by Harper and Brothers, and her sister Edith Greenough, a practitioner who performed rites like funerals and weddings for the church over several decades. These sisters had been friends of the Rankin daughters, part of the social whirl in the Rankin home.[42] In 1902 their father, Thomas Greenough, had given land to create a city park. When Olive came to believe that she had a breast cancer forming, she went to these sisters and decided that they cured her by helping her to move beyond the physical world. As two of Jeannette's biographers claimed, Olive became the "mother superior of the family" in regards to this religion, which offered her more solace than the Congregationalist faith of her childhood or the Presbyterian faith of her married life.[43]

This commitment soon also involved Wellington's siblings. Their brother and mother influencing them, Harriet, Mary, and Edna joined the church, and Christian Science became a key part of their lives.

Harriet's husband, Oscar Sedman, died in Cochise, Arizona, in October 1917, of lobar pneumonia, which he contracted in the mines from gases containing nitric oxide. Before he died, he was sick for five months with emphysema, doctors unable to cure him. What Wellington and Harriet's brother-in-law Ellis Sedman told her about the efficacy of Christian Science as well as her experience with doctors during her husband's illness made her into an adherent. Harriet met with the Greenough sisters when she returned to her mother's home in Missoula after her husband's death. When Harriet went on to Washington at the end of 1917, the capital housed practitioners from all over the country, there to work with soldiers and government employees, and Harriet made connections with several of them as she coped with the death of her husband and supported her two daughters. After she returned to Missoula and later in London, she continued to meet with local practitioners to deal with both mental and physical difficulties.

Like Wellington and Harriet and their mother, Edna also relied on healers during all the hectic travel that she undertook as she worked for birth control rights. When her marriage ended in divorce, she went to see a psychiatrist in New York, in what Wellington judged to be a waste of time even though he was willing to pay for the sessions, for him another snobbish part of eastern society that Edna became involved in through her marriage.[44] He encouraged her instead to rely on Christian Science practitioners, which she began to do after moving to Washington, D.C.

As part of a long association with this faith, Edna met with a healer and missionary, Adele Blok, for help in Jakarta when she was exhausted from her travel and meetings. Edna found Blok's story inspirational, an indicator of the power of Christian Science. Blok, from Holland, had been living in Indonesia when World War II began. She was imprisoned by military police and interrogated by the Japanese, put into conditions that made her feel she would go insane. "I was crowded into a tiny cell with seven other women," Blok wrote in a testimony statement that became a key Christian Science document. "Vermin crawling over everything, I came close to the mental breaking point, going through all the stages of despair, revulsion, self-pity, with one argument repeating itself: Give in." But she found solace in *Science and Health*, through which she began "to open the door of my thought to the understanding of the Christ." When Edna later knew Blok as a prominent practitioner, this story of devotion and curing helped to sustain her as she stood up to local authorities concerning women's health and freedom of choice.[45]

As Edna traveled the globe, she continued to meet with practitioners to cope with problems both small and large. In India, Edna had a detached retina and permanently lost the sight in her left eye. When she first suffered flashes of light and blurred vision, she asked Wellington to pray and to envision her as well. "It will help if you can see me as young, vigorous and without physical handicap," she told him, a means of reconnecting to the image of herself created by God. She also sought out practitioners in India to help her as she adjusted to the change in her vision.[46]

Through the decades, these siblings wrote back and forth about their religious commitment. Mary told Wellington about the deep satisfaction that Christian Science instruction gave her and about the healing help it had provided to her husband, who suffered from crippling arthritis. Edna wrote to her siblings, about how a practitioner had saved her life: "When I returned from Bali, I lost my voice and even the ability to breathe to the point that I thought I was passing on. She worked steadily until 3 a.m.... [The] next morning I was well." Edna told Mary that having a roommate when she traveled did not interfere with her commitment to Christian Science: "I usually read my lesson in the bathroom sometime during the night. I wonder sometimes just how I could cope ... if it were not for my daily study of the lesson.... What a blessing we have." Edna realized that her biographer Wilma Dykeman didn't want to consider this part of her life—as she wrote to Dykeman, "You have carefully refrained from indicating my most consuming interest and concern and study—My Religion." But she did have the support of her siblings concerning this key element of her health and well-being.

Just as other Americans had strong opinions, positive and negative, about this form of curative religion, so did members of the Rankin family. While their mother and siblings relied on Christian Science, religion was not a priority for Jeannette or Grace. Jeannette opposed Christianity, did not believe in God or an afterlife; she judged such faith as a means of escaping responsibility for behavior in the here and now. She stayed with missionaries when she traveled and spoke at church services about the anti-war movement, but she believed that Christianity had repeatedly been used to defend and glorify war and thus she could not endorse any version of it. She used the hymn title "Onward Christian Soldiers" to claim that "forward into battle" was indeed a Christian tradition and all too often citizens could "see His banners go" when war could have been avoided. She referred to Christians as "christers," and did not want, as she said, any goddamn Christian words spoken at her grave. And, especially to Christian Science, she had "a visceral, bitterly negative reaction" since she viewed this approach to healing as a hoax.[47]

Edna and Olive tried more than once to convert Jeannette as she contended with pain that doctors could not cure, just as they could not fix John Rankin's tick fever, Philena Rankin's appendicitis, or Oscar Sedman's pneumonia. Jeannette suffered through the decades with tic douloureux or trigeminal neuralgia, a condition that was intermittently severe. This disorder, involving a nerve that supplies sensation to the face, created a stabbing pain on her right cheek and her forehead. The pain usually lasted from a few seconds to a few minutes, the level of it worsened by stress. It could be so intense that she winced involuntarily, hence the term "tic." When Jeannette was in severe pain in Jakarta, Edna begged her to meet with Adele Blok, but Jeannette wouldn't go.[48]

What Jeannette relied on instead of Christian Science practitioners were prescription drugs of the era, which she seems to have abused, needing more over time. In July 1917, she wrote to Dr. Sample in Saginaw, Michigan, reminding him that he had helped her by prescribing a "little black pill," presumably morphine, when she was sick in a hotel, there working for suffrage in 1913. Four years later, she told him that she did not want to live without these pills, but she was having trouble getting access to them in Washington. While in previous decades opiates had been sold in "an unregulated medical marketplace," with physicians prescribing them for a wide range of ailments, the Harrison Narcotics Tax Act of 1914 had led to their regulation. By 1917, New York and Washington had placed restrictions on repeated use while other areas enforced the law more slowly.[49] In 1917, Dr. Sample again helped Jeannette, and he did so perhaps repeatedly while Michigan delayed compliance with the new restrictions. In September of 1917, she wrote to the Weeks Drug Store in Saginaw to get the drug renewed, 300 pills for two dollars.[50] Through the years, she kept relying on morphine and other pain killers, going to different doctors and pharmacies, trying to avoid the surgery that she deemed would end her career: having the cranial nerve removed, the only treatment then available, left the face disfigured. After suffering with this illness to age eighty-nine, Jeannette finally did have her right cranial nerve removed, which eliminated the pain but left her with a sagging face. She did not, however, turn to Christian Science for help.

Depictions of the frontier and of early western town life often dwell on the risks created by Indian attack, mining and cattle ranching, and severe weather. But another reality of life was the constant presence of illness, before the development of penicillin or other basic drugs, when doctors and hospitals and mental asylums were beginning to have a national presence but lacked effective cures. This attraction to a metaphysical alternative would soon lessen. By the first decades of the twentieth century, accusations of fraud had weakened the credibility of the spiritualist movement. After World War II, the increased efficacy of medicine heralded a decline in the popularity of Christian Science. Cases that secured the label of child abuse also damaged the reputation of this faith. Between 1980 and 1990, concerning decisions made regarding their children's health, seven Christian Science parents in the United States were prosecuted on charges ranging from murder and manslaughter to neglect.[51] In a fractious period for the church, the number of members in the United States fell from 106,000 in 1990 to under 50,000 in 2009. Although their popularity would not continue, for many decades Spiritualism and Christian Science attracted Americans like the Rankins, turning them toward the eternal as life seemed challenging and risky and often beyond bearing, with few other forms of healing available. These religious choices created a means of dealing with what might otherwise have been impossible to withstand.

Four

Progressivism and American Politics

Olive and John left their families' farms in the east, journeyed to the wilderness, and embraced new and often harsh realities. They had seven children and raised them while meeting the challenges of the frontier, the ranch, and the western city. With so many types of risk undertaken, these parents and their children persisted in a dangerous world, finding their own purposes and means of security.

Jeannette and Wellington would make different choices than their parents. Neither had children or entered the social and business life in Missoula for which they had been prepared. In young adulthood, while dealing with their own health issues and uncertainties, they took on new forms of risk, with variations by gender, not as early pioneers or as Victorian city builders but as reformers in the Progressive Era.

The purposes and impact of the progressive movement are still under evaluation. With its ultimate significance up for debate, historian Alonzo L. Hamby asks, "What were the central themes that emerged from the cacophony? Democracy or elitism? Social justice or social control? Small entrepreneurship or concentrated capitalism?"[1] Whatever the answers to these complex questions, with contrasting viewpoints asserted then and afterwards, progressivism was certainly a major emphasis of the beginning of the twentieth century.

In response to a developing America, with less frontier, growing cities, and more immigrants arriving each month, progressives argued that the escalating problems—poverty, violence, greed, racism, class divides—could best be addressed not by trusting in the munificence of a few entrepreneurs, factory owners, or city bosses but by a government providing good education, safe neighborhoods, and equitable workplaces for all Americans. Progressivism is thought of as a city response to an industrializing America of factories and slums, with social reformers, like Jane Addams in Chicago, attempting to improve housing and education while exposing corporate greed. Activists encouraged Americans to register to vote, choose honest representatives, and fight all manner of corruption. Especially at the local level, this movement involved clubs and other organizations through which women could improve their communities, creating a natural and acceptable extension of their role of housekeepers and nurturers.[2]

This belief in the government's role in establishing a better democracy could lead to destructive extremes. As they worked for reforms, progressives often ignored the rights of those minorities deemed less worthy. Many suffragists, for example, argued that white southerners could keep African American women from voting by continuing to enforce Jim Crow laws: white women could more than counteract any increase in minority votes. "White supremacy," Carrie Chapman Catt declared as she worked for the vote in Mississippi and South Carolina, "will be strengthened, not weakened, by women's suffrage."[3] In an attempt to create an America led by the best, some progressives endorsed involuntary sterilization, as a eugenic solution to excessively large or under-performing families. Progressives also advocated for restrictions on immigration to control the entrance of undesirables, another scientific means of ensuring the best America.[4]

While the Progressive Era has generally been studied in its relationship to the east, to big cities and factory towns, the rural west also provided a prime space for this movement, in Montana because of the power of railroads and mining, industries that at the beginning of the twentieth century came close to owning the state.

For both Jeannette and Wellington as young adults, progressivism in Montana and beyond created a space to make a name for themselves, just as frontier ranching and construction had done for their father. This movement provided a platform for their ambitions, for their risk taking, and they often worked together to achieve their goals. Of his oldest sister, Wellington once told an interviewer that "I was the closest person to her in the world."[5] And Jeannette relied on his support throughout her adulthood even though she often made decisions with which he didn't agree.

In the Progressive Era, Jeannette moved beyond family requirements in Missoula to a state and national campaign for suffrage and elected office. And Wellington opposed large corporations and local governments in court, also speaking for the disenfranchised, while building his own reputation and land holdings. Both siblings thus participated in the complexities and contradictions and risks of American progressivism—in its western and eastern, rural and urban varieties.

Two Siblings Starting Out as Progressives

Wellington received preparation for progressive courtroom battles at Harvard Law School. Christopher Columbus Langdell, Harvard's dean from 1870 to 1895, introduced the case system, with professors calling on students to explain the legal reasoning behind specific decisions; what became an influential teaching style provided fine preparation for Wellington. After three years, only half of his class graduated, but Wellington certainly did. His appearance and delivery, deemed "whiz like," often became the focus of class questioning and moot-court cases: he had thought about becoming an actor during college but found an outlet for his dramatic skills in the law.[6]

In 1909, Wellington came home from Cambridge and began practicing law in Helena at the firm of Nolan and Walsh. The partners Colonel C.B. Nolan and Thomas J. Walsh, both political powers in the state, hired the young lawyer because of his Harvard degree, his considerable skill level, and his membership in an established Montana family. Within a year, Wellington opened his own firm buoyed by his growing reputation as one the state's best litigators. As "an individual driven by the need for prestige and power," he was more comfortable working for himself.[7]

While Wellington pursued a steady course that led to power, his equally intelligent and ambitious sister had a harder path to finding a meaningful future in the Progressive Era, beyond the confines of teaching and sewing and tending children, indeed beyond the world of her mother. After college, Jeannette taught in Montana, worked as a tailor, and helped her mother at home with the younger children, none of this particularly fulfilling to her though it was an appropriate precursor to marriage and a family, as helping Billy Berry and teaching in Missoula had been for her mother. But such a future would not be what Jeannette sought. In the Progressive Era, in which women extended the traditional respect for housekeeping to create their own role in society, a combination of the old and new, Jeannette sought not a social life and marriage in Missoula but meaningful and risky work, buoyed by money increasingly earned by Wellington. As a biographer commented, Jeannette "had no patience for charming the male ego," and she sought not a life like her mother's but an entirely different future.[8]

In 1908, with the younger children needing less help, when Edna, the youngest, was fifteen, Jeannette went to Manhattan to study at the New York School of Philanthropy, where suffragist Alice Paul had enrolled in 1905, both women considering charity commitments as a possible life's work. This school had been established in 1898 as a six-week summer program and had expanded to a full-year program in 1904. It was the first higher-education program in the theory and practice of philanthropy: a type of study and work deemed acceptable for young, middle-class women. There Jeannette learned about the role of state and private organizations in the care of needy families, the treatment of convicted criminals from different classes, and the rights of labor. In New York in 1909, as Jeannette sought her own meaningful involvements, she also began to work for the New York Woman Suffrage Party. She served as a sidewalk campaigner in what was a frustrating state effort: suffrage would not pass in New York until 1917.

Seeking challenging work and positive results, Jeannette came home to Missoula and then left for the west coast, where she worked at the Children's Home Societies of Spokane and Seattle, and then in San Francisco at a settlement house. The settlement movement had begun in the 1880s to bring middle and working class women together and provide services such as daycare, education, and healthcare. By 1913, in thirty-two states, there were 413 settlements, including Chicago's Hull House, founded by Jane Addams in 1889.[9]

After Jeannette entered these progressive spaces, she concluded that what women needed was not charity or choices made for them by the more affluent but their own source of power. Like Alice Paul who did settlement work in New York and London, Jeannette found the situation "suffocating." "I couldn't take it," Jeannette claimed. "I saw, that if we were to have decent laws for children, sanitary jails, and safe food supplies, women would have to vote."[10] Only the presence of women voters and legislators, she believed, would change the conditions in factories and end child labor; thus she decided "to give her fulltime attention to suffrage."[11]

In Seattle, Jeannette joined the state suffrage campaign, speaking on street corners, as she had in New York City. To increase her skill level, she began studying oral expression at the University of Washington, following a suggestion made by Wellington, who certainly recognized the impact of forceful oral persuasion, and his Harvard training in it, on his own career. Jeannette announced in newspapers a time and place for a street meeting, brought a few suffrage workers with her to create a small, positive crowd, asked passersby to stop, and then started to speak. When the state approved women's suffrage in 1910, Jeannette was a key part of that effort, engaging in a progressive model of grassroots organizing and rhetoric to spur positive change.

After this victory, Jeannette became a field secretary for the National American Woman Suffrage Association (NAWSA), traveling to ten states to teach street-by-street campaigning techniques. She also lobbied U.S. congressmen for a federal suffrage amendment, working with Alice Paul, who had become head of NAWSA's congressional committee. Between 1910 and 1915, Jeannette "turned into a political dynamo," speaking to a wide range of audiences for the cause.¹² In state after state and in Washington, D.C., as she took on the risky choices of travel and speaking, colleagues noted her attractive youthful appearance, strong voice, fearlessness, and organizing skills.

Progressive Chops: Wellington

While Wellington was establishing himself in the state capital and building his career as a well-connected progressive crusader, he married Elizabeth Floweree Wallace, known as "Helena's society queen." Her mother's family, the Flowerees, had built a huge cattle business outside of Great Falls. The father of the bride, William Wallace, Jr., was a prominent lawyer at Nolan and Walsh, the firm where Wellington began his career. As newspapers reported, Elizabeth's parents opposed this match, given Wellington's lack of ties to Helena society and their daughter's youth: Wellington was then twenty-five, and Elizabeth nineteen. But she threatened to elope if she didn't get their permission, and so her mother and father "capitulated to Cupid," as a newspaper reported. Only her parents came to the quickly planned wedding.[13]

Although this marriage helped Wellington to establish himself in Helena, the father was right that it wouldn't last. The society wife did not fit this constantly working young man. Her social engagements regularly made Helena newspapers as did her visits to other cities, including regular shopping excursions to the east coast. Two years after their marriage, in June 1912, Wellington secured a divorce, citing incapacity of temperament. Elizabeth had told him that, given her love of fashion, society, and theater, she would never be happy outside of New York, and she might have stayed with him longer if he had moved there: "I should never be able to live west."[14] Wellington later had female companions, but he would not marry again until 1956 when he was seventy-two. Through all of the years of a busy career, his energy equaling his father's, he had no wife and no children to lay claim to his time.

At the law firm of Nolan and Walsh and then on his own, Wellington established his willingness to take on difficult cases against powerful institutions such as gold and copper mines, railroads, and the city governments that these industries often controlled. These were the entities in his state against which a young lawyer could make his name as a progressive.

Across the state, Wellington quickly gained a reputation as a defender of the underdog, a legal hero with fiery courtroom skills. He often referred in court to his wrestling and boxing prowess from Harvard and to fighting lessons that he offered young men in his office. Among these pugilists

Wellington Rankin and Elizabeth Wallace Rankin in Helena, 1911 (Schlesinger Library, Radcliffe Institute, Harvard University).

was a young Gary Cooper, whose father Charles was a prominent Helena lawyer and rancher. Along with teaching Gary to box and helping him gain strength after he suffered a hip injury in a car accident, Wellington encouraged him to become an actor, one of his own goals. He also taught Roy Glover, who became chairman of the board at Anaconda, a frequent

Four. Progressivism and American Politics 61

legal opponent that he could claim had come to the master for fighting lessons.[15]

In establishing his reputation as the fighting progressive, Wellington took on personal injury lawsuits as well as criminal cases. Lawsuits were uncommon before the Progressive Era even though dangerous industries, such as petroleum refining and steel manufacturing, and thus workplace accidents, increased dramatically in the late nineteenth century. While workers injured on the job could sue employers for damages, winning proved difficult. When employers could show that the worker had assumed the risk, or had been injured by the actions of a fellow employee, or had been partly at fault, courts allowed them to deny liability. Surveys from 1900 showed that families of only half of the workers who died on the job received compensation, the average being just half a year's pay; workers who were crippled or otherwise injured generally received a small sum or nothing at all. Because accidents cost a company so little, industries developed with little concern for safety.[16] With workers' compensation not available to Montana laborers and with industries expanding without much concern for safety, it might be only the personal injury lawyer who protected the worker. And by winning, especially in a well-publicized way, a lawyer like Wellington could bring attention not just to one injustice but to the plight of a group—and to himself.

One major power that Wellington opposed was the railroad, the Northern Pacific, operating from Minnesota to the Pacific Northwest. This company received nearly forty million acres of land, from federal and state governments, to develop train lines and stations and to sell as a means of increasing profits. Headquartered in Missoula, the Rocky Mountain Division of this line encompassed 892 route miles, over which it shipped wheat, cattle, timber, and minerals; transported consumer goods; and carried passengers.[17]

What was a wonder when construction began in 1870 soon became a monolith, constituting a monopoly in Missoula as other railroads went for only short distances, further north and south. As the Northern Pacific pursued an aggressive policy of line expansion, it twice went bankrupt and dealt with shortfalls by charging higher rates, requesting additional land from the government, and using land grants as security to borrow money. With expanding powers, the Northern Pacific could "squeeze out competitors, force down prices paid for labor and raw materials, charge customers more ... and get special favors and treatment from national and state governments."[18] And to further wield capital and influence, the railroad financed and controlled political campaigns.

Wellington frequently sued the Northern Pacific, as a progressive quite publicly attempting to curb a major monopoly power in his state. He represented farmers and cattlemen who protested the prices charged for transporting their harvests, landowners who opposed the railroad's land grabs, and pedestrians injured in accidents as poorly maintained trains jumped the tracks. In doing so, he called upon his ability to dominate a courtroom and the news. When the railroad failed to pay what it owed after he prosecuted a suit for an injured man, Frank Korol, Rankin went to court to get a judge to cede him a locomotive in lieu of a cash settlement, and he then stopped a full train in the Helena station, claiming that he would hold onto it until he received what a judge had deemed equitable. As one strong man standing up against a train company and even a train, he created a well-reported triumphant moment.[19]

In these cases, Wellington employed an extreme of risky courtroom theatrics and even the fisticuffs of his Harvard boxing and office lessons. In a civil case against the Helena Light and Railway Company, owned by the Northern Pacific, Wellington represented the widow of a barber, John P. McDonnell, who had been killed when he leaned against a streetcar door that suddenly opened, causing him to fall out and be cut in half by the wheels. Under what Wellington assumed to be pressure from the railway, the doctor who treated McDonnell, Ben Brooke, changed his testimony and declared that McDonnell had died of a heart attack. When Wellington asserted in court that the doctor had lied, Brooke called him a prevaricator. Then Wellington "struck him full in the face with his fist," a blow immediately returned, an exchange that "set the town a-buzzin." Wellington spent less than forty minutes in jail for this mutual attack. Back in the courtroom, he strongly depicted his violence as a necessary blow for the individual and the community, against a corrupt doctor in league with a powerful and mercenary corporation, and he won his case.[20] While critics labeled him as hot-headed, no one missed the fact that Rankin had gone the distance for a client and for justice.

Along with the railroad, the powerful copper mining industry became Wellington's "long time nemesis"; in response, the company and its newspapers "viciously attacked Rankin at every opportunity."[21] Anaconda Copper Mining Company, founded in 1881 near Butte when miners discovered huge amounts of copper where silver had "played out," would eventually own all the mines in the area. Butte became one of the most prosperous cities in the country, called "the Richest Hill on Earth," replacing the Upper Peninsula of Michigan as the world's largest producer of copper. The company also owned smelters in East Helena, Great Falls, and Anaconda as well as Montana's only power company, a large lumber operation, coal fields, banks, hotels, a chain of newspapers that included almost every daily in Montana—and many politicians. At a time when legislatures in each state chose U.S. senators, mining interests could influence the election of local and state officials and ultimately the state's leaders in Washington. As Jeannette controversially described the stranglehold of mining interests to a reporter, "They own the State. They own the government. They own the press."[22] Given this increasing profit and power, investors flocked to copper mining, including William Rockefeller, Jr., co-founder of Standard Oil.[23]

In opposition to the Rockefellers and Standard Oil, Ida Tarbell published a series of articles in *McClure's Magazine* that became her 1904 book, *The History of the Standard Oil Company*, her muckraking leading to the Clayton Antitrust Act. In a state without such a magazine and with newspapers owned by Anaconda, it would be a lawyer who launched an attack on the power of mining. In February 1912, Wellington represented Frank Anderson, who had been offered a job for life after being crippled in a mine in Pennsylvania: he had been hit by falling lumber in an area that workers had reported as dangerous. When it purchased this mine, Anaconda refused to honor the agreement. Before a jury, Wellington had Anderson testify at length, piteously, about his life before and after the accident, with his children adding to the sad courtroom scene. The company ultimately acceded to continuing Anderson's office employment and providing a pension.[24]

Wellington also stood up to city governments that might be prone to protecting powerful, established citizens as well as businesses like mining and the railroads. In 1900, 27.6 percent of the population of Montana was foreign born, with only four states having a higher percentage. In the state's towns and courts, a more positive evaluation accrued to descendants of white pioneers along with newly arrived immigrants from northern Europe. Those from southern and eastern Europe, or from Mexico or China or Africa, might find themselves at a disadvantage, as certainly Native Americans did also.[25]

As Wellington advocated for the rights of the vulnerable individual, he involved himself in criminal law and the local realities of race and class. When Austrian immigrant Frank Jackleh was killed in 1911 in Townsend, the sheriff immediately arrested an ethnic Serbian, Mike Rodoman, from Montenegro, assumed to be a lawless, swarthy attacker of a blameless northern European. The editor of the *Townsend Star* described the stellar qualities of the native-born white male jury that heard the case: "men of mature age, possessing analytical minds and the degree of discretion which counts for the conservation of justice." Only such rational men could protect the citizenry from "wanton conduct by a carelessly disposed citizen."[26] In front of the jury, Wellington carefully reviewed the facts while intimating that a Serbian had been assumed to be guilty even though he was protecting himself against a drunken aggressor and that, with the crime occurring on the Fourth of July, the police had sought out a seemingly anti–American criminal to prosecute. In November of 1911, against difficult odds, Wellington won the case, a well-publicized victory for the progressive champion.

Taking on governmental power, like the railroad and mines, also involved Wellington in civil cases. When he represented Velma Riggs against the county commission, the case concerned a car driven at night by Riley Doore, carrying his family as well as Riggs. The car went into a ten-foot creek where a bridge was out, without guard rails or posted warnings. The other passengers escaped with bruises, but Riggs had severe wounds: she was "thrown with great force and violence … torn, hurt, bruised, crippled, and otherwise injured, and she was greatly shocked thereby."

The county's lawyers claimed that these people shouldn't have been out at night, a ridiculous claim that Wellington quickly countered. Commissioners testified that they didn't know that the bridge had fallen down, but Wellington had witnesses to prove otherwise. He went on to prove a pattern of poor maintenance on this bridge and at other county facilities by brandishing record books with missing pages, claiming that these administrators had stolen funds, ignored safety concerns, and ruined lives. To create a further emotional appeal, Riggs' husband, who had been working on the night of the accident, testified that because of her injuries his wife could no longer care for their children. At the trial, even though the commission had friends on the bench and in the jury, Wellington won.[27]

As he represented the individual against the government, Wellington deployed his risky courtroom theatrics. In December 1912, when the city of Helena dug a water main through Bessie Whitcomb's ranch without her permission, he sued the city for her. After the judge decided to allow the ditch digging to continue without her agreement or any compensation, Wellington's "choleric disposition" led him to hit the city attorney on the jaw: as a newspaper article reported, "fisticuffs follow heated argument." Wellington apologized, and then he got the city to pay damages to the widow even though he could not stop the water main's progress.[28]

Wellington certainly didn't win every case, but he did secure the reputation of a dedicated progressive warrior, willing to take on established interests, flamboyant and even violent as he employed his skills for the downtrodden and fought against attorneys who served the rich.

As he developed his legal practice, Wellington took on running for office with the same progressive agenda, taking advantage of his status as a major power in the state. Theodore Roosevelt's new Bull Moose or Progressive Party seemed a perfect vehicle for this young, ambitious, anti-institutional man. Roosevelt decided to seek a third presidential term in 1912, permissible under the Constitution prior to the ratification of the Twenty-second Amendment in 1951. In 1909, Taft had entered office determined to advance Roosevelt's agenda, but he stumbled badly as a progressive when he failed to decrease tariffs and extend Roosevelt's land conservation efforts. At the 1912 Republican National Convention, Taft narrowly defeated Roosevelt for the party's presidential nomination. Roosevelt then formed a Progressive, or Bull Moose, Party: he often said that he felt "strong as a bull moose" both before and after an assassination attempt on the campaign trail. The party's platform, as Roosevelt asserted, centered on progressive reforms that could "dissolve the unholy alliance between corrupt business and corrupt politics."[29] These priorities included campaign finance restrictions, a social insurance system, an eight-hour workday, woman suffrage, and regulation of large corporations, with adherents varying on how far to venture into "trust-busting" and other reform efforts.

In the 1912 election, Roosevelt won 27.4 percent of the popular vote compared to Taft's 23.2 percent, making Roosevelt the only third-party presidential nominee to finish with a higher share of the popular vote than a major party's presidential nominee. Both Taft and Roosevelt finished behind Democrat Woodrow Wilson, who secured 41.8 percent of the popular vote and the vast majority of the electoral college vote. In an election marked primarily by Democratic gains, progressives elected some candidates to the U.S. Congress and to state legislatures, but not a president.

In Montana, Wellington organized the new state Progressive Party, taking this risky chance to become a leader, not by fitting in with establishment Republicans but by moving out on his own, as he also preferred to do as an attorney. He addressed "mass meetings" in many counties, urging citizens to think for themselves, oppose entrenched institutions, and embrace the power inherent in a new people's party. In July 1912, at a party convention, his group went on record as supporting Roosevelt and opposing the control exercised by Anaconda and the Northern Pacific while advocating for the election of U.S. senators by popular referendum—all priorities of Wellington Rankin.

Even though Roosevelt lost to Wilson, progressives continued to organize in Montana, with Wellington becoming their candidate. In 1914, he sought one of two at-large seats in the U.S. House, both then held by Democrats. From statehood in 1889 until the creation of districts in 1918, members elected at large, requiring the vote of the entire state, represented Montana in the House. As Wellington attempted to establish himself as the state's main progressive, his large ads posted in business windows noted that he was president of the Men's Equal Suffrage League, a popular cause in the state. As Wellington later told an interviewer, "morally, I was for women's suffrage," but it was also part of his bid for acceptance and prominence.[30] In this campaign, Wellington continued his criticisms of Anaconda from his courtroom arguments. In a *Missoulian* article with the headline "Wellington Rankin Lets Loose," he claimed that the company had refused to aid accident victims, its corrupt control over Governor Sam V. Stewart limiting its liability.[31] His party motto further reflected opposition to the state monolith: "Put the Anaconda Company Out of Montana Politics." In response, Anaconda newspapers went on the attack, one describing Wellington as having "all the dignity of a baboon, all the self-restraint and poise of a tomcat, all the calm deliberation and judicial decision of a jack-ass, all the finer emotions and sentiments of a yellow dog, all the nobility and character of a snake."[32]

Given his courtroom expertise, in the 1914 election, Wellington thought that not just ads and slogans but debates would provide his best means of prevailing. In September, he challenged the Republican candidate, Washington J. McCormick, who sought only to debate the two Democratic incumbents holding the at-large seats. As the *Billings Tribune* and the *Missoulian* commented, all three men wanted to avoid taking the stage with Wellington, "something of a fighter."[33]

Though these candidates feared Wellington's verbal powers, his reputation for fiery rhetoric and even courtroom violence became liabilities for a politic career. As Wellington ran in the fall of 1914, he seemed to represent too much of the wild west. Some articles mentioned his temper, one declaring that he "went into a tirade" while speaking about the railroads and Anaconda mining.[34] Articles also claimed that he only cared about overwhelming the opposition, not about one-to-one interaction with voters or their needs. The edginess of his law practice as well as his opposition to the primary state employers turned off voters as did his abandonment of the Republican Party. Wellington secured only 6,600 of 80,000 votes.[35]

Although his career ceded him wealth and power, Wellington's personal traits and shifting loyalties continued to make electoral success elusive. Returning to the Republicans, he ran for office eight more times, seeking election to the U.S. House, the U.S. Senate, and the governor's office, in elections spanning 1914 to 1952, but he had to settle for the elected position of attorney general of Montana, in 1920. Though Wellington won only one election, he had access to political power: for many years he directed the state Republican Party, managed campaigns, and influenced governmental appointments. In 1924 Republican governor Joseph M. Dixon appointed him associate justice of the Supreme Court of Montana. Wellington found the court to be a dull space, a site where he could not create change on his own, and he quit after a year. In 1928 President Coolidge appointed him as U.S. district attorney for Montana, and in 1930 Herbert Hoover reappointed him to that post, which he held until 1934, finding it more applicable to his talents than a seat on the supreme court.

Wellington Rankin used the national opposition to corporations and their treatment of workers to establish his own reputation—as a fierce and winning attorney. His legal and political progressivism, however, would not signal a long-range commitment, but rather a young man's choice to establish a career. With a growing legal presence, he did not remain within the progressive pantheon. As an attorney, he began to handle divorces, wills, and real estate transactions. Wellington opened additional law offices in Butte and Havre, as the top criminal lawyer in the state, his cases also increasingly involving the rights of business and industry, including railroads and mines, progressivism for him having been a temporary expedient relied upon at the right place and time.

Progressive Chops: Jeannette

While the progressivism of fighting mines, railroads, and city bosses helped Wellington to establish his career, this philosophy and movement would mean much more to Jeannette, her principles coming between them as she stuck to them when they were popular and when they were not.

Jeannette Rankin first involved herself in an appropriately gendered version of progressivism through her study of philanthropy and her work at settlement houses. She then devoted herself to the suffrage campaign, labeled as women's best means of working to enact reforms in schools, in community government, and in child labor practices. After working in New York and Washington on state campaigns and serving as a national field secretary, Jeannette turned her attention to where she knew that she could make a difference, taking a leadership role in Montana. On a visit home for Christmas in 1910, she realized that the state legislature was only bringing suffrage up pro forma, almost as a joke, a situation that had to change.

In response to this unfair treatment, Jeannette planned a meeting at a Missoula high school to start the Equal Franchise Society, of which she served as secretary while supporting men for the roles of chair and vice-chair since an all-male legislature would have to approve the legislation to be voted on by an all-male electorate. In the 1911 session, D.J. Donohue of Glendive introduced a woman suffrage amendment, with Jeannette there as the society's representative.[36] As she prepared to speak at this session, Wellington reviewed her text and performance, as she later recalled: "So, I came back to Helena and with the help of my brother, Wellington Rankin, worked out a speech. (I would try out the speech, and he would say it was a very important occasion and correct some of my errors to make it more effective, etc.)."[37] As she also mentioned, Wellington would "scare me to death" along with providing assistance. Their ongoing mutual critique, which included her regular commentary on his opening and closing arguments for court cases, helped Jeannette to become a "spellbinding orator" in the volatile space of political meetings while he excelled in the courtroom.[38]

In her speech before the legislature, Jeannette lauded Montana as a leader in democracy, beginning in the frontier days of her parents, while also reviewing women's contributions to the state. In this talk and others given at schools and club meetings, she couched her arguments in terms of progressive civic housekeeping: women would help make laws insuring better medical care as well as access to safe food and water.[39] Colonel C.B. Nolan, who had been her brother's law partner, joined Jeannette at some of these meetings and talked about what his mother and so many women had done for Montana and what voting women would do for families in the future.

Jeannette Rankin in one of her favorite wide-brimmed hats, 1910–1912 (Schlesinger Library, Radcliffe Institute, Harvard University).

In 1911, with pressure from Jeannette and the Equal Franchise Society, a majority in the Montana legislature endorsed a suffrage referendum, but it didn't attain the necessary two-thirds vote. As she later recalled, some legislators used the debate to make what they thought to be funny speeches about women voting, about pots burning on the stove as they left home inappropriately. In fact, as she later recalled, "they did that until all of us felt we had dropped through a hole."[40]

Although the amendment failed to achieve sufficient support in 1911, suffrage activists were gaining the attention that ultimately propelled them to victory. As they mounted another campaign in 1912, Jeannette and her colleagues secured endorsements from the major parties, including the newly forming Progressives led by her brother. In 1913, working from Missoula, the effort also directed by Belle Fligelman of Helena and Margaret Smith Hathaway of Stevensville, Jeannette formed a central committee of fifty influential women, the effort spurred by her speaking skills, superior organization, and "breeze of contagious enthusiasm."[41]

To make a difference in the Montana suffrage campaign, Jeannette employed a variety of techniques: she asked candidates for office to endorse suffrage; she spoke at women's clubs about the social whirl in which she grew up, as preparation for women taking an active civic role; she created suffrage booths at fairs; she marched with her supporters in city parades; she sent literature to women all over the state as well as sashes for their children that said, "I want my Mother to vote"; she courted powerful men's groups and engaged the influential in Wellington's Men's Equal Suffrage League. At each event, Jeannette crafted her message carefully for the particular audience: she appealed to prohibition supporters, for example, but made clear to opponents of the legislation that suffrage was a separate issue. And, using the example of Olive Rankin, she kept emphasizing women's history in the state, what they had done as teachers, ranchers, wives, and mothers. Helping her with planning and appearing with her, as evidence of an established family supporting the rights of the state's women, were Harriet, Mary, Grace, Edna, and Wellington.

While making strong arguments about the state and its history, Jeannette used her Washington connections to strengthen the Montana campaign. In March of 1913, she participated in a suffrage parade in Washington, D.C., that boosted her reputation and gave her practical experience with large events. On the day before Woodrow Wilson's inauguration, Alice Paul and NAWSA staged a huge parade down Pennsylvania Avenue, from the Capitol to the White House, a route that Paul worked assiduously to secure. The theme she chose was not suffrage but the inherently positive Ideals and Virtues of American Womanhood. At the front of the long parade, a model of the liberty bell, brought from Philadelphia, started things off. Following immediately behind was Inez Milholland, a labor lawyer from New York, dressed in white robes and riding a white horse. To achieve a spectacular staging, Paul arranged for twenty-six floats, six golden chariots, ten bands, forty-five captains, two hundred marshals, and marching groups representing states, professions, and organizations.[42]

Organized by Jeannette, the Montana contingent decided to dress as Native Americans, led by a woman portraying Sacajawea, the Shoshone who guided Lewis and Clark through the wilderness. Montana suffragists maintained that she was the nation's first woman voter, following the "generally accepted myth" that Sacajawea voted, along with other members of the expedition, concerning the best route to the west. As one of the vividly dressed participants in white buckskin, Edna Rankin marched as part of the Native American group.[43]

Then, on July 31, Jeannette participated in a national effort to emphasize the dual involvement of the states and the federal government in the quest for suffrage. Committees that Alice Paul and others created in each state took on the daunting task of securing thousands of signatures in support of federal legislation—by circulating letters at women's colleges, women's clubs, suffrage associations, and party meetings. Using this method, activists collected 250,000 signatures on petition sheets in less than five weeks. In each state, they chose representatives to bring the petitions to Washington. Jeannette organized the collection of signatures in Montana, an effort that helped invigorate the state campaign, and then drove across the country with other women, a controversial choice for the time and one that secured press attention.[44] The cars convened in Hyattsville, Maryland, five miles northeast of Washington, and proceeded to the Capitol to present their petitions to Congress, accompanied by members of the press, making a "strong and effective ocular demonstration of the wide spread demand for woman suffrage through a National Constitutional Amendment."[45]

After her return to Montana from Washington, Jeannette launched a speaking blitz for the state amendment in which she employed her national reputation and experience as well as her family connections; the legislature passed the bill in its fall 1913 session. Ultimately, there were just two votes against it in the state Senate and two in the House. Then the considerable effort began to secure a positive vote from male citizens. In March 1914, as the recognized suffrage leader in the state, Jeannette was again "blazing the suffrage trail," relying on her well-honed speaking skills: as the *Missoulian* reported, "everywhere she is stirring press and people."[46]

Jeannette crafted her arguments to persuade the various groups with whom she met. To audiences primarily of men, she spoke of women as workers in the home, employing their vote to improve that essential space: "When women have the power to use their superior knowledge of matters which concern them most they will be able to increase their efficiency." In front of women's clubs and other women's groups, she spoke about the progressive role that voting women could play in the community. At the State Federation of Women's Clubs in June, for example, she argued that well educated and politically empowered women could take control of orphanages, making recommendations not just based on cost per child but on "the principles of education, the effect of work and play and idleness and character building." She also claimed that, given all that women like her mother dealt with as care givers, leaders might begin training professional women "who could assist the woman in her home in caring for her children."[47]

On September 26, 1914, reporters around the state focused on a big suffrage parade in Helena, the "most significant ever seen in the northwest," led by Jeannette and distinguished visitor Anna Howard Shaw, with Wellington at the front of the Men's Equal Suffrage League. This event took place during the state fair, with large crowds thus assured, as had occurred at the NAWSA parade before Woodrow Wilson's inauguration. Borrowing from the Washington event, Jeannette arranged for bands, floats, and groups of marchers carrying banners for their cities, described as a mile-long demonstration appearing before a crowd of 20,000, as Shaw later recalled the circumstances:

> On this occasion the suffragists wished me to wear my cap and gown and my doctor's hood, but as I had not brought those garments with me, we borrowed and I proudly wore the cap and gown of the Unitarian minister. It was a small but really beautiful parade, and all the costumes for it were designed by the state president, Miss Jeannette Rankin, to whose fine work, by the way, combined with the work of her friends, the winning of Montana was largely due.[48]

All of this positive progress appeared in the state's newspapers as well as the *Suffrage Daily News*, published in Helena, to spur state efforts, between September and November 1914.

Suffrage became law in Montana in November 1914, in the election in which Wellington ran unsuccessfully for the U.S. House. The male electorate passed the amendment by a vote of 41,302 to 37,588.[49]

With the state campaign won, in December 1914 Jeannette returned to Washington, to work as a lobbyist for a federal amendment while also traveling to eastern states to help with their state campaigns. In April 1915, in a letter, suffragist Mary O'Neill claimed that Jeannette was "always on the jump" and then "in a frazzle" when she finally returned to her apartment in the capital.[50]

Still interested in participating in big suffrage events, Jeannette sent a design to Anna Howard Shaw to be used at the Panama-Pacific Exposition held in San Francisco in 1915. Shaw adopted Jeannette's idea and printed "several million" buttons inscribed with "I Am a Voter," in black type on a metallic gold background, for women from western suffrage states to wear at the fair. For the eleven months of the exposition that 18.9 million people visited, suffrage created quite a presence.[51] Suffrage speakers held forth in a long hall-like area decorated with Susan B. Anthony's portrait, American and suffrage flags, photographs of campaign events, and a large banner reading, "We demand an amendment to the United States Constitution enfranchising women."[52] Each day, workers at the booth informed visitors about their campaign, asked them to sign a petition, invited them to hear special speakers such as Helen Keller, and gave them Jeannette's buttons. When Anna Howard Shaw spoke there, she commented that Jeannette could wear this button, but she could not because the men in her home state of Pennsylvania were withholding the vote from women. When Jeannette visited the booth in May 1915 and gave a well-attended talk, describing the successful state campaigns and her work in Washington, D.C., she emphasized the electoral injustice still occurring in the majority of states.[53]

By the end of 1915, with so many organizing sessions and events but little progress, Jeannette began to recognize the seemingly unsurmountable difficulties of succeeding with federal legislation or with forty-eight separate state votes. Since 1914, when Montana and Nevada had passed referenda, no other state had granted suffrage to women and, especially with the nation's attention turning to war in Europe, none seemed likely to do so without much more hard work.

Exhausted from her suffrage efforts, Jeannette left on a trip to New Zealand and Australia to witness the results of full suffrage. The Electoral Act of 1893 had given women in New Zealand the right to vote, the first country to endorse woman suffrage. Then in 1902, the newly established Australian Parliament passed legislation that enabled women, except "aboriginal natives," to vote and stand for election to parliament. This trip renewed Jeannette's commitment to political activism. She felt that in both countries the presence of women voters had led to better laws. In New Zealand, women had pressed successfully for improved medical care, leading to a Department of Public Health in 1900 and laws concerning patent medicines, infant care, and the training of doctors, dentists, and midwives. In Australia, by 1915, women voters had successfully pushed for acts enacting invalid and old-age pensions, proper quarantining for illnesses, care for pregnant women, and workmen's compensation.[54]

When Jeannette returned home, she did so with her faith confirmed concerning all that women could enable the United States to achieve once they became involved in politics. But she no longer wanted to invest her time in frustrating suffrage campaigns. Instead, she believed, American women in suffrage states should begin proving what they could bring to the country. A letter in April 1916 from fellow suffragist Mary Stewart listed Jeannette's new activities: meeting with women across Montana, forming good government clubs and civic leagues, planning state meetings of women voters, and asking Jane Addams to join them in urging Montana women to become active citizens and legislators.[55] And Jeannette also envisioned a further goal of civic engagement: taking the decided risk of running for federal office—for the U.S. House of Representatives—the presence of the first victor preparing the way for more and indicating the role that women could play in securing progressive legislation. As she told an interviewer, "I wanted women to accept their responsibilities, and I felt the best way to draw their attention to the fact that Congress directly affected their homes and their lives was to have women—many women—acting and speaking as their representatives in Congress."[56] Suffragists in Montana opposed Jeannette's candidacy at first: many women thought that her chances of being elected would be much greater in the state legislature. As state suffrage activists recognized her determination, they quickly changed their response, as Jeannette later recalled: "They were delighted that I was going to run for Congress. They never hesitated in working for my election after that."[57] Some NAWSA leaders, like Carrie Chapman Catt and Anna Howard Shaw, advised Jeannette to begin by seeking a minor post, claiming that a woman with a law degree and more civic experience would be better prepared to be the first House or Senate victor: a loser would set a bad precedent.[58] After Jeannette won in November of 1916, Anna Howard Shaw waited until March of 1917 to send a congratulatory letter, in which she claimed that she had not supported the campaign to spare her friend humiliation and ridicule.[59]

Along with suffragists who discouraged her, Republican Party officials scoffed at the idea of Jeannette's candidacy, and they appealed to Wellington as presumably his sister's controller. Past U.S. senator and fellow Bull Moose supporter Joseph M. Dixon suggested that Wellington refuse to "let" his sister run. He said further that Jeannette "would be considered freakish" if she made the attempt and it could make her a laughing stock, something no brother would want.[60]

While lacking support from suffrage leaders and from the Republican Party, Jeannette had her siblings' backing and access to Wellington's substantial influence. In response to Republican leaders, he used a positive civic-housekeeping argument: "The way to protect the home," he answered them, was for dedicated women "to have a place in government and equal recognition with men."[61] With his sister, he emphasized the appalling difficulties that she would face as a woman candidate: "I am shocked at the prejudice that exists against a woman going to Congress ... the biggest campaign of education that is going to be required is to the effect that a woman can do the work there and should probably be sent there, rather than the question of you, individually, going.... The prejudice is substantial."[62] But he told her that they could prevail. Wellington argued that suffrage campaigning had been a good career move for entering politics, better than social work. And this highly publicized success would help her whether or not prominent suffragists supported her campaign: "Well, now, you're going to run for Congress," he told her, "and I'm not very much interested in whether these women go along with it or not, and you are going to be elected."[63] He eschewed their claims that Jeannette needed to start at the state level, as she later recalled: "But my brother came in one day after a meeting of these women and he said: 'You can run for Congress—you can win for Congress just as well as for the legislature.... I'll manage your campaign and you'll be elected.' So I announced."[64]

Once Jeannette made her decision, she and Wellington began

organizing across the state. With her friend Belle Fligelman, Jeannette opened her campaign headquarters in Wellington's law office. She then went to see prominent women from around the state, many of whom she had met during the suffrage campaign, thus becoming what Wellington labeled as the "best known person in the whole state." She next began traveling by car and train to meet with any group that would host her, her sisters Mary, Edna, Grace, and Harriet speaking along with her, while Wellington kept track of public sentiment from Helena. The sisters also began asking influential women, as Wellington later recalled, to the Missoula home "where we had lived all our lives" to emphasize the family's history and standing in the state. As Jeannette energized voters, she asked them to mail postcards, to make phone calls, and to bring friends to meetings. Additionally, the siblings established the Jeannette Rankin for Congress Club, with units across the state. Given prejudices entrenched against her, they recognized that a meeting-by-meeting approach would be their only means of securing positive public notice for this campaign.

As Wellington ran Jeannette's headquarters, he conducted research about the needs of men and women voters around the state and the best means of appealing to them. Wellington began the campaign knowing Missoula, Helena, and the rest of the western part of the state, and he immediately started studying the eastern section. He frequently wrote to his sisters while they were traveling, reminding them to study and speak about key issues in each community:

> In Sheridan, Richland, and Dawson counties prohibition will be an excellent plan; in Billings you will be confronted with the tariff on wool, and you will have to bear in mind that the Republican Party has been based upon tariff issues chiefly, and in those sections where they are dependent upon a tariff on wool for prosperity they will not vote for anyone that does not favor protection.[65]

As Jeannette considered the priorities of local communities, she honed her platform by speaking on street corners as she had for suffrage, attempting to reach out to passersby and draw a crowd, something that other candidates wouldn't do: "My opponents," she later declared, "had too much dignity."[66] In her speeches and campaign literature, Jeannette emphasized a platform that her friend, journalist Mary O'Neill, described as "messianic maternalism."[67] Jeannette informed the *New York Times* that she sought election "to represent the women and children of the West, to work for an eight hour day for women, and for laws providing that women shall receive the same wages as men for equal amounts of work" and certainly to advocate for suffrage and for peace.[68] In her campaign, she opposed the all-powerful Anaconda Mining Company, using research that Wellington had done for his law suits concerning abuse of workers and

Four. Progressivism and American Politics 75

unreasonable profits. In response to this attack, Jeannette's coverage by the Anaconda-owned newspapers could have been worse; they ignored her because the company didn't feel that she could win. As Wellington later indicated, "She got a lot of silent treatment."[69]

As sister and brother extended her reputation, employing Jeannette's campaigning skills along with Wellington's research and state-wide strategy, he began to introduce her to the power brokers of the state's Republican Party. The Rankins already knew the price of leaving a major for a minority party, as Wellington had with the Bull Moose Party; they sought to avoid this pitfall in 1916. Even though Jeannette was not a Republican Party member, she needed this support that Wellington helped her to obtain, as she later noted: "I was never a Republican. I ran on the Republican ticket."[70] As she said about herself after she ran for Congress again, in the fall of 1940, she was an American first, a progressive next, and a Republican "somewhere down the line."[71]

While meeting with influential groups, considering key issues, and seeking party support, Jeannette and Wellington planned to take advantage of the legislative situation in their state. In 1916 as in 1914, Montanans would elect two representatives to the U.S. House, both at-large members since no districts had been designated. Seven men and Jeannette formed a field of eight in the Republican primary, from which two would be selected to run against two Democrats. To take advantage of this situation, Jeannette and Wellington made a definite plan: at each campaign stop, as she discussed the issues, Jeannette assured Republicans that they could choose any male candidate and still vote for her, thus backing a traditional party leader while honoring her preparation and the right of women to participate in government. As Jeannette explained this strategy in an interview, "I, as anyone would do, urged them to vote for their local man and for me."[72]

By early August, just three weeks into the campaign, the Rankins had gained considerable momentum. Jeannette easily won the primary, with 22,549 votes against 15,429 for the next contender. Then there were two Democrats and two Republicans in the general election, including the Democratic incumbent John M. Evans, a lawyer who had been mayor of Missoula and would serve in the House from 1913 to 1921 and from 1923 to 1933. In this election, the siblings argued that Montanans could further the power of both parties and genders if they voted for her and their favorite Democrat, presumably Evans. With this argument, Jeannette angered her fellow Republican nominee George Farr because she wouldn't campaign for him—he was "beside himself" with fury—and the Republican Party gave her limited support. Wellington later claimed that the party "did almost nothing for her ... we were conducting an individual campaign."[73]

With a close vote, the newspapers for two days after the election reported that Jeannette had lost. But Wellington told her to wait to concede, as Jeannette later recalled: "My brother's analysis of the vote was perfectly correct. He knew from the history of a certain county what their trend had always been and when the vote started to come in he could tell that they were going in a certain direction and that I had won." After having been labeled as a loser, she described the final verdict as a "doubtful joy." She had won by 6300 votes.[74] Of this election, Jeannette recalled that "the first time I voted, I voted for myself."[75]

Jeannette presented an ethos not seen before, one that led to the first woman being elected to the U.S. House: as a well-educated, well-connected leader in the suffrage movement, a progressive in support of labor rights and peace, from a respected family, and with sisters and especially a brother who could make a difference for her. As biographers James J. Lopach and Jean A. Luckowski have noted concerning Jeannette and Wellington, "There's a lot written about women in politics historically, and the barriers, and often it was a husband or a father who gave them a leg up, and in this case it was her brother. He helped her overcome the barriers."[76] Biographer Kevin S. Giles recognized Jeannette's formidable campaigning skills and her supportive network of activist women, including her sisters, but he also concluded that Wellington "had been a godsend in Jeannette's election to Congress, for without his political intuition and astute engineering she probably would not have won."[77] Wellington's biographer Volney Steele contended that he was "the man who twice propelled his controversial sister, Jeannette, into Congress."[78] This claim went too far because Jeannette propelled herself through hard work and dedication, and with the help of her sisters, but Wellington certainly helped her with funding and party connections and knowledge of issues across the state.

This campaign highlighted the strengths of both siblings as well as their ability to understand and help each other. Jeannette demonstrated a level of concern and humility in her interactions with voters that Wellington could not muster in his own campaigns.[79] She cautioned him about this connection to the state's citizens that he disdained: "I know your ideas and mine on campaigning are not the same, but I am thoroughly convinced you cannot win unless you go out among the people yourself and find out how they feel.… Your chances to win would increase tremendously if you would meet the people. Your aloofness is your greatest handicap."[80] Wellington recognized that, while he possessed greater knowledge of a range of issues and of mounting a state campaign, she had the superior level of skill at meetings with individuals and small groups. In an interview, he claimed that she was "one of the best single-handed campaigners I've ever seen. 'Cause she likes people.… And enjoys them and is interested in their welfare. She could go in any kitchen in any farmhouse and the people were

Jeannette Rankin, speaking from the balcony of the National American Woman Suffrage Association headquarters, as a new member of Congress, April 2, 1917 (C.T. Chapman, photographer, Women of Protest: Photographs from the Records of the National Woman's Party, Manuscript Division, Library of Congress).

at home with her and glad to have her there." As he said further, "She had a great affection, a great love of people and their problems. She was a very unselfish person."[81] Her biographer Norma Smith further described their differences: "He was not the politician she was. He was aloof, even arrogant, though, in Jeannette's words, he could 'pour on the charm' when he chose. Jeannette understood people better, she knew the complex technicalities of politics as well as he, and she was trusted."[82]

Having achieved what no one but the Rankins had thought that Jeannette should or could do, she quickly became a nationally prominent figure, interviewed and sought after. Jeannette realized that some of this attention came as a reaction to a woman's election, as one journalist expressed the general opinion of the time: "Women policemen, yes; women doctors, yes; women lawyers, umm-m, yes: but women congress-men—appalling! Had Montana voters gone plumb crazy? What sort of joke were they putting over on the rest of the nation?"[83] For Jeannette, the publicity and astonishment surrounding her election came as a "great shock": "It was very hard for me to comprehend—to realize that it made a difference what I did do and didn't do from then on."[84]

After her election, Jeannette continued with her progressive priorities, which had begun for her with settlement houses and suffrage. Though she is best known for her position on war, in her two years in office she worked on many issues affecting the needs of the oppressed or exploited, with whom Wellington had begun his law career. She immediately began attempting to secure better health care for infants and mothers, with help from Julia Lathrop at the Children's Bureau. As she later recalled, "I introduced the first bill for instruction in hygiene and maternity and infant care which later passed after the war, because you know nothing constructive is done during war. Later it became the Sheppard-Towner Bill."[85]

Jeannette also began an investigation, much noted in the press, concerning the working conditions in the Bureau of Printing and Engraving, involving mostly women workers who had been added quickly to meet the production of paper money needed as the country geared up for war. She telegrammed Wellington that she was investigating the bureau at the request of a woman in Montana whose sister worked there. Jeannette told him further that she wished he could come and help: she planned to introduce a resolution concerning the treatment of workers and thought he could help her to handle several administrators and congressmen who needed "pasting."[86] On June 8, 1917, she sent out an invitation for the women at the bureau to meet with her, either at the office or at her home. After speaking with them, she wrote letters to Secretary of the Treasury William Gibbs McAdoo, to assistant secretary Oscar T. Crosby, and to the bureau's director Joseph E. Ralph, requesting an investigation into excessive overtime, a lack of pay equity, uneven assignment of hours, and unfair hiring practices. Her dogged efforts caused the director to resign, helped the workers form a union, and resulted in fairer policies concerning hours and overtime.[87]

To keep working for the rights of women, in true progressive fashion, Jeannette introduced a bill in the fall of 1917 to protect American women from having their citizenship revoked when they married foreign men. Section 3 of the Expatriation Act of 1907 mandated loss of citizenship when American women married "aliens," a law that did not apply to American men. With the declaration of war and increased fear of foreigners, Jeannette's bill did not pass although it "netted women's organizations their first formal audience before the House Committee on Immigration and Naturalization to discuss the issue of marital naturalization."[88] Jeannette was ahead of her time: the Cable Act of 1922 reversed former immigration laws concerning married women.

While she was in office, Jeannette also continued her advocacy of women's suffrage and especially a federal amendment. She was instrumental in the creation of the House's Committee on Woman Suffrage. In January 1918, the committee delivered its report to Congress, and Jeannette spoke for suffrage on the floor of the House, serving as acting floor leader for the Republicans. She described the extension of suffrage during wartime as essential to a world-leading democracy. She argued further that women as voters could stand up against corporations and their monopolies to do what was best for the country at war and afterwards: "Might it not be that the men who have spent their lives thinking in terms of commercial profit find it hard to adjust themselves to thinking in terms of human needs? Might it not be that a great force that has always been thinking in terms of human needs, and that always will think in terms of human needs, has not been mobilized?" As Jeannette said further, women had "an intelligence, a feeling, a spiritual force peculiar to themselves," with which they could help solve the nation's complex problems.[89] That year a suffrage resolution passed the House with exactly a two-thirds vote but lost in the Senate by two votes. The following year—after Jeannette's congressional term had ended—the same resolution passed in both chambers. Although she could not secure the vote for women in 1918, she said proudly, concerning a federal amendment, that she was "the only woman who ever voted to give women the right to vote."[90]

As a member of Congress, Jeannette made progressive legislative choices to help vulnerable men as well as women. Some of these priorities extended Wellington's power base in Montana, particularly as she joined him in opposing the Anaconda Mining Company. On June 8, 1917, a fire in a mine shaft in Butte led to the worst metal-mining disaster in American history, causing the death of 168 men. Three days after the accident, a general strike erupted, with better working conditions and wages sought as key demands.[91] Workers also protested the mine's policies intended to curb unionization: as a permit to seek employment, the company required rustling cards, which it would not give to any activists. As tensions built, company stalwarts turned to murder to curb union power: on August 1, masked vigilantes took labor leader Frank Little from his boarding house, tied him to a car bumper, drug him through the streets, and hung him from a railway trestle in Butte.[92]

Jeannette's reaction to the mining accident and resulting violence was risky and immediate. She spoke to the newspapers about the "cowardly murder" of Frank Little, horrible and un–American, dangerous to all citizens, whatever their view of these strikers: "No one is safe where lynching is sanctioned."[93] She immediately tried to gather all the information that she could, writing to activists in Montana and to the mine workers' union. She met with Red Cross officials to assess their plans for helping out in Butte, but found that they were focused on war in Europe. On June 23, 1917, she wrote to several friends that she had been to see Samuel Gompers, founder and president of the American Federation of Labor, as well as William B. Wilson, the Secretary of Labor—and that she was ready to take action at once because of the extreme circumstances.[94] Through this process, she repeatedly wrote to her brother's law clerk Helena Stellway, asking her to double-check the available information and secure more particulars; if Helena couldn't get the facts, Jeannette told her, she could "have Wellington get them."[95] As Jeannette investigated, she recognized that some mining officials viewed her negatively as an extension of her fiery brother: as Wellington recalled about this time period, "she suffered quite a little because of my activities." She was soon "getting the run-a-round" from a series of officials due to both the power of Anaconda and strong feelings about Wellington.[96]

As the strike continued with no government response, Jeannette decided on a visit to the mines, a choice that she knew would raise national attention, given the press' interest in her. Wellington advised her not to take on this entrenched power in such a direct manner, but he met her train in Miles City and escorted her west, to Butte, on August 14. There police did not allow her to speak to a group that gathered at the station. The next day in town at Columbia Gardens, however, accompanied by union leaders, Jeannette addressed a large crowd, which Wellington estimated at over 10,000. In this speech, she objected to the miners being called wobblies or socialists as a means of denouncing them and spoke of their needs as American workers. As her speech ended, the audience stood and cheered for fifteen minutes. Wellington said afterwards that the response was the most enthusiastic anyone had received in the state: "And it wasn't the miners alone. It was all the people.... I never saw such a crowd, the enthusiasm."[97] Even though Wellington had opposed his sister's decision to speak in Butte, her campaign for the miners extended the reach of his power. As his widely publicized narrative claimed, he brought her to the state to stand up to his enemies, a construction of events that Jeannette never countered.

Going beyond speeches and publicity concerning the situation in Butte would prove difficult. In August, Jeannette introduced legislation asking Congress to authorize the president to nationalize the mines. But given the power of Anaconda and the complications of a federal takeover, Congress failed to act. Jeannette tried in August and September to see Woodrow Wilson, writing repeatedly to Joseph Tumulty, his private secretary, who failed to reply. She repeatedly tried to forge a compromise, which would at least include better working conditions if not higher wages, but the miners finally went back to work without achieving much of anything.

While she was in Congress, as she continued to enact her progressivism, Jeannette also introduced a resolution for the people of Ireland. In April 1916, Irish republicans had launched the Easter Rising against British rule and proclaimed an Irish Republic. Although the rising failed after a week of fighting, it led to support for Irish independence. In Congress in December 1917, Jeannette introduced a resolution for the United States to recognize Ireland as a free and independent country. Jeannette argued that this decision to liberate a country would prove that England was really fighting for democracy. Though Irish Americans lauded Jeannette's statement of support, many Americans deemed such criticism of an ally to be a disloyal choice during wartime.[98]

While Jeannette spoke for many oppressed groups, like many other progressives she had a mixed record concerning non-white minorities. Along with Senator Bob LaFollette of Wisconsin, she worked extensively in 1917 with Helen Pierce Gray, who in 1908 had begun to criticize the federal management of funds for the Crow reservation in southern Montana.[99] In September 1917, she approached the Department of the Interior to secure funds that had been promised to the Flathead Indian Reservation.[100] But then in January 1918, she worked out plans for irrigation on the reservation, supporting white homesteaders who were increasingly being ceded these lands. After several seasons of light rainfall and failing crops, she enabled white farmers to gain $750,000 from the Indian appropriation bill. She argued somewhat vaguely that these farmers' development of the land would ultimately help Native Americans: "By using the water from this project the white men will hasten the time when this money will be returned to the Indian funds."[101]

Before World War I, Jeannette Rankin and Wellington Rankin took the risk of standing in progressive opposition to the combined power in

Montana of mining, railroads, and politicians that kowtowed to them. As he established himself in the state, Wellington made his name opposing those powers, stepping outside of the establishment, as a hard-working man of frontier stock advocating for the rights of individual citizens. And this creed of progressive reform also propelled Jeannette, leading to her activism for suffrage, women's rights, better working conditions for miners, Irish freedom, and sometimes for Native American rights.

The progressive movement created opportunities for both siblings to get started on careers not available to their parents, moving well beyond one ranch or a home in Missoula, to steer the development of their state and nation as they advocated for the rights of the citizenry—and for themselves. They took the risk of standing up to established powers, part of the opportunity of America's Progressive Era. In this time period, the first decades of the twentieth century, both siblings engaged in a fight against the fierce grip of capitalism while recognizing the needs of immigrants, the nation's workers, and women. World War I would alter this emphasis on the individual and the outsider along with the lives of the Rankins.

FIVE

Pacifism and American Wars, Changing and Deepening Views

Progressivism was a response to rapid industrialization and the movement into cities of American workers and immigrants. Progressives rejected the Social Darwinism of the late nineteenth century: the strongest did not need to prevail to create the best version of the nation. Instead, they believed that the problems society faced—poverty, violence, greed, class struggle, racism—could best be addressed by providing a good education, a safe environment, and an efficient workplace that recognized the worth and needs of workers and families—though especially white families. Progressives also concentrated on exposing the evils of corporate greed and political corruption, entwined forces that detracted from democracy and the rights of the individual. These activists generally supported suffrage for women, who presumably would vote to ensure better health care, education, and neighborhoods.

In the late nineteenth century and into the Progressive Era, the belief that human beings in a democracy could do better involved not just efforts to achieve suffrage and workplace safety but to keep the nation out of war. Given different labels, of pacifism, nonviolence, and isolationism, the peace movement had varying judgments attached to it through the decades, in different parts of the country. And in the twentieth century, this commitment would be judged as both right and wrong, as both patriotic and traitorous.

In the nineteenth century, many Americans voiced their determination to stay out of wars and especially those occurring across the ocean. This judgment and a movement it engendered had connections to religious groups and to the east coast. Pacifism, an opposition to militarism, violence, and especially war, was a key belief of the Quakers, who first came to the Massachusetts Bay Colony, and of William Penn, who settled land that became Pennsylvania and Delaware, a gift from King Charles II to his father. He wrote to local tribal chiefs declaring that "I am very sensible of the Unkindness and Injustice that hath been too much exercised towards you by the People of these Parts of the World.... But I am not such a Man, as is well known in my own Country; I have great Love and Regard towards you, and I desire to win and gain your Love and Friendship, by a kind, Just, and Peaceable Life."[1] During the American Revolution and the War of 1812, Quakers generally respected their faith's injunctions against bearing arms or paying for soldier-substitutes. When the Civil War was declared, most Quakers refused to serve, but some joined in the Union's cause as they faced the need "to choose between two evils"—war or the continuation of slavery.[2] Other historical peace churches moving from Europe to east coast settlements included the Church of the Brethren, the Mennonites, and the Anabaptists.

The foundation in 1828 of an American Peace Society, with New England as its center, engaged those who opposed war but not from a set religious perspective. This group merged state and local societies, of which the oldest, the New York Peace Society, dated from 1815. The Society opposed wars between nation states, but not the American Civil War since members deemed it a "police action" against "criminals" of the Confederacy.[3]

The pacifist movement in the west had less influence from religious sects or the Civil War than in the east. Like the forms of Victorianism and progressivism, pacifism had its own western story, as certainly it did for Jeannette Rankin.

When the nation shifted to support for World War I, Wellington went along with the national judgment, as he would also in the 1940s. But when Jeannette saw the tide turning she was willing to pay a steep price for her opposition: it was one thing to oppose corruption as a progressive in the early 1910s or in the 1920s, but to oppose the drive to war would be something else, the acceptable becoming unacceptable. Jeannette took the risk of continuing to fight for her own independent principles as she voiced her highly public opposition not just in 1917 but in 1941: to two world wars.

For Jeannette, Early Influences Toward Pacifism

The ongoing warfare against Native Americans led to a different experience with violence and warfare in the west than in the east. Certainly white settlers sought the land that they secured in Indian wars, but generations of western families lived and died with the reality amid bloody conflict, more a part of western consciousness and history than was the Civil War.

Jeannette Rankin grew up with a recognition of the futility of violence, in the attack and counterattack by which her state dealt with Native Americans, part of her family's history. This brutality came with miners to the west. In California, "the widespread random killing of Indians by individual miners" along with "well armed death squads" resulted in thousands of deaths in the first two years of the gold rush and perhaps fifteen thousand between 1849 and 1870.[4] John Rankin's story of his journey from Canada, repeated to his children, included tales of violence: in late 1869 in Montana, a group of Crows attacked a small wagon train and killed two white men; in retribution, explorers at Fort Benton killed two Indians who had not been involved in the attack. Then in January 1870, U.S. soldiers stormed a Blackfeet camp on the Marias River to exact revenge for the murder of Malcolm Clarke, a prominent rancher. According to a company commander, the resulting massacre of 200 Piegan Indians, mostly women and children, was "the greatest slaughter of Indians ever made by U.S. troops." This ongoing history of conflict also included the infamous Battle of the Little Bighorn in 1876, in which warriors from the Lakota, Cheyenne, and Arapaho tribes opposed the 7th Cavalry, killing commander George Armstrong Custer along with 267 soldiers.[5] While these stories did not involve John Rankin directly, the Fort Fizzle affair of 1877 did. Occurring three years before Jeannette's birth, this failed attack embarrassed her father as it became a much repeated story in town, involving the intelligent plans and movements of Native Americans, the frustrations of warfare, and the ongoing need for a western solution.

During Jeannette's childhood, this warfare continued. In July 1882, the Battle of Big Dry Wash involved Apaches. In September 1886, Geronimo and his troops surrendered to Brigadier General Nelson Miles at Skeleton Canyon. In January 1891, the Pine Ridge Campaign, a lopsided engagement involving a huge regiment of both infantry and cavalry, caused Sioux warriors to lay down their arms and retreat. In December 1890, in the Wounded Knee Massacre, some 200 Sioux were killed by the U.S. 7th Cavalry.

Besides growing up with awareness of the ongoing slaughter of Indian wars, Jeannette knew about the often disreputable vigilante justice. In the late nineteenth century, the Montana Vigilantes, patterned after a group in San Francisco, meted out swift retributions, including whippings and banishments from town as well as lynchings. These vigilantes took over where legal authority didn't exist and even where it did. With such overweening power, they could become nothing more than ruthless mobs.

Jeannette knew this vigilante tradition from repeated tales about the west but also from her great-uncle Billy Berry, who died when she was seventeen. Jeannette had certainly heard his stories about an Indian's arrow passing through his beard. She also knew that after Billy was robbed, he had rounded up a posse and chased the robbers. After their capture by the local sheriff, Billy and his men stormed the jail, overpowered the guards, and took the robbers "into custody." The accused were found dead the next morning, "hanging by the neck" in a barn. After this raid, Billy became a sheriff in a dangerous gold-mining area, the whole story casting him as the toughest of marauders and heroes.

As was true of Billy Berry, many vigilantes found employment in sheriffs' offices, their illegal lynchings becoming legal hangings, deemed a proper punishment for serious crimes like theft, rape, and murder, a highly visible deterrent and spectacle. Prisoners' deaths were unusually painful: most executioners did not know how to calculate the correct drop of the hangman's noose to ensure that the neck would break, so the victim usually died slowly, by strangulation.

Jeannette witnessed the violent justice of capital punishment, mostly of foreigners, in her neighborhood. In 1883, Billy Berry oversaw the first legal execution in the county, of a Chinese man named Ah Yung, his death witnessed by a hundred people, including Billy's niece and her family, who came to town from Grant Creek for the event. Then in December 1890, when Jeannette was ten, four Native Americans, convicted of murdering white men, were hung on a tree between the jail and the courthouse, on a hill right above the Rankins' Madison Street home. As newspapers reported, these men, tied by their legs, ankles, and arms, appeared all dressed in black, with black caps over their faces. Hundreds of people, including several tribal chiefs and the Rankins, saw the men hang there for an hour. The newspaper described this execution as "one of the neatest ones ever done in the north-west."[6]

Jeannette's biographers recorded her dismay at this hanging as well as at the much repeated stories of Indian attack and counter-attack. As hangings continued behind the house, she later told an interviewer, she recognized this violent form of "justice" as something horrendous, as a terrifying local show of death.[7] By the time that she entered college, Jeannette demonstrated a strong reaction to any glorification of violence and warfare. In an article that she wrote in 1958, she recalled what was clearly a memorable educational moment for her: while studying at the University of Montana, she was asked to read Tennyson's poem "The Charge of the Light Brigade" at a student assembly. She refused because she viewed the six hundred's fateful decision to ride into the valley of Death, with the commander demanding "half a league onward" and "charge for the guns!," as not a rational choice, but instead as a cruel and stupid instance of what patriotism might require. In 1958, she still remembered the incident as well as her response: "But this is hideous. I can't read it."[8] She believed that in the ongoing Indian wars, as well as the violence of vigilantes and sheriffs, the individual's judgment was overwhelmed by mass fear and momentum.

Though easterners are credited with forming the pacifist movement, this American belief system also had western leaders, both women and men, from the first pioneer states of Michigan and Ohio all the way to the west coast. As Indian wars became less common by the end of the nineteenth century, pacifist critics began to tally the violence and death caused by the military. Criticism also arose concerning the vigilante tradition of justice and injustice.[9] Western pacifists, building their theories from this history, included Lillian Wald and Evan Thomas from Ohio, Olympia Brown from Michigan, Dorothy Detzer and C. Mervin Palmer from Indiana, Lola Maverick Lloyd from Texas, Genevieve Fiore from Wyoming, Ammon Hennacy from Utah, Ava Helen Miller from Oregon, Mary Wilhelmine Williams from California, and Jeannette Rankin from Montana. They came to the movement influenced by harsh realities of ranches and farms, vigilante justice, and long-term, bloody warfare against Native Americans.

War and Money and Government Power

Jeannette developed an abhorrence to warfare from the west where she grew up, but she also considered the realities of violence and death through her studies during the Progressive Era. She did not go to the New York School of Philanthropy to study war, but there she learned more about what it meant, especially for new immigrants, for industries and their profits, and for campaigns concerning human rights.

Of her education in college, she later declared that "no one had ever seriously taught us about the nature of war." But in New York she had progressive leader Louis Brandeis as a teacher. As he asserted in essays collected in *Other People's Money and How the Bankers Use It*, Americans needed to guard against powerful corporations, large banks, monopolies, public corruption, and mass consumerism so that democracy and the individual could flourish, his analysis involving many of the issues of Wellington's court cases. As Brandeis further indicated, capitalists with the kind of power that mines and railroads held in Montana might seek an extended war since all the equipment and transportation that one required could lead to huge profits.[10]

Jeannette also had the influence of progressive Jane Addams who connected war to the extremes of a government system that required adherence to unjust laws. Addams had visited Leo Tolstoy's home in Yasnaya Polyana in 1896 and read all of his works that she could find in French and English.[11] In *The Kingdom of God Is Within You*, Tolstoy argues that people can become stuck in a violent, unjust government system ruled by corporate greed and thus ruin their basic nature.[12] Besides being an inspiration in forming Hull House, a site where residents could live better values, Tolstoy's ideas helped shape Addams' view of war: as how powerful leaders, deploying their poorest young men as soldiers, sought to colonize groups deemed as Other, while controlling their own populace through cynically deployed appeals to patriotism. In 1898, Addams joined the Anti-Imperialist League, in opposition to the U.S. annexation of the Philippines, and in 1906 published *Newer Ideals of Peace*, in which she concentrates on industrialists and imperialists who seek war and ignore human rights.[13]

After Jeannette Rankin read Tolstoy and Addams, she visited Hull House and became involved with Addams in the Women's Peace Union and the Women's International League, organizations that sought an end to colonialism and war. Their closeness continued after the First World War when they toured the damage in Europe together. When Jeannette worked for the National Consumers' League in the 1920s, her base of operations was Hull House. With both Brandeis and Addams, Jeannette moved beyond realities of her state and region and to an international perspective on the unchecked power of corrupt governments and industries.[14]

Suffrage, Nonviolence and the Anti-War Movement

Before World War I, support for an end to war came from the suffrage movement and its positive view of what women with full citizenry could contribute. Gender essentialism, the attribution of innate qualities to women and men, provided grounding for women who sought to extend their role as caregivers—as they studied home economics, became teachers, and helped reform city governments. The suffrage movement similarly involved the argument that women could refine and humanize their nations, leading them to a better means of settling local and international disputes.[15]

Along with Jane Addams, Alice Paul became a key influence on Jeannette, helping her to consider the appropriate connection between suffrage campaigning, women's role as voters, and peace advocacy. After graduating from Swarthmore, Paul spent 1905 and 1906 at a settlement house in New York City. Like Jeannette Rankin, Paul decided that philanthropy would not spur social change. "I knew in a very short time, I was never going to be a social worker," she later recalled, "because I could see that social workers were not doing much good in the world … you knew you couldn't change the situation by social work."[16]

During 1908 and 1909, Paul attended the School of Economics in London and became involved with the Pankhursts and the English suffrage movement, which was moving from nonviolent marches and boycotts to violence. The first violence occurred as suffragists threw stones through a window of the prime minister's house in August 1908. As time passed without their demands being met, the Pankhursts initiated more violent alternatives. In July of 1912, their adherents began setting fire to empty buildings, such as Nuneham House, the residence of anti-suffrage minister Lewis Harcourt. Then they set fire to the Theatre Royal, where Prime Minister Henry Asquith was slated to speak.[17]

For Alice Paul, these choices were not appropriate for demonstrating the best of what women could bring to government and society: she adhered to the Quaker belief that the nonviolent confrontation of evil is always superior to violent measures, both as an approach to activism and to foreign wars. In England in 1909, Paul met with Mohandas Gandhi, when he traveled there to stay with Emmeline Pankhurst and discuss the status of Indians in the new Union of South Africa.[18] The widespread press coverage of violent protest in England provided Gandhi with an opportunity for publicly defining his own nonviolence: he praised the suffragists' determination to secure equal rights but criticized their methods, as lacking a tie to the best of human choices and thus having no chance for success.[19] Paul made similar judgments as she crafted her own approach to activism: when she returned home, her involvement in England gave her a public presence, but she repeatedly defined herself in opposition to the choices of the English campaign.[20]

Jeannette got to know Alice Paul when they worked on the suffrage parade in 1913 to proceed Wilson's inauguration. Then they collaborated in Washington, in lobbying members of the House and Senate. Though Jeannette was planning a campaign for Montana and worked for NAWSA in Pennsylvania, New Hampshire, and other states, she agreed with Paul about the priority of seeking a federal amendment. They also spoke frequently about nonviolence as the right method of making effective appeals for change, about opposition to war, and about the role of women, as voters and activists, in curbing the male will to violence and combat. As Jeannette recalled in 1958, suffrage and opposition to war became "integrally related in my youthful thoughts and activities."[21] As she claimed, about an essentialist difference and women as natural protectors of children and American communities, "One of the very main things that we talked about in woman suffrage in every campaign was that it was women's job to get rid of war."[22]

Quickly Altering Views of War

When Jeannette ran for office in 1916, her opposition to war, formed from her western childhood, her study in New York, and the suffrage movement, was acceptable in her state. In the *Literary Digest*, Jeannette said of local residents at the time: "I judged the sentiment in Montana was overwhelmingly against war."[23] By World War I, nearly half of the Montana population was foreign-born, with immigrants from Germany and Austria as well as Canada, Ireland, Norway, Sweden, Mexico, and England. In 1916, 10 percent of Montanans spoke German and another 10 percent were of German descent. When news of the war reached the United States in August 1914, immigrants who had come from all over Europe reacted with sympathy and concern for the citizens of their home countries: German-Americans in Montana and elsewhere held patriotic meetings and collected war-relief funds. In Butte, a multi-ethnic community with a significant immigrant population, the Metal Mine Workers' Union opposed war as primarily a profit source for large industries and a cruel exploitation of poor young men.

Like Jeannette, progressives generally felt that this war would just extend older, irrational conflicts in Europe while increasing industrial profits and sacrificing workers. Woodrow Wilson had witnessed the Civil War firsthand as a boy, which contributed to his desire to avoid sending men into battle. After the German attack on the British liner *Lusitania* in 1915, in which 128 Americans died, Wilson withstood the pressure to declare war. As he ran for reelection in 1916, he employed the popular slogan "he kept us out of war" to appeal to voters who wanted to avoid engagement in Europe or with Mexico. Republican candidate Charles Evans Hughes criticized Wilson for not taking the "necessary preparations" to prepare for a contracted conflict, which only served to strengthen Wilson's image as an anti-war candidate.[24] He won in Montana with 56 percent of the vote in 1916, with the more bellicose Hughes at 37 percent. Wilson had only secured 35 percent of the vote in 1912 when he ran against Roosevelt and Taft.

As the country moved toward war after the 1916 election, with Germany declaring its intention to pursue unrestricted submarine warfare and telegramming Mexico to suggest an alliance, Americans still sought to avoid entering the European conflict. To appeal to progressives, Wilson began in January 1917 to depict the war as a form of idealistic progress. He insisted that the United States would participate not as an ally of the British and the French, but as an "associated power": Americans would be fighting not to enact the discredited goals of other nations, but to change values, to "make the world safe for democracy" and end war permanently. On April 2 as he urged a declaration of war in Congress, expanding on themes he established through the spring, he made the case for a glorious battle for the "right," a term that he kept repeating: "the right is more precious than peace, and we shall fight for the things which we have always carried nearest our hearts—for democracy, for the right of those who submit to authority to have a voice in their own governments, for the rights and liberties of small nations, for a universal dominion of right by such a concert of free peoples as shall bring peace and safety to all nations and make the world itself at last free."[25] He began and ended by addressing "gentlemen of the Congress," which described everyone there except for Jeannette Rankin.

Moving into 1917, although many unionists continued to protest, most Americans and especially those with political aspirations acquiesced to war. Indeed, most NAWSA activists joined the preparedness campaign and backed America's entry into war: whether they actually supported this decision or not, they believed that their participation would lead to respect in the political arena and to suffrage as a reward. Both Carrie Chapman Catt and Anna Howard Shaw, neither of them actually war supporters, accepted appointments on the Women's Committee of the Council on National Defense. As they responded to the call of patriotism that made opposition into traitorous activity, they would not be joined by Alice Paul or Jeannette Rankin.

The Vote in Congress

After Jeannette entered Congress in March of 1917, even though she wanted to work on so many progressive issues, all of her focus had to concern war. This vote for American involvement was not what she expected to be the first, and in some ways the only, focus of her term in Congress.

As Jeannette considered her own decision, she demonstrated strength and self-reliance, what it took to stand up against the rush to war. As Wellington later noted, Jeannette could be "disgustingly independent." She admired people who were willing to sacrifice for their principles. "She'd just blow up," Wellington said, at the suggestion of making decisions for more selfish reasons. She "would consider it more dishonest not to vote your conviction than to rob a bank or steal something."[26] He recalled, in comparison, that a number of times during his own career he didn't follow his convictions: it is a low thing not to have the courage of your convictions, he concluded, and she had eight or ten times more of it than he did. But he also thought that her inability to compromise or accommodate could be a limitation: "She just won't pretend, which is stupid in my view, in a way."[27]

While Jeannette made up her mind, Wellington sought to persuade her for war, his progressive beginnings not extending this far, to opposing the president and the changing tide of public opinion. He wanted her to decide on what he called "a man's vote": she was on trial with America, he argued, and must make the patriotic choice, showing that women could cope with the hardest circumstances of governing.[28] As he later described the impact on her career of how Jeannette might vote, "I knew she couldn't be elected again if she did vote against the war. I didn't want to see her destroy herself."[29] And Jeannette later recalled his logic: Wellington "couldn't bear to think of all that I had done and built up and the recognition I had received being torn down if I voted against war. He knew the hysteria of the people."[30]

Realizing that the vote was coming, Wellington asked her to meet with others who might persuade her. He took Jeannette to Oyster Bay to see Theodore Roosevelt, whom Wellington knew from the Bull Moose days, what would be, as Wellington recalled, "the most wonderful evening 'til midnight" though it started badly when the driver got lost on the way. The night featured the surprising complexities of what Roosevelt told Jeannette as he agreed that war could have been avoidable: he said of Woodrow Wilson, as Wellington recalled, "if he had a lick of sense, this war wouldn't need to be." Roosevelt brought out pictures of himself with Kaiser Wilhelm II from when they planned a conference of thirteen nations in 1906 and went on military maneuvers together in 1910. He told the Rankins that if he were president, he could have warned the Kaiser not to start a conflict that he couldn't win, especially if Americans came into it: "He'd know I meant it."[31]

That night, though Roosevelt recognized that a smart president could have controlled the situation, he told Jeannette that once diplomacy efforts had failed, he was all for the United States entering the conflict. As he campaigned for Wilson's opponent, Republican Charles Evans Hughes, in 1916, Roosevelt had blasted Wilson as cowardly for not going to war over the sinking of the *Lusitania*, and after war was declared he tried to sell the president on reconstituting the Rough Riders from the charge up San Juan Hill. Though Roosevelt thought that war was inevitable by April of 1917, he declined Wellington's request to tell Jeannette how to vote. As she recalled, "I felt very much honored and I appreciated that he thought the situation in Europe by then required war, but he said nothing to me to indicate that he wanted to influence my vote. At the time, he realized that I was a symbol of democracy and he didn't want that symbol destroyed."[32]

When Roosevelt did not convince Jeannette to support the war, Wellington brought suffragist Harriet Laidlaw to Washington to describe the damage that would be done to the suffrage cause by the first woman in office voting against war, seemingly unable or unwilling to contribute to the defense of the nation.[33] As Wellington and Harriet talked to Jeannette, they argued that she would be harming the careers and political participation of other women, perhaps for decades to come. As Jeannette later recalled of other similar persuaders who sent letters and telegrams, "many of my loved friends told me I would ruin the suffrage movement if I voted against war."[34]

Five. Pacifism and American Wars, Changing Views 93

On the day before the vote, after an argument lasting until midnight, Wellington once again tried to convince her. He told her to vote for war since it would be approved anyway and the vote would determine her chance at reelection. As he recalled his logic, "I didn't want to see her destroy herself."³⁵ And then he finally said that she had heard it all and "You just vote your conscience."³⁶ She told him that she could not vote for war to extend her own career: "But never for one second could I face the idea that I would send young men to be killed for no other reason than to save my seat in Congress."³⁷ She did tell him that she would not vote no, or at all, on the first ballot, but would wait to see how the arguments progressed. Wellington later reflected on all he had done to persuade her and the cost to both of them: "I was the closest person to her in the world, and today.... I think that my pressure did more harm to her than anybody else.... I put all kinds of pressure on her.... I've been kind of ashamed of it since."³⁸

While almost everyone spoke to Jeannette about voting yes, Alice Paul made a final visit to lobby for pacifism and a no vote. While the debate went on in the House, she came to the Capitol with Hazel Hunkins, a friend of Jeannette from Montana, to say, as Paul later recalled, that "we thought it would be a tragedy for the first woman ever in Congress to vote for war." Paul and Hunkins argued further that since women were "the peace-loving half of the world," they needed to demonstrate their commitment to their country and the future by opposing war no matter what the personal cost.³⁹

In the Senate, six senators, led by Robert LaFollette of Wisconsin, voted against a declaration of war. Then the legislation went to the foreign affairs committee of the House and on to the floor for a vote. Members debated all of Thursday, April 5, and up until Good Friday morning. As she had promised Wellington, Jeannette did not vote on the first roll call. Speaker Joseph Cannon, who then assumed she would not vote at all, walked over to her seat. "Little woman, you cannot afford not to vote," he said. "You represent the womanhood of the country in the American Congress. I shall not advise you how to vote but you should vote one way or another—as your conscience dictates." There was silence in the chamber after Jeannette's name was called a second time, and everyone turned to look at her. She rose slowly, clutching the chair in front of her. Softly, she said, "I want to stand by my country, but I cannot vote for war." And then she added, "I vote no." In speaking in this manner before voting, Jeannette violated a House rule that forbade comment on a vote.⁴⁰ Wellington later told an interviewer that she had not planned to speak: "I'm satisfied that five minutes before she didn't know she was going to say that. It always broke her up when she hated not to be standing by the country."⁴¹ Jeannette recalled concerning what she said as she voted, "Of course, if I had thought it out I wouldn't have said a thing like that." As she commented further, the congressmen had all yelled "vote," creating "an awful commotion," and she spoke without planning to do so.[42]

The vote in the House was 374 for declaring war, 50 against, and 9 not voting.[43]

As Jeannette later recalled, tears ran down the cheeks of hundreds of members of Congress as they spoke and then as they voted. "Very few of the men wanted to vote for war," she said. "They were stampeded. They didn't know what else to do and so they voted for it.... All the Civil War veterans voted against it."[44] She later regretted that she hadn't shared her doubts or her ultimate decision with her congressional colleagues because some of them later told her if they had known how she planned to vote they would have joined her.

Afterwards, Jeannette met Wellington in the hallway of the Capitol to walk home together, and Wellington told her that "You know you are not going to be reelected. You know there will be a lot of feeling," and she replied that "I am not interested in that. All I am interested in [is] what they will say fifty years from now. That's all I'm thinking about.... They can go to Hell. I don't care what they think."[45]

And then Wellington said the more general "Think what you've done," a line he repeated when Belle Fligelman, in Washington to serve as Jeannette's secretary, let them into the house. The next week, in a letter to her brother, Jeannette wrote that "I am sorry to disappoint you. I still feel that this was the only way I could go." Jeannette later reflected on making the decision: "It was easy to stand against the propaganda of the militarists, but very difficult to go against friends and dear ones who felt that I was making a needless sacrifice." As she stated further, she wanted to demonstrate the power of a woman in Congress standing up against male bullying and the drive to war: for her, it was "a most significant vote and a most significant act on the part of women, because women are going to have to stop war."[46]

Jeannette judged her risk-taking vote as principled; her brother thought of it as principled but foolish; others viewed it as hysterical and weak. Fifty members of Congress voted no, but the *New York Times*, in the main article concerning the decision, led with the headline of "Seek to Explain Miss Rankin's 'No,'" a much smaller fifth headline mentioning the other forty-nine representatives.[47] A subheading in the article called hers "purely a woman's vote." The text focused on her emotional reaction right afterwards: she "threw her head back and sobbed … her appearance was that of a woman on the verge of a breakdown." Jeannette admitted to crying during the debate, an action she defended: "I have more respect for a woman who cries before she votes upon whether or not we shall have war than [for] the man who goes to a saloon and takes three highballs in a similar situation." While the *New York Times* and newspapers across the country depicted her as bordering on

Five. Pacifism and American Wars, Changing Views

hysterical, witnesses said she was dry-eyed and controlled, as Jeannette also recalled: "I had wept so much that week that my tears were all gone by the time the vote came."[48] When her close friend and fellow freshman representative Fiorello LaGuardia was asked if she cried, he said that he didn't know because he couldn't see through the tears in his own eyes.[49]

In the weeks and months after the vote, Jeannette dealt with strong criticism. The Montana state women's club passed a resolution against her. Letters sent to her that she kept, signed and unsigned, accused her of being un–American, a traitor, a weak-willed woman.[50] Some state newspapers depicted Jeannette as an undesirable and impeachable member of Congress. Newspapers from other states labeled her as ineffectual and childlike in her logic, more stupid than traitorous: the *Lincoln* (Nebraska) *Star*, for example, excused this faulty maiden vote because of her sex and thus her ignorance concerning harsh, male political realities.[51]

Through it all, while many articles and letters made Jeannette into a dupe or a villain and only a few depicted her as a moral, independent American, she had the support of her siblings, including Wellington even though he disagreed with her choice, and of her friends. Along with other letters to her sisters, she wrote one of many pages to Harriet in May 1917, to explain her reasons for the vote and what happened in the Congress on that day. She also often corresponded with Cornelia Swinnerton, called Nina, an activist and nurse that Jeannette met when she went to the New York School of Philanthropy. They exchanged long handwritten letters, sharing chit chat and dreams and gossip as well as political and emotional support. Nina had sent a wire and letters urging Jeannette to vote against war and not follow along with other suffragists: "Jeannette, dear, don't sell us out as Mrs. Catt and all the rest of them have done. We count on you to vote for peace."[52] She sent supportive letters afterwards, urging her friend to continue focusing on the future of humanity. On May 22, 1917, Jeannette wrote to Nina that women supporters were pulling away; her friend wrote back that she never would. Other friends stood by her and tried to help her remain positive. At Christmas 1917, her friend and Wellington's associate Helena Stellway wrote to Jeannette that she had sent her dainty pink undergarments and "garterettes" with cunning French bows to help her feel a little better about all that she had endured.[53]

In the Following Months—and Seeking Re-Election

Wellington continued to support Jeannette, but he faced difficulties after her vote, their careers continuing to be entwined and her anti-war vote making him seem unpatriotic. Right afterwards, he sought out interview opportunities to report that he believed in his sister but opposed her decision.⁵⁴ To further defend himself, Wellington joined the Tank Corps. He ultimately entered the armed forces on November 4, 1918, one day before that fall's election, in which his sister was again running, and seven days before the signing of the armistice. He earned the rank of corporal on December 9 and was discharged four days later. An anonymous opponent, in a radio broadcast, spoke derisively of his seven days of service: "There may be soldiers listening to me tonight who were chloroformed longer than Rankin was uniformed. Perhaps paraphrasing Nathan Hale, Wellington's only regret is he did not have another week to give to his country."⁵⁵ Though Wellington tried to demonstrate his dedication to war and the nation, many people in Montana never forgave him for being Jeannette's brother: eleven years later, when he ran for governor, newspapers across the state reminded voters of Jeannette's pacifism and thus the entire family's seeming lack of patriotism.⁵⁶

After the declaration of war, it was not just Jeannette and Wellington who became suspect in the state. Anti-German and anti-labor sentiment increased in Montana and led, in the following February, to passage of the Montana Sedition Act, legislation that served as the model for the federal Sedition Act of 1918. The Montana act prohibited the teaching of German in high schools and universities, banned the sale of works in German, required the removal from library shelves of books in German and about Germany, and prohibited the speaking of German in public. This legislation led to the arrest of over two hundred people, mostly recent immigrants, and the conviction of seventy-eight. An instant sort of patriotic zeal also drove the state's response to army recruitment efforts. In 1917–18, approximately 40,000 Montanans, 10 percent of the state's population, either volunteered or were drafted into the armed forces, a manpower contribution to the war that was 25 percent higher than any other state's on a per capita basis.⁵⁷

In this climate, Jeannette did not return to office in 1918. That year Jeannette and Wellington judged that she could not be reelected to the House. Since 1916, Montana had been split into two districts, each with one representative. The new western district, including their hometown of Missoula, was heavily Democratic, supportive of Wilson and the war effort, and not supportive of any Republican. Both Wellington and Jeannette felt that Anaconda and other state powers had forwarded this division to gerrymander her into a district where she could not win.⁵⁸

When Wellington wrote a long letter to Jeannette in July 1917, about eastern and western districts for 1918, he was beginning to think that attempting to attain another office, presumably the U.S. Senate, would be a better choice. Given their shared analysis of the new political landscape, Jeannette decided to run in the Republican primary for a U.S. Senate seat. Hampered by her anti-war vote and her support of miners against the all-powerful Anaconda, she was defeated by Dr. Oscar M. Lanstrum, a former state representative and publisher of the *Montana Record-Herald*, by the close vote of 18,805 to 17,091. To oppose him, the Democrats nominated incumbent Thomas J. Walsh, who had first entered the Senate in 1912, a supporter of Wilson and a skillful and popular politician, the lawyer who hired Wellington when he first returned from Harvard.[59]

After Jeannette lost the Republican primary, her vote against war certainly a prime reason, Wellington began negotiating with the Democrats, threatening that she might run against Walsh and Lanstrum as a third-party candidate. Because of her opposition to Anaconda, Democratic Party officials feared that if she ran she would siphon off labor votes and thus hurt Walsh. In sexist terms that highlighted Wellington's power, Colonel C.B. Nolan, Walsh's law partner, wrote to Walsh on August 30, 1918, urging that "every influence possible be brought to bear on Wellington not to have her run."[60] Nolan and Walsh proposed to Wellington that a position be created for Jeannette, perhaps overseas, so that she could retire from the field gracefully. Walsh's campaign manager, A.E. Spriggs, also suggested that the Democratic Party might offer cash.

This discussion, of payment and an overseas appointment, soon hit the state's newspapers, something that Jeannette found an anathema. Such rumors, in fact, may have led her to stay in the race.[61] That fall, Jeannette became a candidate of the National Party, an organization founded by socialists, as she later recalled the situation: "I was offered bribes not to run on the Independent ticket. In order to prove I didn't accept bribes I had to run. So I ran."[62] She knew that representing a minority party, as her brother had done in 1914, would be unlikely to lead to victory.[63] For this campaign, to assert her differences from other candidates and position her antiwar vote versus all that Wilson had claimed as he declared war, she chose the slogan "make the world safe for humanity."[64]

Her sources of support in 1918, after the war vote, were different, and lesser, than in 1916. Dr. Karl Weiss, president of the Montana German Press of Helena, wrote to her in January to say that she would certainly get the German vote. But many groups were less positive. Union organizer L.C. Butterfield of Fortina wrote in May about her "struggles against the powers of darkness," but claimed that she still had the support of mine workers. Supporter Mary Dean from Helena wrote to her in July to claim that "the men politicians" were creating "prejudice and fear."[65] During that month, as she sent out fundraising letters to women in Montana, many of them responded that they planned to vote for her but did not want any public association with the campaign. She was also warned that her national connections, to suffragists and peace advocates—deemed suspicious outsiders during wartime—would no longer help her in the state. And some of these long-time associates openly opposed her: Carrie Chapman Catt quite publicly supported Walsh. On November 5, the vote totals were Walsh 46,160; Lanstrum 40,229; Rankin 26,013.[66] Lanstrum did not run for office again.

Jeannette's Changing View of War

In 1916, Jeannette voted against war as a progressive, viewing it as an anathema to democracy, a symbol of colonial aggression and industrial corruption. These ideas had been influenced by Tolstoy and Gandhi. Like Jane Addams and Alice Paul, she believed that the votes of women could temper ancient, bitter tendencies of men. She believed additionally that Wilson had defrauded voters in 1916 as he ran for office, his "kept us out of war" slogan being disingenuous since after the election he advocated for a national commitment to it.

Jeannette's view of Americans at war changed after 1918. After this first American engagement abroad, she moved into a deeper analysis of the cause and effect of war, of the inevitability of repeated conflicts, with even the winners becoming losers in the war system or method, a continuing pattern of death and destruction and vengeance. In the 1920s and 1930s, with a change of presidential administrations and Americans well aware of what war had cost in just a year of engagement, advocates of peace like Jeannette could question American involvement in World War I—indeed they could argue against Americans ever entering into the European sphere of power and hate again, without being labeled as traitors or naïve hysterics.

For Jeannette, the Treaty of Versailles demonstrated the absolute power and destructiveness of victors as well as the inevitable anger of losers. In June 1919, when German leaders asked for changes to the drafted treaty terms, the Allies issued an ultimatum stating that Germany would have to accept them or face an invasion within twenty-four hours. On June 28, the peace treaty was signed. For Jeannette, its specifics reeked of despotic vengeance, of a war's ending that would cause the next one. The treaty stripped Germany of 25,000 square miles of territory and seven million citizens: the treaty "restored" Alsace-Lorraine to France; recognized the independence of Czechoslovakia and Poland; allocated the Ruanda-Urundi territory of Africa to Belgium; and ceded German East Africa to England. Japan was granted all German realms in the Pacific north of the equator and Australia those south of the equator, except for German Samoa, which New Zealand acquired. The treaty additionally placed strict limits on the size of the German army and navy, disbanded the air force, and dismissed the general military staff. Additionally, and for Jeannette most egregiously, the allies required Germany to compensate them for the damage caused. While a commission would determine the final amount in 1921, in the interim, Germany had to pay an equivalent of $5 billion in gold, commodities, ships, and securities. To ensure compliance to these demands, Allied troops were to occupy the Rhineland and bridgeheads east of the Rhine for fifteen years.

The inequity of the treaty and the instability it engendered caused Jeannette to deepen her analysis of warfare. As she traveled in Europe directly after the war for various peace organizations, she saw firsthand the effect of war and of this treaty's form of peace: bombed buildings, a lack of health care, the unemployed living in the streets, and long lines for food. She also studied all available data: with the country in political chaos, the government was trying ineffectually to deal with 2.7 million disabled veterans, a million war orphans, and half a million widows along with a disheartened and desperate populace.

When Jeannette returned to Germany in the 1930s, during the summers from 1931 to 1937, she saw that in a dire situation party leaders and the people were willing to listen to anyone, even Adolf Hitler, who promised better days and a return to prominence. Jeannette wrote to Eleanor Roosevelt in 1935 about the German arms build-up of which Americans seemed unaware. She urged Eleanor to use her influence to educate the public about American defensive preparedness and Nazi military might. In the summer of 1937, Jeannette spoke again with the first lady and once again tried to reach the president through her.[67]

While Jeannette realized that aggression and war might appeal to Germans as a means of regaining land, financial stability, and status, she also judged a new conflict as potentially restorative to a United States mired in depression. War created a future for military leaders as well as huge profits for industrialists, from steel to shirt manufacturers. In her speeches, Jeannette described an American "military organization that want to keep their jobs by expanding their production." As she said repeatedly in speeches in the 1930s, while war enriches the coffers of industrialists, it also improves the reputation of military and political leaders, who staunch the opposition by labeling them as unpatriotic, as traitorous, a process she knew well. In 1933, before the House Foreign Affairs Committee, she argued that "we are walking in the direction of war and we can get a war anytime the munition makers and profit makers demand it."[68]

As Jeannette responded to what she saw occurring in Europe and the United States, what she believed would inexorably lead to the next war, she developed her thinking about a "war system" overwhelming the twentieth century, a vengeful victory leading inexorably to the next attack. As she looked at childhood playgrounds and Indian removals, the atrocity and aftermath of World War I, and what was occurring in Germany in the

1930s, she argued that "war is a method that has nothing whatever to do with the dispute," leading inexorably to death and more war, chosen instead of careful analysis, diplomacy, and compromise.[69] Jeannette argued in radio addresses and before civic groups that the war system had been the cause and effect of problems in Europe for 1000 years, what our forefathers had left to get away from. Europeans might decide to continue fighting, relying on the wrong systems, but by entering these fights we would make no real change abroad while wasting the lives of our own young men: like the 116,516 who died there in 1917–1918.[70]

As Jeannette witnessed all that was occurring in Europe, she argued in the early 1930s that the United States had to begin planning its own thoughtful response, learning from the first war experience in Europe. Instead of planning to invade, the United States should prepare to defend itself, primarily through what she described as a "shore defense." As she claimed, "A foreign invader could not win a guerrilla war fighting on our own soil."[71] She argued that Americans could defend our shores with a well-developed navy, with a string of bases and sufficient sailors to staff them—to keep any attack from reaching the United States. She recognized that the nation might be bombed, but it would take millions of men to launch the ground attack that would have to follow in order to defeat us. Canada and Mexico would not allow any sort of staging to occur from their territories: they would not choose to offer up their countries as a battlefield against the United States.

In this judgment, Jeannette was moving from absolute pacifism to isolationism based in international diplomacy, a change from 1917. She thus reasoned within a long-held American tradition, dating back to the colonial period. Indeed, the colonists took comfort in being "isolated" from Europe by the Atlantic Ocean. In his Farewell Address, George Washington memorably spelled out the intent of this American creed: "The great rule of conduct for us, in regard to foreign nations, is in extending our commercial relations, to have with them as little political connection as possible. Europe has a set of primary interests, which to us have none, or a very remote relation. Hence she must be engaged in frequent controversies the causes of which are essentially foreign to our concerns."[72] Thomas Jefferson, in his inaugural address, summed up American isolationism as a doctrine of "peace, commerce, and honest friendship, with all nations—entangling alliances with none."[73] President James Monroe gave voice to the same priorities as he established the Monroe Doctrine: "In the wars of the European powers, in matters relating to themselves, we have never taken part, nor does it comport with our policy, so to do."[74] During the 1800s, the United States fought the War of 1812, the Mexican War, and the Spanish-American War, whether admirable choices or not, without forming foreign alliances or fighting in Europe.

Five. Pacifism and American Wars, Changing Views

As Jeannette studied this history of American isolationism, she began investing her time in its possible applications to the twentieth century, at a time when her activism for peace was more acceptable than in 1917. Though she remained a resident of Montana, she bought a farm in Watkinsville, Georgia, outside of Athens, in 1923, with money from Wellington, seeking to remove herself from capitalism and corruption. But she was often in Washington and on the road advocating for peace.[75] While also working for the National Consumers' League, she began lobbying for the National Council for the Prevention of War, her work centered in Washington. She also became an officer of the Women's International League for Peace and Freedom, established in 1915 by Jane Addams. She worked on the Kellogg-Briand Pact, which renounced war as an instrument of national policy. Jeannette then devoted time to lobbying for the Neutrality Acts, in 1935, 1937, and 1939, legislation that she believed would bar the nation from investing further in the "war method." These acts banned munitions exports and loans to belligerents, restricted American travel on belligerent ships. and banned U.S. ships from carrying goods or passengers to belligerent ports.[76]

With war raging in Europe, the progress made in the 1920s and 1930s began to fade. In the fall of 1939, Roosevelt secured a revision to the Neutrality Act, to allow allies to buy arms in the United States, a provision called "cash and carry." And Jeannette decided to run for office again instead of continuing to work for peace organizations. As she viewed the situation, Montanans had no great appetite to enter into another war against Germany and would welcome a more thoughtful and diplomatic approach.[77]

Jeannette Rankin's home in Watkinsville, Georgia, in the 1920s (Schlesinger Library, Radcliffe Institute, Harvard University).

Interior of the bedroom in Jeannette Rankin's home in Watkinsville, Georgia. Her photograph is on the dressing stand (Schlesinger Library, Radcliffe Institute, Harvard University).

That fall, she talked to students at 52 of the 56 high schools in the western part of the state, in the same difficult district in which she ran in 1918.[78] She asked students and their parents to write their congressmen and the president, to create a strong message against war at a time when it was still acceptable to oppose it.

As she had done in 1916 when she sought election, Jeannette began to make campaign plans with Wellington, as she later recalled: "Of course, I wouldn't have run without the advice of my brother."[79] Wellington wasn't sure if she could win in the Republican primary against the current congressman, or whether she could beat a Democrat in the general election; he feared that Roosevelt's popularity would sweep Democrats to victory. But certainly Wellington told Jeannette that he would back her if she made the decision to run, and he began working with her on a plan for success.

This election presented opportunities in the form of weak candidates opposing her. In the Republican primary, she beat Jacob Thorkelson, from Butte, who had entered the House in January of 1939. In July 1940, the *Christian Science Monitor* labeled him as a Nazi sympathizer who had "built up a reputation of having filled the Congressional Record with anti–Semitic diatribes."[80] Then in the general election, she faced Democrat Jerry O'Connell, a divorced Catholic widely discussed in Montana as having communist sympathies. In "An Election Special—A Voter's Guide," issued during the campaign, Republicans labeled O'Connell as "a moral coward and a mental pervert as crooked as a python's track through a primeval forest."[81] Fortunately for Jeannette, Anaconda Mining didn't endorse O'Connell and so, though the company didn't support her, it did not mount an opposition campaign. In the fall election, she secured 54 percent of the vote. In a district with a majority of 12,000 Democrats, she won with over 9000 votes.[82]

Jeannette Rankin wearing a corsage, in Helena, as she ran for office in fall 1940 (Schlesinger Library, Radcliffe Institute, Harvard University).

Soon after entering office in January, Jeannette opposed the Lend Lease policy, which passed in March to provide warships and warplanes, along with other weaponry, to the allies, what she viewed as a first step toward war and an abandonment of the Neutrality Acts. In the summer she worked in support of the Flood Control Act, which authorized civil engineering projects such as dams, levees, and dikes. And then there was the attack on Pearl Harbor.

Concerning this declaration of war, with a direct attack on Americans involved, Wellington knew that the reaction to a no vote would be more severe than in 1917 and would not garner the positive response given to peace advocacy in the 1920s and 1930s. On the night of the attack, Wellington began desperately trying to reach Jeannette. He called Edna to see if she was hiding their sister from him. Edna said that Jeannette was on her way to Buffalo to give a speech for peace and that she didn't know what her sister planned to do when the vote occurred. Wellington later recalled telling Edna, "Well, keep her on that train—or be sure how she's going to vote. She can't be for peace again—after Pearl Harbor!" As he remembered further, "The second war was coming. I couldn't—she wouldn't talk to me on the phone. She wouldn't answer the phone. I'd get my sisters to talk to her, but I couldn't do much with them."[83]

But, regardless of Wellington's efforts and what the decision would cost her, Jeannette once again voted against war. At the same time that Edna was in the White House making a speech on improving the nation's birth-control programs, Jeannette stood and cast the sole no vote in both houses of Congress. She later said in comparison that concerning World War I the members of the House discussed the resolution for a full day and night, but this time everything was rushed, denying the right for full democratic debate and consideration. The president made an eight-minute speech, and there was a short positive discussion. After each member spoke, she requested to do so but Speaker of the House Sam Rayburn would not recognize her. During the roll call, she again broke protocol, as she had with her World War I vote, saying that "as a woman I can't go to war, and I refuse to send anyone else." Her "no" brought on hisses and boos, as she recalled, the atmosphere un-parliamentary and irregular.[84] Afterwards she stayed in a phone booth waiting for police to take her back to her office.

Her vote brought immediate vilification in the newspapers, her complex anti-war stance, developed from 1920 to 1940, no longer acceptable or properly American. Much of this response involved gender. On December 9, the *New York Times* reported that Montana's Republican leaders had denounced her and that she needed to publicly renounce her own weak-willed, feminine decision so as "to redeem Montana's honor and loyalty."[85] The *Washington Post* concentrated on the response of rational male leaders to a weak woman: "After she voted, there was a small procession of solemn-faced colleagues back up the aisle to her seat. They spoke earnestly to her, in the benign manner of men who strive to change a woman's mind ... but at the end of each conversation, she always shook her head."[86] Henry McLemore, a columnist for the Hearst Corporation, claimed that Jeannette would make everybody's dream wife: she was all sweetness and light, with a complete inability to see what is going on, a dupe who dismissed a bomb like a run in her stocking, so pacific that she couldn't see trouble in the Pacific. Her husband could do any mean thing, of which the article gave many examples, and she wouldn't even notice. He would marry her, McLemore claimed further, if there weren't laws against bigamy, and she would be voted Miss Tokyo of 1941 by the Japanese.[87] Other newspapers branded her as a "skunk," a "traitor," and a "Nazi," although William Allen White wrote in the *Emporia Gazette* that "probably 100 men in Congress would have liked to do what she did. Not one of them had the courage to do it. The *Gazette* entirely disagrees with the wisdom of her position. But Lord,

5. Pacifism and American Wars, Changing and Deepening Views

Jeannette Rankin sitting in a telephone booth in the Capitol, waiting for Capitol police to escort her back to her office after she cast the sole vote against war with Japan, December 8, 1941 (Bettmann/Getty Images).

it was a brave thing!"[88] Many letters and telegrams condemned her, branding her a traitor or a coward and mentioning the possibility of a recall. One letter sent from Albuquerque, for example, addressed her as "traitoress"; another claimed that "if you had a man, you would be different"; a third said that she had entered the phone booth after the vote to pray for the Japanese to win.[89]

After her brave and independent vote, even as her nation began to wage war, Jeannette continued to analyze American involvement in foreign conflicts. In December of 1942, in articles published in the *New York Sun* and the *Christian Science Monitor* and reprinted across the country, she concentrated on the often deadly complications of foreign allegiances. She encouraged readers to analyze the last year's events, moving beyond what the president expected them to believe. In the summer of 1941, after Japan moved to take Indochina, the United States had completely frozen all trade with Japan. At the Atlantic Conference in August 1941, Churchill had urged Roosevelt to instate extreme sanctions to weaken Japan and thus preserve the English empire, including Hong Kong, Fiji, New Zealand, the Solomon Islands, Malaysia, Ceylon, Myanmar, and North Borneo.[90] This embargo led to a drop of 75 percent in imports, creating a severe lack of food, iron and steel, gasoline, coal, and textiles, leaving the country near to "economic collapse." Jeannette felt that sanctions bolstering English colonial power had led inexorably to Japanese retaliation, intended to ensure that the United States would not only defend English property in Asia but become one of the allies fighting Hitler. As she argued, "The Japanese situation was created to force Congress to go to war with Germany. That was done to satisfy England's desire for us to go to war in Europe." Citing research that appeared in state department bulletins and newspapers, Jeannette argued further that Roosevelt had anticipated an attack in the Pacific that would allow him to declare war on Japan and thus on Germany. That he failed to warn commanders, not of a particular date but of a coming attack, she referred to as traitorous. In this argument, Jeannette quoted Charles Beard, Harry Elmer Barnes, and other sources who agreed with her assessment of Roosevelt.[91]

Her letters to the more thoughtful people who wrote to her gave her a chance to explain her thinking further. In April 1942, responding to several correspondents, she described the purpose of a declaration of war: we did not need this act "to defend ourselves and to protect the Philippines, Guam, Wake and other possessions and to fight, defensively and offensively, any enemy who attacked us." She then turned to what she judged to be the act's real purpose: "We DID need a declaration of war to send men to die in Europe, Africa and the Far East." Indeed the troops sent to Europe in January 1942 demonstrated the true emphasis of the declaration of war. With so much attention on Europe, she claimed with some exaggeration, "We didn't send one gun or one boat to protect the Philippines. We did absolutely nothing."[92]

After the war ended, Jeannette Rankin continued her analysis of world war's cause and effect. If we had taken diplomatic measures and remained on our own continent, we could have avoided 116,516 deaths in the First World War and 405,399 in the second.[93] Had we remained on the sidelines in World War I, she argued further, perhaps World War II could have been avoided: a German monarchy might have blocked the creation of a Hitler. Additionally the cruel revenge of the powerful victor, Woodrow Wilson, led to Hitler's appeal. Though the choice of helping to rebuild Europe after

World War II was better than the post–World War I vengeance, the 13 billion dollars spent on the Marshall Plan, an equivalent of 104 billion today, could have been avoided if we had not engaged in war. As one critic reviewing her arguments in the 1960s commented, after evaluating the history of war in the twentieth century, "What if Jeannette Rankin, once assailed as an over-emotional fuddy-duddy, happened to have been right all along? We can never know."[94]

In her evolving opposition to two world wars, what Jeannette Rankin emphasized in her articles, speeches, interviews, and votes was the right of every American politician and indeed every American to judge the choices that government officials presented as unavoidable and right. By her rhetoric and action, she stood up for the right to question, maintaining that there was nothing traitorous in doing so. Indeed, she deemed it more traitorous, irrational, and unpatriotic to mindlessly acquiesce to what could be dangerous for the country. She especially opposed the bullying that often accompanies a rush to war. In her arguments, she echoed Wilson's claims about making the world safe for democracy—it would not be war that would do so but the freedom to think and act independently, and certainly for legislators to vote not by party or by fear of reprisal but by the dictates of their conscience.

Through two world wars and the intervening years, Jeannette Rankin willingly paid the price required to enact her own vision of patriotism. After both votes, she would be unelectable, a pariah, especially after the 1941 decision, but she remained determined to make her own risky decisions. She believed that in the democracy for which women had fought, all citizens had the responsibility, regardless of the consequences, to speak and act independently for the best American values and future.

Six

Twentieth-Century Stages of Acceptance
The Educated Woman

Through her education and then as she worked in settlement houses and for suffrage, Jeannette formed ideas about individual rights and about peace that she continued to develop throughout her career. Beyond the years in which progressive arguments seemed acceptable, she had the strength to continue to analyze her country's choices and take action. And she embraced education as not just as a preparation for a better form of motherhood, but for a bigger contribution to the nation.

While Jeannette worked against war through the decades, her sister Harriet dedicated her time to women's education and work opportunities, especially in two key periods. In the 1920s and the 1940s, Harriet served young women as they first attained an education in large numbers and then as they used their college education and their skills to support their nation during World War II. In these two periods, with repeated focus on women's assumed need for protection and their movement toward independence, women showed what they could learn and do.

The history of university education rarely includes what it took for students to move beyond a few eastern seminaries and women's colleges to equal participation at co-educational state universities across the nation. That story involves deans of women, who helped parents in the 1920s to overcome their fears and more confidently send their daughters to college. Deans of women dealt with the realities of students occupying a much more open space than their homes or women's colleges. They both oversaw and fought back against the making of special majors for women and helped students to consider more choices of careers in an era when college was defended less frequently as preparation for motherhood but might be viewed as just a place to have a bit of fun, prepare for teaching, or find a husband.

Six. Twentieth-Century Stages of Acceptance 109

Harriet's career involved a key period in women's education as well as the first decade in which women secured widespread positive notice for their work. During World War II, especially in the Red Cross, educated women proved what they could do to utilize their own skills and thus serve the nation.

Harriet's Own Education

As she took on these two key challenges in the 1920s and 1940s, Harriet's career followed the pattern of many women of her generation. Harriet taught before she married, with more education for teaching than her mother had, but, like her mother, she quit her job after marriage, moving with her husband as he established a career and starting a family. Harriet did not work again until she was a widow, the supporter of her family. In these involvements, Harriet's choices reveal twentieth-century patterns for women, of intermittent work but impactful careers.

Harriet was born in 1883, in the first group of Rankin children, on the ranch, age eleven when her father died. Like the others, she took part in the social whirl in Missoula, with the newspaper including notices of her singing at school and town events and reading an essay on the American flag. Many well-publicized occasions involved her with her siblings: in March 1902, Harriet and Jeannette went to Bonner with a friend for a masquerade party featuring costumes from history; in January and February of 1902, Harriet helped to host progressive dinners, convening at several houses, for which she served as one of the entertainers.[1]

Like Jeannette, Harriet went to the University of Montana. When she graduated in June 1903, with a BA in psychology and pedagogy, the newspaper reported that her thesis title was "The Ideal

Harriet Rankin Sedman, at age seventeen, in Missoula, 1900 (Schlesinger Library, Radcliffe Institute, Harvard University).

School." At the graduation, she was "easily the feature of the day's exercises," as the class phrenologist, reading bumps on the skulls of the graduates to judge their mental traits. The newspaper further reported that she planned to travel during the next year and then begin graduate work.[2] While Harriet was at college, there was little extra-curricular involvement for women at the university. She lived at home and often spent her time with friends from her social group in Missoula.

Through the nineteenth century, state universities made no provision for housing women students or involving them in campus social life. At the University of Kansas and the University of Montana, an association of faculty wives and women faculty offered the only assistance to the few women students.[3] The University of California waited until 1896 to begin considering the housing and social needs of women students, first admitted in 1871.

While she was living in Missoula and finishing college, Harriet began a career in education by filling in at the Grant Creek School, on land and in a building donated by her father, where teachers seemed to come and go. This first school there had opened in 1897 with a curriculum of singing, drawing, handwriting, and spelling: "keeping busy the hand, heart, brain, and tongue." Teachers who were "young, inexperienced and had a minimum of training," like her mother had been, often from families living nearby, usually worked for a year or two. The teacher made a fire in the morning with wood contributed by parents and dealt with children from grade one to eight by herself. About Harriet's tenure, a state school visitor commented, "discipline good."

To extend her training for a teaching career, Harriet next went to Winona Normal School, Minnesota's first teacher-training academy and the oldest normal school west of the Mississippi. The well-regarded Winona Normal fostered many innovations, including a "model school" program, a laboratory school for training teachers. After she graduated, Harriet came home and passed the new state teacher's exam. Without a normal school in the state and with a revolving door of qualified and unqualified teachers, school superintendents had begun instituting oral and written exams to assess content knowledge and moral character. Harriet lived at her parents' house on Madison Street while teaching in town.[4]

Harriet married the brother of Ellis Sedman, Wellington's close friend. Oscar Sedman, a mining engineer, was six years older than Ellis, age seven when their father died. Harriet and Oscar married in Missoula in October 1907 when he was thirty-three and she was twenty-four; the newspaper's wedding announcement described the couple as "members of two of the most prominent families in Montana during pioneer days." Her sister Mary was her maid of honor.

After the wedding Harriet and Oscar moved to Murray, Idaho, where Oscar and his partners invested in gold mines. Her teaching career ended

Harriet Rankin Sedman in the middle, with her husband, Oscar Sedman, on the right, and her sister, Mary Rankin Bragg, on the left (Schlesinger Library, Radcliffe Institute, Harvard University).

with her marriage, just as her mother's had. This small town where Harriet kept house and began having children existed for mining and logging, a few buildings only. From there Oscar went on the Copper Queen Mining Company and the most prosperous mine in Arizona, in another small town, Cochise. Then, in October 1917, Oscar Sedman died of lobar pneumonia, which he contracted from mine gases containing nitric oxide. Before his death, he had been sick for five months, from an unsafe industry and from the resulting emphysema that doctors could not cure. Though Harriet had not worked since her marriage, their two daughters, Virginia and Mary Elizabeth, at ages eight and seven, were Harriet's to support, the mine contributing almost nothing.

In a pattern that continued through much of the twentieth century, women supported themselves and their families in intermittent periods. In 1900, almost half of single women held jobs. About a third of widowed and divorced women worked, a figure that increased with the decades, with single and widowed women working at much higher percentages than wives: only 6 percent of married women worked outside the home in 1900. Between 1918 and 1940, years of so much social change, the overall rate of labor force participation by married women went up only from 9 percent to 14 percent. As in Harriet's case, American women often worked after high school and college and again as widows but less commonly as married women with children, generally out of economic necessity.

To gain employment as a widow, Harriet took her children to Washington and went to work for Jeannette, in her congressional office, using her experience from Jeannette's campaigns. During the state suffrage effort, Harriet had traveled with her sisters and spoken at a variety of venues and especially to organizations of teachers. She had also helped Jeannette when she ran for office. In 1917, Jeannette's friend and initial Washington assistant Belle Fligelman, who had participated in the suffrage campaign, had met her future husband, Norman Winestine, and moved with him to New York where they both wrote for *The Nation*. After Harriet took over as her sister's assistant, she dealt with a huge volume of mail, about the war vote but also about suffrage and other legislation.

Besides dealing with letter writing and scheduling, Harriet became central to the 1918 campaign. Wellington wrote to her daily concerning its progress, the two organizing together while Jeannette served in Congress and met with groups in Montana. Through the summer of 1918, Harriet wrote to supporters across the country. She included a personal note at the end of many of these letters, reminding recipients of how much they mattered to Jeannette and to the future of the nation. As she requested financial support, she referenced woman suffrage, the rights of labor, and the transition to peace: whatever was most important to the donor. She also

Six. Twentieth-Century Stages of Acceptance   113

Working in the congressional office of Jeannette Rankin, from right to left, are Florence Leech Murray of Dupuyer, Montana; Harriet Rankin Sedman; Elizabeth Puffer of Massachusetts; and an unidentified woman at far left. At right is a poster of a soldier standing over a dead German soldier, used to sell liberty bonds, 1917 (Schlesinger Library, Radcliffe Institute, Harvard University).

explained how Montana's division into legislative districts had been a gerrymandering effort intended to injure her sister's chances for reelection.

As Jeannette prepared to leave Washington after losing the 1918 election, she knew that a final requirement would be to help her sister find another job. Jeannette wrote to her friend Jane Thomson in New York City to ask for her help there though Harriet preferred to stay in Washington. Then Jeannette secured a position for her at the Bureau of War Risk Insurance. The War Risk Insurance Act had passed in 1914 to ensure the availability of insurance for shipping vessels during the war as well as life insurance coverage for sailors in the Merchant Marines who transported supplies across the Atlantic for the Expeditionary Force. With war benefits eventually being paid, this office provided Harriet with employment for just two years. Since by then Jeannette no longer had the same level of influence in Washington, Harriet and her children returned home to Missoula and her mother's house. She began working in the Missoula public schools, as one of twelve new teachers, the turnover high since so many women still taught just until marriage.

Harriet was soon looking for a better paying and more challenging job, with her education, experience, and family opening doors for her in Missoula. In August 1921, she was named dean of women at the university.

She then moved out of her mother's house and into the Randall Apartments though her mother still helped her with the children and with campus events. By July 1931, Harriet was living with both of her daughters at 105 Connell Avenue, a large home in the university district.

Harriet Rankin Sedman and a Changing Educational Culture

Harriet entered into a changing culture of higher education for women, a second stage of participation. Higher education for women had occurred first at female seminaries in the east, including Litchfield Female Academy (which opened in 1792), Troy Female Seminary (1821), and Hartford Female Seminary (1823). In defense of women's education, these institutions stressed that they prepared women for motherhood and teaching, acceptable goals. In a sheltered site, as at Troy Female Seminary, women could study basic science, history, and literature as well as sewing and household skills.

In the east, some seminaries eventually transformed into four-year colleges. In 1837, Mary Lyon founded Mount Holyoke Female Seminary, which became Mount Holyoke College in 1893. Wellesley College began as the Wellesley Female Seminary, renamed in 1873. Other private colleges for women formed, first in the east, without a beginning as seminaries. Vassar, the first of the Seven Sisters to be chartered, opened to students in 1875 as did Smith College, with Bryn Mawr following in 1885. Some eastern women's colleges opened as extensions of men's colleges. Barnard College affiliated with Columbia University at its founding in 1888. Radcliffe, chartered in 1894, was informally called The Harvard Annex because Harvard professors also lectured there.[5]

While the majority of women's colleges were private institutions, a few were public. Southern state schools established separate campuses for women instead of incorporating them in existing institutions. In 1884, the Mississippi legislature established the Industrial Institute & College (later Mississippi University for Women), the first public women's college. Other states soon followed: in Georgia, the Georgia State College for Women in 1889; in North Carolina, the North Carolina Women's College in 1891; and Florida converted its co-educational Florida State College into a women-only school in 1905, called Florida Female College until 1909 and then Florida State College for Women.

The earliest co-educational institutions in the United States were private, most with religious affiliations. Of the 195 private institutions founded before 1860, 50 (or 26 percent) enrolled some women students at their founding or within a decade afterwards. Oberlin College became a model for co-education, and, after a decision in 1835 to accept African American students, a proponent of racial equality. Co-educational Antioch College also opened in Ohio, in 1853, with reformer Horace Mann as its president. Public universities endorsed co-education slowly. In the sparsely settled west, women attended the new state universities since separate campuses were not feasible. Women enrolled at the University of Montana, in very small numbers, when it opened in 1895.

The most influential accelerators of co-education in state schools were the Morrill Acts of 1862 and 1890, intended to improve the country by providing education in practical professions. The first land-grant act gave each state 30,000 acres of public land for each senator and representative. The land could be sold, with the proceeds to fund university education. According to prescribed gender roles, women did not belong in agriculture and mechanical arts classes. In the west as elsewhere, they found themselves routed toward home economics or education, in a semi-separate college space: "Although western women were educated by the sides of men, the content of their education reflected their domestic roles."[6]

Even with this extension of opportunity, small percentages of the population attended and graduated from college at the turn of the century. The percentage of men and women ages eighteen to twenty-four who were attending college was just 1.3 in 1870, 1.8 in 1890, 2.8 in 1910, and 4.7 in 1920. Though only a small number of women enrolled, these students created an intense reaction, beginning in "medically" based judgments.

In the late nineteenth century, Harvard Medical School's Dr. Edward Clarke, in his *Sex in Education* and other works, helped to spur negative "diagnoses." His popular book asserted that college education was harmful to women's reproductive organs and general health: a girl could study and learn, he admitted, "but it is not true that she can do all this and retain uninjured health and a future secure from neuralgia, uterine disease, hysteria, and other derangements of the nervous system."[7] Other opponents declared women intellectually inferior to men and higher education socially undesirable because it would render women "manly" and unmarriable: a college education was for future male leaders of the country, not future wives and mothers. Historian Henry Adams, writing about women's intellectual ambitions in 1875, commented on "the pathetic impossibility of improving those poor little, hard, thin, wiry, one-stringed instruments which they call their minds."[8] Such staunch critics could argue from data as well as prejudice and tradition: between 1880 and 1900, 50 percent of those with a college degree remained single while only 10 percent of American women did.[9]

At the beginning of the century, though the overall percentages didn't greatly increase, with an expanding population the numbers of women in college went up quickly, and the most common sites of their enrollment began to change. There were 127,000 more women enrolled in 1910 than in 1870, and then 142,000 more in 1920 than in 1910. By 1920, 47 percent of college students were women, and over 80 percent of those attended co-educational public universities, many with Morrill Act funding, across the country. With this explosion, the reactions to the presence of women students changed somewhat: fewer critics argued that they should go home, but new negative judgments and potential problems replaced the old.

Into the twentieth century, there were more single women between the ages of fifteen and twenty-four than ever before, with the delay in marriage caused by high school and college attendance part of what was creating this trend. These young women came into a different world from their mothers and grandmothers. Women on college campuses by 1920 enjoyed the new freedoms ushered in at the end of the war, in an era of prosperity, urbanism, and consumerism. In the stereotypes that frightened their mothers, the flapper, a slang term for a prostitute or a young girl "trained to vice," had a short "bob" hairstyle, cigarette dangling from her painted lips, drinking alcohol during Prohibition, dancing to a jazz band, surrounded by male suitors, unfazed by previous social conventions or taboos.[10] Leaving unescorted from college dormitories or rooming houses, she went on dates—in cars—with much less supervision than occurred in family parlors. This freedom had limits, however, and marriage remained the ultimate goal, and so an old-fashioned type of reputation still mattered, as historian Lynn Dumenil points out: "There's a sense that you have to be really careful about your sexual activity, for fear that you'll lose your reputation and won't get married.... So the flapper's wildness is always, I would say, contained by that."[11] The historical section of the University of Montana web site declares that "the '20s were about more than flapper girls, speakeasies and endless Great Gatsby–style partying. People went to school, too." But though such a description makes the era sound like tons of fun, the reality was more complicated for students and their parents.

Even with so much change, as in earlier decades, women might come into adulthood with little preparation. In *What Young People Should Know*, from 1875, Cornell zoologist Burt Wilder marveled that parents could send young women away to a university, or out to work, without talking to them about dating and pregnancy. In *Eve's Daughters*, in 1881, Marion Harland decried the "criminal reserve" and "pseudo delicacy" that kept mothers from preparing their girls for adulthood. And while times were changing, some customs did not: of women who attended Stanford between 1892 and 1920, surveyed by Clelie Mosher, slightly more than half claimed to have known nothing of sex prior to marriage; the better informed said they had

Six. Twentieth-Century Stages of Acceptance

gotten their information from books they "read surreptitiously" in libraries, from talks with older women, generally not their mothers, and from observations like "seeing the farm animals during all processes of breeding."[12] These students and their families might be ill prepared for the frightening situations inherent in dormitory spaces and boarding houses, what Horace Mann referred to fearfully as "association together without supervision."[13]

These realities, of women entering schools that had been instituted for men, with an enlarging population and new questions about their attendance, led to the position of dean of women. The first was Adelia Johnston in 1869 at Oberlin College, with the job title of lady principal, the catalog speaking of her responsibility for morality: young ladies were "placed under the superintendence of a judicious lady, whose duty it is to correct their habits and mold the female character."[14] By the first decades of the twentieth century, almost all co-educational colleges and universities had deans of women. At many campuses, the excesses of behavior that led to the appointment—at fraternity rushes, parties in town, and athletics— were those of men.[15] And women on affiliated campuses caused some men's schools to suddenly acquire deans of men. The first one was LeBaron Russell Briggs at Harvard University in 1890, who took on a position seemingly not needed for the college's first 253 years but suddenly required after the arrival of women at Radcliffe.

With women newly arriving at co-educational institutions, deans of women took on a multi-faceted job. They oversaw dorm floors where women were living, to insure their safety and morality. With an inadequate number of rooms generally available on campuses, they also dealt with off-campus landlords who had to be approved and monitored by the university. Through the decades, they also dispensed advice and discipline, the presence of this campus officer easing fears over the enrollment of women and enabling them to feel safe and to succeed even if such supervision was not always appreciated.

The dean of women position began at the University of Montana in 1907, with Mary Stewart, who had the limited role of supervising the few women students in the dormitory. Harriet Rankin Sedman took the position in 1921 and served until 1935, in a confusing time for an enlarging student population. By 1920 the university had a women's gymnasium and residence hall and departments of education and home economics: in 1922 the university had 625 women students and 725 men students and a faculty of 16 women and 64 men. Of the women students, 200 stayed with family, 200 in residence halls, 100 in nine sororities, 75 in rented rooms in homes, and 50 in homes where they did housework in exchange for a room.[16] During Harriet's tenure, the dean became responsible for administering social and sports activities, counseling women students, overseeing discipline, and many other key tasks.

With little experience when she began this job, Harriet immediately tried to get help. She went to Helena to confer with architects concerning possible designs of new dormitories for women. At the Montana State College in Bozeman, she spoke with her counterpart there, Una Herrick, who, like Harriet, had taken on this job as a widow with a family to support. As Herrick discussed her varied work on campus, she told Harriet about her new project: in 1921, Herrick patented a brassiere that fit the wearer snugly without shoulder straps. In her campus talks and with Harriet, she equated the bra to their task—of providing the secure support that could insure a young woman's confident movement forward.[17]

When school started in September 1921, Harriet was a busy administrator. In October, she was officially welcomed at the fall convocation, along with the new president Charles H. Clapp, a geologist who had directed the School of Mines at Butte. He served as president from 1921 to 1935, the same years that Harriet was there, during what he called the university's "stage of adolescent growth."[18]

As she frequently spoke about a new system for Missoula students, Harriet sought to reflect her view of the modern young woman. She recognized the common criticism of the young: that they "make light of the value of appearance," of established codes of moral behavior and dress. But, Harriet argued, those who told such stories about the few were unfairly condemning the whole. As she spoke to high school students, to parents, to business and professional women's clubs, to first-year students, and to graduating classes, she developed her thesis concerning young women's intelligence and morality—that their education, career goals, and new freedoms combined with traditional values to form the best of adulthood.

As Harriet reviewed the actual high quality of young women of the 1920s, she frequently spoke about her childhood to emphasize the need for early independence—and the difficulty of being mothers. She told audiences about being born on the Grant Creek ranch, where she only lived to age two but afterwards spent her summers, learning to ride horses, from the old plough horse to a wild bucking bronco. As Harriet described her siblings, she joked about her mother's difficulty with both quiet and openly rebellious daughters, challenges that spanned the generations, certainly not beginning in the 1920s. She said that too much authority from a mother could weaken either type of child. Because her own mother had a ranch and then a town home and big family to care for, she had to allow her daughters to make their own decisions and monitor each other. In discussing Olive's choices, Harriet cast the independence and difficulties of a 1920s daughter as something not so new or unprecedented, and she constructed her mother's withdrawal as a means of growth for girls.[19]

In her frequent speeches, as Harriet moved through time considering mothers and daughters, she also spoke of her own daughters. In this swirl of generations, she talked about Virginia and Mary Elizabeth as bringing her up, especially during their teen years, when she was their only parent. They had taught her that young women needed attention not just to their safety or morality but to their opinions, their point of view. This Harriet explained through an example that she often repeated: on the phone, she told her audiences, she had said to a suitor of her teen daughter, "Virginia has gone to a debate with the girls, John," a choice that later infuriated Virginia because it indicated to John that she didn't have a date and that she was seeing so few boys that her mother knew his voice. Though the moment seemed a trifling one, their conversations concerning it led to frank talk, about why some girls base their self-image on the approval of one boy and why Virginia did not. As Harriet further discussed the development of young women, she spoke of mothers as needing to offer comradeship, patience, and understanding. Girls, she claimed, should learn to make their own decisions year by year so that when they came to college and adulthood they would be prepared to think for themselves and thus forgo the shock and problems of gaining freedom suddenly. Harriet insisted that the actual changes occurring for women in college did not concern drinking or acting sinfully, but instead feeling homesick, learning to budget time and money, adjusting to different styles of teaching, and coping with academic competition: a college girl considered the choice of "gainful occupation" more than just running wild or finding a husband.[20]

As she constructed the modern young woman in positive terms, Harriet further assuaged families by discussing the protective role of the dean of women, which was short-term, a bridge to full adulthood. She wanted families and the students themselves to enter college with full awareness of a well-developed system, which could alleviate fear of the moral and physical degradation described in the news.[21] In one radio talk, from January 1926, Harriet described the system created for first-year women living in North Hall and Corbin Hall, which probably appealed to parents more than their daughters. These students had to sign out to leave the dorm after dinner and then sign back in, by 10:30 curfew: the dorm social director "never retires at night without knowing that every girl is in her own room." The first-year woman could go out overnight only with family; she could have social engagements with men only on weekends, with a curfew of 12:15; her lights had to be out at eleven on study nights "in the interest of health and scholarship." She needed to report any illness to the dorm social director and then to the nurse. She could secure no permission to enter male rooms of any type: "if she enters fraternity houses unchaperoned it is without the knowledge of the director or the dean of women." She could not go to public, off-campus dances or smoke on campus: "If they must smoke it is done elsewhere." In summarizing this system in her talks and articles, Harriet alluded to the unlikely possibility of young people drinking, out of control, but claimed that the system of dormitories and well-planned campus events led "toward right thought followed by right action," beginning in habits formed in the first year, with the emphasis not on reining in bad girls but allowing a positive group to thrive.[22]

In this system, as women moved beyond their structured first year, they could begin regulating themselves. In the second year students could move into sororities or approved rooming houses, but if they still needed more assistance, viewed a bit pejoratively in campus documents, they could remain in a dorm with Mrs. Frank Turner as the social director. By sophomore year, student associations took over the monitoring of behavior, a sign of respect for the women's abilities and growth, in line with suffrage rights just achieved.

In her time as dean of women, Harriet encouraged the growth of sororities as a site that could create community for women students. In 1959, her sister Mary wrote from her home in San Marino, California, to the current sorority leaders who had invited her to a golden anniversary banquet, which she would have to miss. As the first Kappa Kappa Gamma to graduate from the university, in 1909, she recalled that this group had helped her to feel like a valued part of the university.[23] After their first years in dormitories, the sororities moved out into rented homes where juniors and seniors could mentor each other and undertake service commitments, all needing approval from the dean of women.

To incorporate women more fully in university life, Harriet established an array of events that could demonstrate women's abilities and positive sense of purpose. The Lantern Parade, the name coming from the motto of the university, "Lux et Veritas," engaged women's clubs and leaders in a night march. This procession came to feature organizations that Harriet initiated, such as the Association of Women Students, which assisted with events and with discipline. Parade participants also came from Harriet's new Big Sister Club, pairing first-year with advanced students, the pairs volunteering to work with high-school girls in town. The organizations also included Spurs, which Harriet founded along with Una Herrick at Montana State to encourage upper-class students to enter an array of majors and move thoughtfully toward careers—to spur them on to a choice that might be teaching but did not have to be. In a university that had been primarily made up of men, these groups fostered a sense of belonging and confidence, well remembered by participants.

To expand the choice of careers, beyond the education and home economics programs encouraged by the university, Harriet opened a vocational bureau for women students, staffing it herself, while a full-time employment secretary helped the men. According to a report that she issued in November of 1931, 25 percent of the women students were working while they attended classes, paying for part or all of their expenses.[24] As Harriet helped these students to attain jobs during college, she also encouraged them to plan for careers afterwards.

Harriet's additional responsibilities as disciplinarian, part of the job that she tended to downplay, can be seen in a court case from 1928: *State ex rel. Ingersoll v. Clapp*. It concerned first-year students on New Year's Eve, partying in the home of a married woman, Janet Thoms Ingersoll, and returning to the dorm drunk, choices certainly not within the prescribed behavior codes or Prohibition restrictions. Both Janet and her husband Rufus were students at the university; he was studying law and she chemistry. When Harriet reported the incident to President Clapp, he suspended both husband and wife. The Ingersolls appealed their suspension, first to campus advocates, and then to the state board of education, a district judge, and the state supreme court, all of which agreed with the initial adjudication.[25] While the Ingersolls' case progressed, beyond her purview, Harriet used the situation to hold special meetings with first-year students about drinking.

Though Harriet did not oversee the men, the dean of women had responsibility for all social functions of the university, arranged through her office, and thus involvement with their behavior. Her office approved dances on campus and at off-campus venues like the Elks Hall. She determined that no dress suits or tuxedoes could be worn by freshmen, the privilege given only to upper-class men, to keep social events from becoming exclusive. "I doubt if there are more than 115 dress suits on campus," Harriet said in one talk in which she delineated regularly occurring decisions that helped her to control campus life.[26] In dealing with male students, Harriet took steps to protect women on campus, at a time when there were no campus police and no clear sense of how to exercise control, issues still not fully resolved at the University of Montana or on other college campuses, as Jon Krakauer has documented.[27] In December 1921, her first fall on the job, women came to Harriet to protest the vulgar dancing of male students, which they found threatening and inappropriate, an effect of heavy drinking occurring even during Prohibition, a prime cause of much worse, even violent behavior. To create a better environment, Harriet met with leaders of male organizations, who declared themselves willing to help, to control their own behavior and monitor their friends. She also regularly attended campus parties, making sure that men as well as women followed appropriate codes of behavior, her choice with the men being persuasion since she had no authority over them.[28]

To help students further, Harriet let some of them live in her home with her daughters. When Marguerite Savage, a home economics sophomore, became ill from toxic goiter, she lived for a time with the Sedmans while her sister, a first-year student, remained in North Hall. Extending the personal connection, Harriet also hosted parties for women students, first at her mother's large home and then also at her own. In January 1926, for example, Harriet gave a reception at her mother's house for two hundred students, with Jeannette, Edna, and Grace serving with her as hostesses along with her daughters.

In 1929–30, Harriet took a leave of absence to seek an extended education in college administration that women were beginning to attain. At Columbia University, she received a master's degree in education, in a program that included classes on the work of deans of women. After Harriet returned to Missoula, she became a professor of education at the university as well as continuing as dean. She then also began teaching personnel administration in the local high school as a class for seniors.

Harriet served as a dean of women at an important time, as women became accepted as appropriate members of the co-education community, soon approaching half of the student body. Women earned 19 percent of bachelor's degrees in 1900, but their share doubled to 40 percent by 1930 and remained at that level in 1940. The presence of a dean of women helped parents to trust the college environment. She helped the students adjust and feel welcome. With this assistance, students made adjustments that led to self-control in the sophomore year and in adulthood.

From this beginning, these first women administrators at co-educational universities established routines that ultimately created the field of student affairs. In 1915, Lois Mathews, at the University of Wisconsin, published the first book on this profession, *The Dean of Women,* In 1916, the new National Association of Deans of Women provided a professional organization, and by 1920 Columbia University and other schools began training programs.[29] Though this position seemed superfluous and old fashioned by the 1960s, deans of women, like Harriet Rankin Sedman, had done essential work with students, families, and the community as women became half of the student body at American universities.

Putting College Education to Work

After fourteen years at the University of Montana, in June 1935, Harriet wed again. She sent a cable to the university in which she announced

Six. Twentieth-Century Stages of Acceptance 123

her wedding and quit her job. She married Alexander Grant McGregor; he was 55, and she was 52. Both were embarking on a second marriage. A former Missoulian, he graduated from the University of Montana, where they met in college, living a few doors down from each other. As an engineer, Alexander McGregor worked in Anaconda and then in Arizona, designing smelting and mining operations, before heading abroad to take on similar projects. With war imminent, he began directing government production in England and designed a smelter in Burma to provide metal for cannons and other weaponry.

For six years in London, Harriet didn't work, and she never returned to a career in education. But she did return to administration, in support of her country, for the Red Cross, an appropriate role in wartime for a married woman who would not otherwise be on the job. Though Harriet agreed with Jeannette about the futility and cost of warfare, she came out of retirement to serve American soldiers abroad.

During World War II, Harriet led and participated in a tremendous involvement of women, much greater than for the shorter period of World War I, involving a more independent and educated work force. The female labor force grew by 6.5 million during the Second World War; the percentage of married women working outside the home increased from 13.9 to 22.5. Women were sought for new jobs in defense plants, but the majority took over factory or office jobs that had been held by men. Approximately 350,000 American women joined the military, working as nurses, driving trucks, repairing airplanes, and doing clerical work.[30] American women also served during the war through the Red Cross, with positions abroad engaging women in independent decision making and action, in administration, more than other war-time positions. In the Red Cross, American women like Harriet demonstrated what their education and work experience could do for the nation.

Focusing on the needs of American soldiers in England were 2700 Red Cross workers from the United States who served three million American soldiers during the war.[31] While Harvey D. Gibson, a retired U.S. Army colonel, became the American Red Cross Commissioner for Great Britain, almost all of the administrators and workers in the field were women. Margaret Mason Colt served as Deputy Commissioner for Great Britain, responsible for British and American volunteers, with a staff of women running individual facilities.

The Red Cross set high standards for recruits: they had to be college graduates, between the ages of twenty-five and thirty-five, with work experience preferred. Recruits needed stellar reference letters; they had to pass physical examinations and demonstrate an outstanding personality in personal interviews. With the rigorous selection process, only one in six applicants made the cut.³² As a booklet about this service noted, they were "former teachers, entertainers, journalists, or business girls.... Some of them have husbands in service; all of them have a love of adventure."³³ With large numbers of applicants interested in using their education and experience to help their country, the Red Cross found a sufficient amount of volunteers. The pay was $150 per month plus maintenance overseas.

The organization's standards were meant to insure that workers could shift easily from serving coffee to creating meal services to planning the housing for hundreds of soldiers each day. Once accepted, new volunteers went to Washington, D.C., to the American Red Cross headquarters at American University. There they received immunizations and underwent two weeks of basic training, which had been intended to take six weeks but was shortened to meet demand overseas. Recruits received health lectures and were warned about getting enough rest and avoiding malaria and other illnesses, including sexually transmitted ones. Mary Thomas Sargent, from Wisconsin, a graduate of Ripon College, noted that her group was not told anything more specific about sex: they were just expected to know better and take care of themselves. These women were also taught how to break the ice with servicemen; Sargent reported learning card tricks and palm reading. She also reported, however, that such techniques were largely unnecessary—all it took to engage a soldier was a kind word and a question about his hometown. Recruits also received uniforms that came with ten pages of specific instructions concerning deportment—no earrings, hair ornaments, "brilliant" nail polish, or "excessive use of cosmetics." Once training was complete, women journeyed to either coast, working locally while they awaited transport to their final destinations. For most, this meant a trip to Brooklyn and travel to the European theater via troop carrier. Once Red Cross workers arrived at their final destinations, more specific training began. These women learned to drive buses, create schedules, secure and run lodgings, and repair the buses and mobile doughnut machines that always seemed to be breaking down.³⁴

The Red Cross also recruited American women already living in London, dropping the age restrictions to seek experienced managers who knew the city. In early 1942, at age fifty-eight, Harriet Rankin Sedman McGregor volunteered and was immediately accepted. With the desire to work full-time for her country, she stepped right into familiar work, administering an array of spaces and programs.

As at the University of Montana, part of Harriet's fulltime Red Cross job in London was to secure lodgings for the women involved, an increasingly difficult task in a city where bombing, during the Blitz in 1941 and afterwards, destroyed 70,000 houses and damaged more than a million. Harriet helped to locate hotel rooms and apartments, with women housed together, often in tight spaces as in college dormitories, rooms shared by WACs, Army nurses, ferry pilots, and Red Cross workers. Along with locating any available apartments, Harriet prevailed on hospitals and banquet halls to provide extra rooms. She also secured space at Strand Palace, Dukes, Flemings, Browns, and other hotels in Mayfair that might have empty rooms for a few nights. Red Cross workers were not allowed to stay, however, in the hotels for servicemen that they began to administer.

Using her skills from the University of Montana, Harriet also administered housing for soldiers on leave. The U.S. army gave men an eight-day furlough every five or six months, and there were not enough lodgings in England to house them, so General Eisenhower requested that the Red Cross establish service clubs, in cities first and later in the countryside. At the peak of the program in England, more than 100,000 men a month stayed in Red Cross lodgings.[35] Harriet served as a director of the Columbia Red Cross Club, across from the Marble Arch and Hyde Park, where 2000 men a night were registered. As she described in letters to Wellington, after she helped to outfit this space "at a breathtaking pace," each day she had responsibility for reservations, for food and clean rooms, and for additional services.[36]

The service club attempted to provide a comfortable, comforting space: "not only a home away from home, but the fraternity house, the Elks Club, the corner drug store and Mom's front parlor all wrapped into one."[37] Soldiers leaving camp on furlough received a card ensuring them a bed at a Red Cross club in the city to which they were traveling. At the Columbia and other clubs, they entered into a reception room that featured a large map of the United States on which flags could be affixed so that a soldier could tell whether someone from his hometown was staying there. Beyond their lodgings, soldiers encountered cafeterias and snack bars with American food, first-aid stations, hot and cold showers, barber shops, tailor shops, shoeshine parlors, game and reading rooms, and less widely advertised prophylactic stations, all staffed by recently trained Red Cross workers. Club administrators like Harriet arranged additional services, such as trips to the theater and concerts, sight-seeing tours, and overnight or weekend visits with British families. They also sponsored dances, concerts, and theatrical productions. Harriet developed a card-catalog system to foster exchanges between American and British farmers, factory workers, social workers, artists, and teachers. Her staff arranged historical tours to Oxford, Cambridge, and Windsor. Additionally, staff members at the Columbia and other clubs planned for displays of art work done by American servicemen; sent out on tour, these exhibits were seen by more than half a million people. The low charge for the room and food as well as for access to many other services was fifty cents per day.[38]

From this site, Harriet also helped to arrange for services in rural areas where men and women were stationed: camp clubs that featured entertainments and meals, everything from the city clubs except for lodging. Additionally, she coordinated the routes of clubmobiles that regularly toured rural service areas to offer coffee and doughnuts, a venture beginning with forty buses acquired from a company that had discontinued its services. These buses offered space for soldiers to relax, with newspapers and magazines, as well as room for Red Cross workers to sleep since they might be out on the road for as much as two weeks at a time. Harriet also helped plan for an additional group called Clubmobile Rangers who served at railway stations, offering coffee and doughnuts in the few minutes between the soldiers' arrival and their departure on a troop train to a post, all of this work occurring "in frantic fashion," as she described it to Wellington. These Red Cross workers served in twelve-hour shifts with push-mobiles that carried 750 doughnuts and 400 cups of coffee. While helping to set up all of these services, Harriet and other directors prepared for the Normandy invasion: on the sixth day after D-Day, the Red Cross followed the troops into France, as part of the invasion force.[39]

Harriet quit a career and moved with a husband twice, leaving her job as a teacher to go with Oscar Sedman to Arizona and her job as a dean of women to move with Alexander McGregor to England. After World War II, like many married women, she did not continue to work.

Harriet's careers occurred at key times of change for women. In the 1920s, deans of women did crucial work as they helped to normalize the presence of the quickly growing number of women in co-educational schools. Their codes protected women who left home and assuaged parents' fears concerning the departure. Some of the rules that deans of women enforced could seem overbearing, indeed as an unfair division of the student body, and by the 1960s they would be outmoded. But these rules did make a place for women students in classrooms, dormitories, and extracurricular activities, in preparation for their adulthood and for the nation's acceptance of their involvement in higher education. At the University of Montana, Harriet created the safety and identity that encouraged women to go to college, that led parents to allow them to do so.

In World War II, women were much more involved in the war effort than in World War I. Though the employment of women in factories has become the icon, women took on administrative and leadership responsibilities in the Red Cross. Harriet sought housing for Red Cross workers and created a place of rest and renewal for servicemen, relying on skills that she developed in Missoula.

At the University of Montana, Harriet's administrative work helped to prove to parents, students, and the public that college education, even at co-educational schools, was right for women. In London, along with other Red Cross employees and volunteers, Harriet demonstrated what educated women, of any age or marriage status, could achieve working together and for their nation. Historian William Chafe called the war a "watershed" event forcing a change in attitudes about women in the workforce, as they entered jobs after securing a high school or college education.[40] Though the 1950s are thought of as an era when women returned to their homes, they continued to go to college and to seek meaningful employment, trends begun primarily at co-educational universities in the 1920s and continued in the 1940s when the nation needed their involvement and skills during war.

Seven

The Campaign for Birth Control, a Pact with the Devil

> "It's a struggle to be a woman and become yourself and work in dignity and receive respect."[1]

As women like Jeannette and Harriet Rankin encountered and caused so much political and educational change, another Rankin sibling greatly affected the status of women and families. Olive and John's youngest daughter, Edna, also embraced a life of activism, devoting herself to the birth control movement, heading down this path not after the death of a husband, as in Harriet's case, but instead after a divorce. After her marriage, she worked in a store to help support her husband and children but sought a more meaningful commitment after her divorce. In her activism, for birth control, she forged a pact with the devil, threading a needle, to achieve what she thought was right for women and families alongside of leaders whose most extreme goals she did not endorse. Edna entered the birth-control movement in the 1930s, after the most restrictive of laws had passed and activists had begun to oppose them, a time when women in this country and internationally sought contraceptive rights as a means of controlling their health, their families, and their destiny.

Edna's Movement Toward a Life's Work

Edna Rankin was born in 1893 in Missoula, three years after Philena died, in the house on Madison Street, the youngest of the Rankin children. She was eleven when her father died, there as her mother began to withdraw, dependent on Jeannette who had responsibilities that she didn't want.

At the end of the second group of Rankin children, separate from the affinity and strength of the first, Edna often felt herself to be lesser. As one of Jeannette's biographers commented, Edna was afraid of Jeannette

Seven. The Campaign for Birth Control, a Pact with the Devil

to some extent and "would dwell in Jeannette's shadow all of her life." She once, in fact, remarked that Jeannette viewed her as an unwanted child.[2] Along with the awe she felt for Wellington, she experienced a "painful childhood inferiority" to him as well.[2] She knew the insecurity and anguish of growing up as the last member of a family that, as she recalled life after the death of her father, was too large. Given the advanced age of her mother at her birth, at age forty, after six other children and several miscarriages, she came to view her birth as more accidental than intentional, a sign of a family out of control.[3]

Even as the last child with a mother who had withdrawn from society, Edna entered

Portrait of Edna Rankin as a child, 1903 (Schlesinger Library, Radcliffe Institute, Harvard University).

into her family's social whirl: the local newspaper included her in the society page articles about parties and other events, but it also highlighted her concern with justice. In high school she served as president of the Political Equality Club. In June 1911, her first-prize speech at her high-school graduation concerned "Modern Slavery," a talk which may have shocked the audience as she discussed child labor and forced marriage as forms of bondage.[4] These articles commented on her finely coiffed hair and dramatic outfits as well as her flair for dramatic discourse, attributes that would make her a memorable personage as she later traveled the nation and globe.

Edna started college at the University of Montana, living at home with her mother. She then left for more education, as her siblings did, continuing her activism from high school. In 1912–1913, at the University of Wisconsin, she studied psychology, sociology, and economics while also taking public speaking at Wellington's insistence, as had Jeannette. There Edna became president of a campus suffrage league. In 1913, Wisconsin's legislature authorized a referendum for full suffrage, with Edna joining in the successful campaign effort, but Governor Francis McGovern ultimately vetoed

Informal portrait of sisters Edna (left) and Grace Rankin (right) as teenagers, ca. 1907–1909 (Schlesinger Library, Radcliffe Institute, Harvard University).

the bill. That year, Edna went to New York and Washington to work with Jeannette, then an organizer for the New York Woman Suffrage Party and a lobbyist in Congress. In March of 1913, for the suffrage parade on the day before Wilson's inaugural, Edna traveled as part of "an imposing contingent" from Wisconsin, but she marched with Jeannette and other suffragists from Montana, dressed as one of Sacajawea's group, in white buckskin. In Wisconsin and in Washington, she met with women who lived in many different situations, a chance to learn more about political and personal needs. As a suffragist campaigner who was becoming a skilled communicator, as she wrote later in an employment application, "I was taught the value of kindliness and sympathy in dealing with people, which releases one's reserve."[5]

Edna's desire to impact social issues continued as she returned home from Wisconsin. She worked with Jeannette on the Montana campaign for suffrage and as she ran for office. Belle Fligelman Winstine, Jeannette's close compatriot, wrote about the House campaign and Edna's special traits: "One of the moments I remember most clearly out of all of that exciting time was when Edna first walked into her sister's campaign office here in Helena. She was the most elegant person I'd ever seen. Such a fine bearing! She appeared to me all golden, shedding warmth and light."[6] Edna also appeared as warmth, light, and enthusiasm as she introduced her sister at

Seven. The Campaign for Birth Control, a Pact with the Devil   131

many meetings and spoke for her at others.

Edna's activism, and especially her concern for the injustice encountered by women and children, continued in her travels, as she recorded in a journal. Concerning a trip to Madeira, undertaken with friends, it was not just the beauty of rural scenery, but the local working conditions that secured her attention: "the intensity of the agriculture is appalling." She commented repeatedly on the large numbers of children laboring in the fields. As she toured a market where mothers made embroidered linens and sold them, she was struck by "the tedious manual labor and the begging cries of the children." In Cadiz, she commented on the women's exhausting work and the "same constant throng of beggar children at your heels." Throughout this cruise and vacation, Edna extended her own commitment to choosing a future through which she could help women and children and ameliorate the conditions she encountered.[7]

Edna Rankin as a teenager, ca. 1910 (Schlesinger Library, Radcliffe Institute, Harvard University).

After attending the University of Wisconsin, Edna graduated from the University of Montana with a B.A. in 1916 and an LL.B. in law in 1918: just one woman had secured a law degree, in 1914, before the three in Edna's class.[8] As the rare woman in law school, Edna dealt with an antagonistic professor who assigned her rape cases to discuss, seeking, Edna believed, to make her uncomfortable as the class considered controversial cases and legal changes in the state. The Montana legislature in 1913 defined rape as a crime, an act necessary because it had been left out of law codes revised in 1907. This legislation set the legal age of consent at eighteen, with many opponents arguing for no law or for a lower minimum. The class considered a controversial and well publicized Missoula case: Frank C. Hall, a former city treasurer and merchant, received a sentence of 14–29 years for the rape of Ellen Lucetta Pruyn, age seventeen. Testimony that damaged her credibility concerned her provocative clothes, her "crocodile tears," and the inconsistencies in her story. Even though Hall had brandished a gun, his many business associates pressed for his sentence to be commuted.[9] This awkward manipulation of Edna to defend the law, this case, and the rights of women and girls may have helped her prepare to speak of sex when she began to work for birth control.

Wellington had insisted that Edna study law, a field in which he could help her succeed, and she worked for a while in his office after she graduated. But she then decided against a legal career, a choice that strained her relationship with him. He claimed that she just enjoyed clothes, travel, banter, and parties and was avoiding a serious commitment.[10]

In 1919, after working for a short time, Edna married John McKinnon, when she was twenty-five and he was twenty-eight. A Harvard graduate from a wealthy Boston family, McKinnon came to the Bitterroot Valley to manage a fruit-growing venture sponsored by eastern businessmen. When this company failed, he took his wife back east, where he worked at a string of jobs, listing himself on census records as an inventor and a salesman. John's lack of success became another source of criticism for Wellington: he thought Edna had married this Bostonian to impress everyone in Montana, but then that decision had gone all wrong.[11]

Because John McKinnon did not earn enough to support a family, Edna joined the minority of married women who worked though she did not attempt to practice law in New York: she was employed as a dry goods sales person at Best and Company department store in Manhattan, beginning in 1919, and later became a manager at this company's stores on Long Island and in East Orange, New Jersey.

This marriage would not last. John and Edna had two children, Dorothy in 1920 and John in 1923. The third pregnancy that followed immediately resulted in a miscarriage and an infection that led to sterility. Edna's son John died at age seven at summer camp, of a "mysterious malady," a sudden loss of a child that her mother had also suffered.[12] After this death, the couple divorced, and John moved to Idaho. Though Edna had involvements with other men, she did not marry again. She saw Harriet enter a second marriage and end her career at the University of Montana; she saw her sisters Grace and Mary enter marriages and halt other activities. And she saw the freedom attained by Jeannette and Wellington in avoiding family ties, a path that she chose.

Just as Jeannette had enabled Harriet to secure employment in Washington, she also used her connections to assist Edna, who sought a more meaningful sort of job, with a teenage daughter to support, and a new

Seven. The Campaign for Birth Control, a Pact with the Devil

home after her marriage ended. Having returned to Washington in the 1930s to lobby for the peace movement, Jeannette was able to help Edna find a job at the Resettlement Administration (RA), a New Deal agency created to move farmers from depleted lands to newly planned cities, an inspirational goal that seemed too socialistic to Congress and faced opposition from land owners who relied on tenant farmers. Congress only allocated enough resources to relocate a few thousand people and build three small "greenbelt" cities. When this program did not expand as had been initially planned, the RA turned its attention to constructing relief camps in California for migratory workers. While Edna enjoyed her employment there, working to relocate American workers, she knew that it would not provide a long-term career.

Edna Rankin McKinnon in her wedding gown, 1919 (Schlesinger Library, Radcliffe Institute, Harvard University).

At a luncheon in Washington in 1936, Edna heard a speech by Mordecai Ezekiel, a New Deal economic advisor who worked for the United Nations Food and Agriculture Organization. He presented the group with data: about the high birth rates in rural areas, which lacked the farm products to support these children, and about maternal mortality, often of malnourished women exhausted from prior births. Ezekiel argued that though there was reluctance to include birth control in federal New Deal programs, the need certainly existed. From that first exposure to the issue, the inadequacy of birth control for American women and their families secured Edna's attention, a cause like suffrage, political engagement, and university education—one that could matter for the future of women and the nation.

As Edna began to investigate further, she realized that rural women having large families in the 1930s might encounter health services no better than what had been available on Grant Creek and in Missoula at the turn of the century—and many of these women lacked the financial security of her mother. Edna also related the birth control movement to her own situation in marriage and afterwards. As a child that grew up in town, as she noted, she missed a basic education around farm animals. As the last child, not there during her mother's many pregnancies, she didn't have any family preparation for sex and children. And she did not learn the basics from her mother, a situation that Harriet also wanted to change for young women. As Edna said about this situation that she thought was all too common, "I was brought up as a Puritanical idiot, untrained in marriage relationships. All my mother ever told me was that I was marrying a darling, fine young man. Well, that darling young man didn't know anything, either." As she later told an interviewer, she didn't find out "where babies came from" until after her third pregnancy.[13]

As she discussed her new commitment with Jeannette, Edna came to see birth control as an extension of what her sister had tried to achieve. When Jeannette was in Congress, she advocated for a bill that provided birth control supplies and information to women as well as health care during maternity and a baby's infancy, the intention being to focus on rural areas first. Jeannette testified for this pending legislation in Congress in January 1919.[14] Her bill did not become law, but it did set the stage for the Sheppard–Towner Act, of 1921, which provided federal funding for maternity and child care while bringing greater access to birth control although it was never a publicly discussed part of the funded services. Edna connected birth control not just to Jeannette's attempt to secure a health care act, but to her efforts for peace since overpopulation led to a lack of resources and a damaged environment, which could trigger unrest and war. As Edna claimed, "birth control and peace are the answers we must give to death control by war and pollution." She came to believe that uncontrolled male aggression led both to warfare and to the subjugation of women inherent in constant pregnancy and child care: "We struggled against the machismo Jeannette encountered," Edna claimed. "I am a man because I can kill" seemed to both of them to be directly related to "I am a man because I can sire twenty children."[15]

From her discussions in Washington, Edna found a lifelong calling, an extension of the activism of her college years, an issue concerning which she could make a difference. To further understand the choices available and the situation of women, Edna went to New York to meet with Margaret Sanger, whom Jeannette had met when she worked for suffrage and attended philanthropy school in New York. Edna told Sanger about her growing commitment to the issue, her education in college and law school, and her connections in Washington through Jeannette. Sanger launched her on a crash course of study, concerning the legal barriers and the few choices for birth control then available, to prepare her to work for the cause.

The Effort That Edna Began to Lead: Birth Control History

The birth control movement that Edna engaged in from the 1930s created a challenging path for her, beginning in Montana, as she tried, like her sisters, to improve the situation of American women.

The use of contraceptives had increased throughout the nineteenth century, contributing to a 40 percent drop in the fertility rate in the United States between 1800 and 1900, particularly in urban regions, family size decreasing from an average of more than seven children, the number that Olive Rankin had, to four children per couple.[16] Birth-control techniques, with varying levels of efficacy, included the rhythm method, prolonged breastfeeding, oiled silk sheaths, sponges, rubber uterine caps, syringes filled with alum, and diaphragms, with more choices available in the east and in cities than on the western frontier.[17]

Toward the end of the century, new legal restrictions began to alter the availability of birth control. In the 1870s, a social purity movement gained adherents, who aimed at outlawing vice. Proponents attacked contraception as an immoral practice that promoted prostitution and venereal disease. Anthony Comstock, a postal inspector and leader of the movement, successfully lobbied for the passage of the 1873 Comstock Act, a federal law that prohibited the mailing of "any article or thing designed or intended for the prevention of conception or procuring of abortion" as well as any form of contraceptive information. Individual states followed by passing their own restrictive laws.[18] At the beginning of the twentieth century, some means of contraception continued to be available but with dissembling involved: drug stores sold condoms as "rubber goods" and cervical caps as "womb supporters." Additionally, by 1910 all but one state had criminalized abortion except where necessary, in a doctor's judgment, to save the woman's life.[19]

In response to these legal restrictions, Margaret Sanger argued that for women to have an equal footing in society and lead healthier lives, they needed to be able to determine whether and when to bear children. She also wanted to prevent back-alley abortions, becoming common with both legal abortion procedures and birth control unavailable. Like Edna, Sanger grew up in a family situation that spurred her efforts: her mother was pregnant eighteen times before dying at age forty-nine. Margaret was the sixth of eleven surviving children, spending her childhood taking care of family members. In 1916, she opened the first birth-control clinic in the United States, in Brooklyn, a decision leading to her arrest under the Comstock laws.

Sanger's subsequent trial and appeal generated controversy in New York and beyond. This publicity led to further consideration of the laws and to a 1918 state court ruling that allowed New York physicians to distribute contraceptive information to women if it was prescribed for medical reasons, presumably for their safety. In 1921, Sanger founded the American Birth Control League, which later became the Planned Parenthood Federation of America, and soon afterwards, she established the Clinical Research Bureau, the first legal birth control clinic, staffed by doctors, its publicly stated mission being to give out information and conduct research on maternal health.

In attempting to open a clinic, Sanger emphasized the health and choice of individual women, who needed release from the repeated births that often led to ill health of a mother and children and to the destitution of a family. She described birth control as a "herald of new freedom," bringing women to the "principle of intelligent and voluntary motherhood."[20] As she presented research in 1920, in her *Woman and the New Race*, she quoted William J. Robinson who wrote that "every physician knows that too frequent childbirth, nursing and the sleepless nights that are required in bringing up a child exhaust the vitality of thousands of mothers, make them prematurely old, or turn them into chronic invalids." And Sanger additionally noted the effects of repeated childbirth on an exhausted father, who becomes a "frantic struggler against the burden of five or six."[21] As Edna studied Sanger's book and spoke with her, she realized that these characterizations related to what many families across the country, including her parents, had encountered after marriage.

Sanger also made arguments, however, that Edna never accepted and that have damaged Sanger's reputation. In *The Pivot of Civilization*, which Sanger published in 1922, she recognized the positive influence of eugenics, a set of beliefs and practices that aimed to improve the genetic quality of human beings through selective breeding. In 1883, Sir Francis Galton coined the word, meaning "well born," and linked it to his cousin Charles Darwin's theory of natural selection. Galton related the perfection of plant and animal species to the possible perfection of especially the white race—attained by furthering the best hereditary traits.

These theories engaged both positive and negative forms of eugenic engineering. Theodore Roosevelt, for example, endorsed positive eugenics, arguing that the best eastern-educated men should have large numbers of children, a choice that would sustain the future. Roosevelt warned in 1903 that immigrants and minorities were too fertile, and that superior

Anglo-Saxons risked committing "race suicide" by using birth control and thus failing to keep up baby for baby. In 1917, in *Metropolitan Magazine*, he discussed race suicide further, bemoaning the low birth rate of Harvard and Yale graduates and suggesting contests and bonuses to alter this trend.[22]

This part of the eugenic plan seemed misguided to Sanger, who argued that all women could be overwhelmed by repeated childbirth, that the universal use of birth control would improve the race, a failing birth rate of all classes being a key step to improving civilization.[23]

While Sanger denied the reasoning behind positive eugenics, she endorsed negative eugenics, aimed at what was judged as the other extreme of the population. The methods intended to control undesirable elements included bans on interracial marriage and on marriage of those with epilepsy and other illnesses as well as immigration restrictions. The Johnson-Reed Immigration Act of 1924, which eugenicists sought, limited the number of immigrants through a national origins quota—no more than two percent of the total number of people of each nationality as recorded in the 1890 national census. The act increased the percentage of visas available to individuals from Western Europe and limited the numbers from Southern and Eastern Europe, more recent sites of emigration. The act completely excluded immigrants from Asia.

Eugenic plans also included involuntary sterilization of those deemed "unfit to reproduce," including through the decades people with mental or physical disabilities, criminals, poor women who were deemed immoral, and members of disfavored minority groups. Many of Sanger's biographers have minimized this association, but she makes it clear in her writing. As she argued in *The Pivot of Civilization*, negative eugenics can curb the "irresponsible and uncontrolled fertility of the 'unfit' and the feeble-minded," their breeding having created "a progressive unbalance in human society." She argued further that social services enabled the poor to have more children and should be eliminated: "Altruism, humanitarianism, and philanthropy have aided and abetted machinery in the destruction of responsibility and self-reliance among the least desirable elements of the proletariat." She continued by claiming that "Every feeble-minded girl or woman of the hereditary type, especially of the moron class, should be segregated during the reproductive period. Otherwise, she is almost certain to bear imbecile children, who in turn are just as certain to breed other defectives." One of the aims of her American Birth Control League was thus "sterilization of the insane and feeble-minded and the encouragement of this operation upon those afflicted with inherited or transmissible diseases."[24] In her speech "My Way to Peace," in 1932, she argued that removal of the unfit, after sterilization, could occur on "farm lands and homesteads where these segregated persons would be taught to work under competent instructors for the period of their entire lives." Further cleansing of the populace, essential to establishing peace and prosperity, could occur through even more stringent immigration policies than those established in 1924: "Open the gates of the USA to those countries whose inhabitants have the inherent talents and national characteristics desirable, eliminating entirely those countries whose subjects have already been difficult to assimilate."[25]

Sanger extended this eugenic shaping of the future to control over the African American population. Her Birth Control Federation of America initiated the Negro Project in 1939 to promote contraception among Black residents in the South, with a purpose beyond extending information to all populations. The proposal for this program, kept within a small group, clarified the reasons for this birth control and sterilization plan: "The mass of negroes, particularly in the South, still breed carelessly and disastrously, with the result that the increase among Negroes, even more than among whites, is from that portion of the population least intelligent and fit, and least able to rear children properly." Of this project, she wrote to Clarence Gamble that "we do not want word to go out that we want to exterminate the Negro population."[26] As her biographer Edwin Black wrote, examining this project as well as her publications and speeches, Sanger had "legendary status as a champion of personal freedom and women's rights" but she was also "an ardent, self-confessed eugenicist, and she would turn her otherwise noble birth control organizations into a tool for eugenics, which advocated for mass sterilization of so-called defectives, mass incarceration of the unfit, and draconian immigration restrictions."[27]

State use of involuntary sterilization to control inferior populations first became law in Indiana in 1907. This act legalized the vasectomies already being mandated for some men at the state hospital. The state court invalidated the law in the 1920s, but Indiana brought it back after the 1927 *Buck v. Bell* ruling, in which the Supreme Court upheld a state's right to practice involuntary eugenic sterilization to improve the white race. This case concerned the Virginia State Colony for Epileptics and Feebleminded, which filed a petition to sterilize Carrie Buck, an eighteen-year-old patient, diagnosed as having a low mental age, deemed a genetic threat to society.[28] With Indiana, Virginia, California, and Illinois starting a national trend, by 1937 two thirds of the states had similar laws, and others performed sterilization procedures without laws having been passed. Roughly 64,000 is a repeated number for involuntary eugenic sterilizations in America up until 1963, but a more realistic figure is now thought to be 80,000, with sterilization common during the Depression, but with more than half of these operations occurring after World War II. Though the first decades involved more white women, with the goal of improving the white race, the proportion of African Americans increased in each decade: it rose in

Seven. The Campaign for Birth Control, a Pact with the Devil 139

North Carolina from 23 percent of the total in the 1930s and 1940s to 64 percent in the 1960s when single Black mothers were commonly blamed for urban plight, poverty, and social unrest. The North Carolina Eugenic Board labeled many of these women as sexually uncontrollable, the state allowing social workers as well as doctors and wardens to recommend involuntary procedures.[29]

This dual focus, on birth control for individual women sought along with a coercive means of controlling the worst of the population, engaged Sanger with Clarence Gamble. An heir to the Procter and Gamble fortune who graduated from Princeton University in 1914 and Harvard Medical School in 1920, Gamble sought to combine birth control planning with both positive and negative eugenics.

When his mother died in 1929, Gamble created a maternal health clinic as a memorial for her in Cincinnati. The clinic dispensed information at a time when few other birth control clinics existed: one in Cleveland, one in Chicago, and Margaret Sanger's Clinical Research Bureau in New York City. From this beginning, Gamble followed a pattern of careful spending, making grants sufficient to allow a clinic to open or a research project to begin. He was both unable to and uninterested in permanently subsidizing every new project, but instead he worked on securing the local support needed for long-range efforts. Gamble and his staff explained and promoted simple methods—not the expensive and often impractical diaphragm, but spermicidal jellies, foam powders, and sponges to be dipped in salt. Harriet also set up clinical trials, with Gamble's visiting nurses collecting data that measured the effectiveness of new contraceptive methods. He conducted testing without telling women of the risks and failure rates of new contraceptive methods, partly because the answers weren't known, but also because he seemed to possess "a cavalier disregard for the health and dignity of the women involved."[30]

While Gamble worked on expanding birth control methods, he also advocated for sterilization, both involuntary and voluntary. Like Roosevelt, he believed that well-educated white couples, especially with husbands from the Ivy League, needed to have larger families, and he dedicated funds for contests and bonuses to achieve this goal. But he also believed in controlling the "lesser" segment of the population. As a biographer noted, he concluded "that it was more efficient to give money to birth control clinics to prevent the production of relief babies than to the Community Chest to care for them."[31] The dire need for large-scale programs of eugenic sterilization, as Gamble claimed, came from "economic underdevelopment, poverty, perceived overpopulation and a demographic otherness."[32] As Clarence Gamble wrote, "students of heredity who were alarmed with the increase in insanity and mental deficiency" had been ushering in eugenic laws across the country. He compared the states that ignored eugenic methods to a government that failed to avail itself of vaccines for smallpox.[33]

Edna Joins the Birth Control Movement

For Edna, who worked with both Sanger and Gamble creating clinics in the United States and abroad, this effort would always be about individual women, about their need and right to control their lives, as she chose to do more fully for herself after her marriage ended and would have chosen for her mother. Edna collaborated with Sanger and with Gamble, but her focus would never be on state law or mental institutions and certainly not on involuntary sterilization, but on creating places for women to get help and improve lives.

After Edna began meeting with Sanger in 1936, she was put to work. She had a first assignment of joining with Morris L. Ernst, a founder of the American Civil Liberties Union, at the end of his long fight to break the hold of Comstock laws, not just in New York but across the nation. Comstock bragged of convicting 3760 people and driving fifteen to suicide; he planned to appeal the changes to New York law and extend the reach of birth-control restrictions.[34] As Edna engaged with Ernst in Washington in the last steps of a crucial legal case, called One Package, together they challenged the Comstock interference in the medical profession and in the lives of individual women.

To create a strong test case, Dr. Hannah Stone, at Sanger's clinic in New York, ordered a new type of diaphragm from a Japanese physician, to be shipped from Tokyo. Upon arrival of the shipment, customs officials seized it. And then activists took the case to court. In December of 1936, Morris Ernst and Edna Rankin McKinnon achieved a landmark decision in the United States Court of Appeals: that Comstock laws had not been intended to, and did not have the purview to, prevent physicians from saving the lives or promoting the well-being of their patients.[35] Following this groundbreaking case, the American Medical Association approved contraception as an integral, protected part of a medical practice.

With this legal success, applying beyond the state of New York, Margaret Sanger decided in 1937 that the time had come to establish clinics across the nation. Impressed by Edna's efforts, Sanger asked her to return to her home state, her first assignment beyond the courtroom, to the locale where her sisters had been a legislator and a dean of women, her brother a major land owner and politician, and her parents well-known pioneers. As she did later in other states, Edna had one preferred option and two secondary ones: first, to encourage the state board of health to include birth control

Seven. The Campaign for Birth Control, a Pact with the Devil   141

care in a public health program or, if that option could not be achieved, to proceed county to county with local health boards and involve charitable groups in starting clinics. As Edna embarked on this work in her home state, she was funded by Sanger and Gamble.

In the spring of 1937, Edna went to Montana with her daughter Dorothy, a student at the University of Wisconsin, to pursue these options. There she found supporters of the birth control movement engaged in "a litany of defeatism," with little progress having being made through the decades.[36] When Edna attempted to distribute contraceptive information, resistance came from state and county health officials, conservative women's groups, and medical professionals. Besides encountering indifference, opposition, and despair over a lack of progress, Edna found one disturbing source of support, caused by concern about the growing number of parents and children from Mexico.

For Edna the most crippling response came from her brother Wellington, whom she regarded as "conservative, proper." He had changed her life, and ultimately led her to birth control advocacy, in his insistence that she study public speaking and law; he was "who she adored, feared, hated, and worshiped." Wellington told her that he was profoundly shocked by what she was intending to do. Her work in their home state, he claimed as soon as she came home, would lead to ridicule that might wreck his reputation and hurt her. As her biographer Wilma Dykeman recorded their testy conversation, it included his forceful reply when she spoke about contraception as a valuable, humane cause:

> "That may be," Wellington finally replied, "but it's not going to be your life's work."
> "And why shouldn't it be?" Edna asked. "It's important."
> "Sewers are important. But you don't have to dig them."

As Dykeman commented further on the disagreement, Edna "had grown up with the pride and burden of being a Rankin in Montana," and she did not want to disappoint her brother or seem disrespectful to the family. His response would "plunge her into despair" and cause her to reconsider her decision to start her new career at home.[37]

In Montana, as Edna dealt with Wellington and tried to get organized, she became aware of the trend toward involuntary sterilization from which she repeatedly separated herself. The strong reaction to this government power in Montana helped her establish her own opinion: that sterilization procedures might be made available to Americans, but never required.[38] Involuntary sterilization had begun in Montana state institutions in the 1910s. The two main "feeder institutions" were the Montana State Training School in Boulder and the Montana State Mental Hospital in Warm

Springs, which housed people with mental illnesses as well as senility, epilepsy, and a history of substance abuse.[39] The 1919 Survey of the Feebleminded in Montana included descriptions of those for whom the procedure had been mandated: "Girl 17 years of age was at Boulder one year. A defective brother is now at Boulder," the survey noted of two patients. Of an additional teenager chosen, the notes said, "Mother is irresponsible for her care. Father is a drunkard," and of another, "Family of children making no progress in school. Father and Mother of low mentality and ne'er-do-well type."[40] A state law that passed in 1923 to institute a Board of Eugenics claimed that a program of well-regulated sterilizations, building on prior efforts, would secure an improved future for Montana.

As early as 1924, newspapers across the state reported on sterilization as part of what was occurring at corrupt institutions. In October, it hit newspapers that the director of the Warm Springs facility, R.J. Hathaway, had been extorting "large amounts of money" from the families of patients and depositing it in his own accounts. Newspapers also stated that "those poor state patients are just treated like dogs," given foods "unfit for human consumption" and inadequate medical care. In fairly vague terms concerning sterilization, reports described "helpless patients," subjected to "mutilation of the bodies," which resulted in future children lost. The worst theft concerned the "robbing of the unfortunate relatives," not of their funds but of their family. As a piteous example, reports focused particularly on Mrs. Kelly and an "operation performed upon her against her will," with no authorization beyond the decision of corrupt hospital officials.[41]

After December 1924, with so much negative publicity, there would be no more sterilizations at Warm Springs.[42] Sterilizations at other Montana institutions began to occur only with consent of patients or their families. As historian Julius Paul judged this situation, in comparison to residents of other states, Montanans had developed a "higher sense of patient's rights" and regarded "consent as mandatory." As Clarence Gamble noted in 1948, the state had undertaken only four sterilizations of "insane patients" while California had approved 141, Kansas 116, and Virginia 102. By 1964, 256 people had been sterilized through the auspices of Montana's eugenics program whereas the number in California was then 20,108.[43] For Edna, Montana became a model concerning sterilization: the procedure should only be for the few and should always be voluntary, a choice of families and not of government.

Although Edna learned from her state's sterilization choices, she found her brother's opposition there difficult to cope with. In September 1937, after six months, Edna wrote to Clarence Gamble and told him that because of Wellington she would need to start working elsewhere. Gamble suggested that she take on another challenging situation, in Tennessee. When her biographer asked her about this change in her plans, Edna replied that "I disliked my experience in Montana so much that I psychologically had buried all memory of it."[44] As she kept working for birth control reform elsewhere, she maintained the support of her sisters and her mother as well as friendly if distant contact with Wellington.

Beginning in Knoxville, Edna's efforts, funded by Clarence Gamble in association with Margaret Sanger, would extend to thirty-two states. In Tennessee, she helped to set up five clinics. As a Knoxville newspaper article reported, as she met with many groups, she stressed the need for not just those with financial wherewithal to have access to services.[45] Over the opposition of some local groups, she began interacting with African American doctors and nurses, especially in Memphis, and insisting on clinic sites that served African American women.

In this first successful state endeavor, Edna relied on her powers of persuasion, like those of her sisters and brother, but she happily operated outside of Wellington's sphere of influence. While she helped to forward the reputation and power of local leaders, she also deployed the reputation of Margaret Sanger where it proved helpful. Sanger came to Tennessee to meet with groups that Edna specified and left impressed by her organization, speeches, and small courtesies that matter to people. To Sanger and other associates, as Dykeman noted, "Edna seemed an indestructible source of physical drive, professional know-how, and supreme confidence."[46]

In the spring of 1938, Edna went on to Kentucky and Alabama and then South Carolina and Georgia, what Dykeman called the "greatest march through the South since Sherman."[47] Next followed work in northern states, up through New England. During these visits, Edna first contacted doctors that could push the work forward. She also formed supportive committees of lay people, by reaching out to the PTA, university professors, welfare organizations, and civic groups. Additionally, she sought financial support from local industries, like the iron works in Birmingham, Alabama, where she spoke of birth control as essential to healthy workers and families. Following Gamble's dictates, she did not try to establish clinics without multiple sources of support: "If I couldn't interest the people there to raise funds themselves, then he'd say to forget about them."[48] Besides working state to state, Edna began to lobby in Washington for federal funding. Because of her connection to Jeannette, Congress members met with her when they would have avoided other birth control advocates.

To her family, Edna frequently wrote letters about her constant travel and work. In February 1942, for example, in typed letters to "Dear Mother and Family" as well as others to Jeannette and Harriet, she spoke of the exhaustion caused by what she repeatedly referred to as the Great Cause. For an immanent trip, like so many ones before and after, she sent a schedule and hotel names. As she told them, she planned to spend a day or two each in Waco, Austin, Dallas, and San Antonio and then go on to Colorado, where she would be taking psychology classes at Denver University and meeting with the chair of Denver Planned Parenthood. She told family members that the next stop would be California where she would speak at several civic organizations, the prospect of addressing a large crowd making her nervous as usual for she preferred little fireside chats. At the end of a letter to Jeannette, she asked in handwriting for Jeannette to send her red coat for the trip but not if she needed it.[49]

In her letters, Edna repeated stories about herself that her sisters might enjoy, that showed her obstinately pursuing her goals, a trait they shared. A retold story was that at a Hollywood party given by Jack Bickel, the actor Fredric March's brother, she told everyone about birth control improvements and brought out a pelvic model to demonstrate how doctors fit a diaphragm. She kept a sample coil IUD in her purse, she told her sisters, and demonstrated it for anyone who showed the slightest interest.

After working doggedly in so many locales and always moving on, Edna decided to focus her efforts in one place although certainly not Montana. In 1946, she became executive director of the birth control clinics in the Chicago area. By that time, Gamble's goals had become too controversial for her, not what she wanted to be involved with, for she was treading the narrow path of developing clinics with his funding but avoiding any connection with eugenics. She had come to Chicago first as a consultant and recognized that the program there had great potential.[50] Local leaders welcomed her: an article from July 25, 1947, titled "A Vet at Fighting for a Cause," noted that she came to the city as an experienced executive, having worked with her sister for suffrage and run a department store before taking on birth control activism across the country.

Part of Edna's attraction to Chicago came from the state's rejection of involuntary sterilization. Illinois had established strong laws for dealing with the infirm. Beginning in December 1915, a newly passed bill titled Commitment and Care for Feeble-Minded Persons allowed courts to permanently institutionalize anyone whom an expert deemed to be grossly inferior. This state power, to keep the objectionable locked up, meant that eugenic sterilization did not seem necessary. The only known victim of involuntary sterilization in the state was a 65-year-old prisoner who in 1916 had been given the choice of going to prison for the crime for which he was convicted or being sterilized. Even this one sentencing decision sparked a negative public reaction.[51]

With the emphasis on voluntary services and birth control, the Chicago Planned Parenthood offices seemed to Edna like a good site for her efforts. She used her administrative and speaking skills to pull this

Seven. The Campaign for Birth Control, a Pact with the Devil   145

organization out of debt, triple the size of its operations, and increase its budget sevenfold. As she assumed responsibility for reproductive, medical, and educational services in the city and beyond, Edna established a board of directors of twenty-two men and women to increase involvement and support. She created a new series of programs for women in public housing. In 1958, she established The Big Push to introduce birth control services into Cook County Hospital and Chicago Board of Health Clinics. Through all of this expansion, Edna insisted on serving unmarried women, African American and Japanese as well as white, at a time when birth control services were officially mandated for married women only. Through each planned expansion, Edna continued to exert her charismatic personality and forceful organizational skills. As the board chair of Planned Parenthood in Chicago commented to an interviewer, if there were an earthquake and everything was in rubble, Edna would rise out of the wreckage and announce "let's get to work," her concern being the rebuilding of neighborhoods first and then the provision of birth control to families.[52]

Growing up in Missoula as the youngest Rankin, observing risky choices made by her siblings, Edna became interested in political activism. After helping Jeannette on the suffrage and political campaigns and attending law school, she became a working wife and mother, and such goals receded. But she then found her own activist commitment, concerning birth control, at a time when the mortality rate of mothers and children were at high levels and women often found their health and needs overwhelmed by pregnancy and childbirth. Like Jeannette and Harriet, Edna sought to change the lives of women and their families. She made compromises as she worked with Sanger and Gamble, attempting to use their funding and contacts as she traveled the country and created a model program in Chicago. At each site, she worked to extend the rights of women, beyond suffrage, political involvement, and education, giving her time to a type of freedom needed to succeed at everything else.

Eight

The Risks and Judgments of the Postwar World

After taking on various means of participation in the Second World War, the Rankin siblings entered the post-war era, encountering a changed environment for women as well as men. In this challenging time, conflicts in the home space, in businesses, and in the political realm engaged the nation and the Rankins.

Change and uncertainty occurred in foreign policy at the end of the war. In August 1949, the Soviets tested their first nuclear weapon, escalating the risk of warfare. Within the United States, the Cold War, a term from a speech by Bernard Baruch, an influential advisor to Democratic presidents, prompted concerns about communist influence. In contrast to Eisenhower's warning about the perils of the military-industrial complex, Kennedy focused on rearmament. He ordered a massive increase in defense spending, a rapid build-up of the nuclear arsenal to restore superiority over the Soviet Union: from 1961 to 1964 the number of American nuclear weapons increased by 50 percent. After the French left Indochina in 1954, the U.S. had begun offering financial and military support to the South Vietnamese to curb communist power in the region. U.S. involvement in Vietnam escalated from just under a thousand military advisors in 1959 to 16,000 in 1963 and to 23,000 in 1964, with advisors turning into soldiers. After the Gulf of Tonkin incident, in which a U.S. destroyer was allegedly twice fired upon by a North Vietnamese torpedo boat, the Congress gave President Johnson broad authorization to increase U.S. military presence, with troop levels soaring to 184,000. The human cost of the war would ultimately include three million Vietnamese soldiers and civilians, 300,000 Cambodians, 60,000 Laotians, and 58,220 U.S. service members.[1]

The transfer from World War II to the Cold War period would bring changes and uncertainties on the home front as well as to American foreign policy. After the war, wives were expected to return home along with their husbands, with a post-war change occurring in the purpose of American

Eight. The Risks and Judgments of the Postwar World   147

women or at least in the public depiction of that purpose. In *Homeward Bound: American Families in the Cold War Era*, Elaine Tyler May concluded that in the 1950s, "Americans turned to the family as a bastion of safety in an insecure world" and thus "cold war ideology and the domestic revival" should be rightly seen "as two sides of the same coin."[2] In *More Work for Mother*, Ruth Schwartz Cowan wrote that psychiatrists, psychologists, and popular writers of the era, influenced by the national emphasis on women returning to their homes, critiqued women who wished to pursue a career, referring to such "unlovely women" as "lost," "suffering from penis envy," "ridden with guilt complexes," or just plain "man-hating." This shaming and seeming banishment of the few did not reflect reality because women of all classes continued to work. In the United States, about 27 percent of women worked in 1940, a percentage that went up to 37 in 1945. In a complicated time for American women as workers, the percentage would be 33 in 1950, decreased from the war years but not to 1940 numbers. By 1960, the percentage would be 38.[3]

Changes in judgments concerning work for women were not the only business alterations of the era. In the decade and a half after World War II, the United States experienced phenomenal economic growth. Gross national product, a measure of all goods and services, jumped from about $200 thousand million in 1940 to $300 in 1950 and to more than $500 in 1960.[4] This growth changed the nature of many industries and the job choices within them. In Montana, for example, many business ventures began at the start of the 1950s, but they certainly didn't involve all residents. With a growing middle class and World War II's rations lifted, Montanans could buy more food, creating a high demand for farming and ranching. But the growing mechanization of agriculture meant that fewer people worked on the larger farms and ranches—and their owners pressured the government to decrease the amount of arable lands reserved for Native Americans. The discovery of oil at Williston Basin near Billings in 1951 dramatically increased production. Other oil fields, including Cat Creek near Lewistown and Kevin-Sunburst near Shelby, also became big producers but with a minimal need for unskilled labor. As businesses boomed, the world's largest copper producer, Anaconda Copper, changed its methods: with underground mining becoming too expensive, the richest deposits having already been extracted, the company adopted open-pit mining, removing low-grade copper with fewer skilled workers and more equipment. This alteration in mining methods, as well as in farming and ranching, caused many residents to lose their jobs and feel the pressure to seek work elsewhere.

As in Montana, across the country not all Americans participated equally in expanding opportunities and economic prosperity. As a consequence, well before the 1960s, many groups began protesting to extend their rights. In the early 1950s, there were hundreds of large-scale labor strikes each year. The peak occurred in 1952, when 470 stoppages involved nearly 2.8 million workers or roughly 4.5 percent of the civilian labor force, compared to .04 percent engaging in strikes in 2013.[5] In December 1955 activist Rosa Parks' refusal to give up her seat to a white man on a bus in Montgomery, Alabama, sparked a sustained bus boycott that inspired mass protests elsewhere. Many groups, including the growing numbers of working women, pressed for the Equal Pay Act, passed by Congress in 1963, promising equitable wages for the same work, regardless of the race, color, religion, national origin or sex of the worker.

The changing environment after World War II engaged the Rankins in new and complex decisions and risks. In an uncertain time, the Rankins dealt with family changes and with their own aging, taking advantages of the opportunities of the period and dealing with its challenges.

For the Rankin Siblings and Their Mother, Women in Post-War Roles

Part of the postwar reality, with families spreading out away from their hometowns and states, was the changed life of the older woman. Women lived longer than men, the life expectancy in 1950 being 65.6 for men and 71.1 for women, the average for women having changed from 37 in 1800 and 48.3 in 1900. In a growing American economy, with emphasis on suburbs and young families, women's later years, especially as widows, often lacked a clear sense of purpose, with children grown and inheritance of land and property going to sons.[6] Harriet came back from England after her husband died after the war. Until she died in October of 1979, she lived on Long Island and stayed with her daughters in Cambridge and in Washington, a widow like her mother. In 1945, Olive had been living without John for forty-one years, and Wellington had long held power over the land and family funds. Through these decades, the responsibilities of Olive's daughters and less so of her son included caring for the mother who lacked other means of support.

By mid-century, the house at 134 Madison Street stood vacant and decaying. Olive had sold it in the 1930s, unable to maintain it on her own, and had begun to stay with her children for varying lengths of time. Ultimately, this house along with a dozen others would be demolished, in the fall of 1958, to make way for a new Madison Street bridge. The article in the *Missoulian* concerning the Rankin home had the title of "Pioneer's Home Wrecked for New Bridge," and it focused on "a bridge builder's home being demolished for a new one."[7]

Eight. The Risks and Judgments of the Postwar World 149

For almost twenty years, Olive had no permanent address, with Wellington in charge of her finances and all the children in charge of her whereabouts. She had help from Harriet in Missoula until she married in 1935 and moved to London. Then, Olive traveled repeatedly to her other children's homes. With this repetition of visits and back bedrooms, she became even more "self-isolated, always with an illness, and easily bored," in Wellington's estimation.[8] In a family of busy independent siblings, the responsibility for the mother would not fall on everyone equally, but primarily on Olive's children who maintained traditional homes, a sore subject in a family spread out across the country. In a changing world, women who undertook traditional family work might feel insecure, indeed lesser, as they cared for children and parents.

Much of the responsibility for Olive fell on Grace whose home in Idaho was a quick drive from Missoula. She was born in 1890, the year that Philena died, and she was fourteen at the time of her father's death, in 1904. A Rankin child who made the more traditional choices of her generation, she married and stayed at home. Wellington later told an interviewer that she was a housewife, a wonderful woman, who in his estimation "did more ... through her children," John, Thomas, and Janet Kinney.[9]

Grace went to the University of Montana. She married Thomas Kinney in August 1913, at home in the yard with white ribbons in the trees and colored lights, the wedding group processing to Mendelssohn's "Wedding March." Mary was one of six bridesmaids and Edna maid of honor, with Harriet's young daughters serving as flower girls. The *Missoulian* described the decorations and dresses of an elaborate family event: "dress was of silk shadowlace with jacket and court train of crepe meteor and a maline veil shirred into a cap of shadowlace."[10] Grace moved to Thompson Falls, Idaho, with her husband after her marriage and later with him to other small towns in eastern Idaho with the shifting focus of his job, in the forestry service, and later as a land owner. Wellington said that Grace "was a million per cent with Jeannette" concerning suffrage and the elections, but she did less campaigning than her sisters. As he said of his sister in Idaho, "I wish she lived in Montana."[11]

Though Grace did not travel abroad with her sisters, they wrote to her from wherever they were. When Edna and Jeannette were together in India, Jeannette told her that they were "going to things people say that you should see" and that "Edna is looking at another palace." Jeannette also said that there was a rug where they were staying just like one in Grace's hall, so she thought of her sister every time she stepped on it.[12]

Many of these letters among siblings concern the mother's movements from house to house where she frequently felt ignored or abandoned, the answer often being another extended stay with Grace. She wrote to her

Grace Rankin Kinney and her three children: clockwise, John, Thomas, and Janet Kinney, 1921–1922 (Colville Studio, Missoula, Montana. Schlesinger Library, Radcliffe Institute, Harvard University).

mother on July 12, 1941, as she did frequently, to check on her health and ask her to come to visit since her mother felt neglected by Wellington when she stayed at his ranch. On July 1, 1942, Jeannette wrote to Olive at Grace's house, recognizing that she was happier away from Washington and wishing her a good, long sojourn there. In April 1942, Jeannette again wrote to her mother in Couer d'Alene to tell her that she couldn't come then to

Eight. The Risks and Judgments of the Postwar World 151

Idaho, which her mother had requested, because she had just returned from Washington to Georgia. On May 14, 1942, the sisters wrote back and forth about the difficulty of securing help because their mother could "get the goat" of someone she knew or someone she didn't. In 1946, Grace wrote to Edna that Mary and her mother were at her house in Couer d'Alene and that Mother was telling her "all that her mean daughters had done to her." In this letter, Grace commented, "Do you forget how murderous one is after caring for her for a few weeks?"[13]

Mary was another sister who made more traditional choices after college, including marriage and family, choices that could seem limited in comparison with all that her siblings were doing. Born in 1888, she participated in the family social whirl before heading to the University of Montana where she graduated in June 1909, winning a prize for the best work in the musical department. In September 1910, she left for a year's further study at Wellesley. In the fall of 1912 while teaching in Colfax, Washington, she met Herbert Bragg, a building contractor, whom she married in July 1916 at her mother's house when she was twenty-seven. The bridesmaids wore "shepherdess gowns of old gold satin" and carried "tall white crooks." Escorted by Wellington, Mary came down the aisle in a "cape of duchess lace, from which depended a net train and a filmy bridal veil," like the heroine of a fairy tale.[14]

In the 1920s, Mary and Herbert Bragg moved to California, first to San Marino and then to Los Angeles. Later, as Wellington told an interviewer, Herbert became "terribly crippled" with arthritis, and Mary was required to care for him while teaching to support their two children, Kenneth and Mary Jane, and repeatedly providing a home for her mother.[15] In Wellington's telling, she was the "saint of the family." Like her sisters, she frequently wrote to her siblings about the everyday while also recording the difficulties of her work and family. In July 1942, she wrote to Jeannette to tell her that she had gotten a book from the library to read more about India where her sisters were traveling and where she wished that she could go with them.[16]

With Wellington and perhaps also with her sisters, Mary had the feeling of being lesser, that becoming a wife and mother was not all that she should have done. Once after Wellington came to visit her in California, clearly a stressful visit for her, she wrote to him about her children and money that he gave her:

> The money will help with the clothes problem. I wish it could do even more, but unfortunately money cannot obliterate unhappy memories of the facts that you firmly impressed upon me—namely that I am the one whom Mother likes to visit the least; that I am your "dumb" sister; that Grace, Edna, and Jeannette have told you that I am very hard to live with; that though you had not seen me for three years you had no time or desire to spend your second day here with me.

Olive Pickering Rankin at the beginning of World War II (Schlesinger Library, Radcliffe Institute, Harvard University).

Eight. The Risks and Judgments of the Postwar World

Olive Rankin with her children and grandchildren. On the back row, from left to right: Harriet, Mary, Wellington, Edna, Dorothy McKinnon Brown in Edna's arms, Grace, Jeannette; 2nd row, both in white blouses: Mary Elizabeth Sedman, Virginia Sedman; 3rd row: Janet Kinney and Olive; 4th row: John Kinney, Thomas E. Kinney (in lap), Kenneth Bragg; in front, Mary Jane Bragg (Schlesinger Library, Radcliffe Institute, Harvard University).

But then in the same letter Mary assures Wellington that she will put their mother's welfare first, that she can't keep up the anger, that she was ill while he was there and thus too concerned about what he thought of her.[17]

As occurred in many families, after World War II, the Rankins had all left their hometown. They had spread out across the country, to new sites but ones where women still had responsibility for ill husbands, for children, and for elderly members of their families. This was by that time a conflicted service, which might cede a sense of inferiority or anger as some siblings moved forward with more freedom than others.

Wellington and Post-War Business

As a busy progressive and then as an established power in the state, Wellington, who had been married from 1910 to 1912, did not marry again until 1956, when he was seventy-two. After the war, as a power broker in Montana, he took advantage of business and real estate opportunities to thrive in an era of big business.

While avoiding married life for most of his career, in 1946 Wellington met Louise Replogle, who beat him in a legal case. He also knew her through his Republican Party connections. After graduating from Fergus County High School, Louise enrolled at the University of Montana where she served as president of the Associated Women Students, an organization that Harriet instituted. In law school she edited the *Montana Law Review*. After graduation, she was elected Fergus County attorney, defeating two men in the Republican primary and another in the general election, becoming the third woman in U.S. history to be selected as a prosecutor. She also became chair of the state's Young Republicans. In 1949, Louise was elected as co-chair of the National Young Republicans, her achievements recognized when she was named a Young Woman of the Year by *Mademoiselle* and *Look* magazine did a feature profile on her. Louise joined Wellington's law firm in 1950, one of the few women to become a partner in a Montana firm, and she married him six years later.

Formal portrait of Wellington Rankin, 1940–1945 (Schlesinger Library, Radcliffe Institute, Harvard University).

At his offices across the state, his business expanding dramatically in the post-war period, Wellington specialized in real estate investments and wills; the legal work needed by companies, ranches, governments, and financial institutions; medical malpractice; and criminal law. He took advantage of his postwar affluence to buy a good percentage of Montana. He ultimately owned a million and a half acres in the state, making him one of the largest land owners in the country, with 25,000 head of cattle. His acquisitions included ranches that he heard about through his work on wills and divorces, sometimes at the edge of what was legal. After owning the Avalanche Ranch near Townsend for years, he bought the Ringling Ranch where the circus once wintered its stock, and then other large properties as they became available. With profits came the ability to secure the larger Miller Bros. Ranch, forty miles across in some places, reaching to

Eight. The Risks and Judgments of the Postwar World

Wellington Rankin at his Avalanche Ranch with Louise Replogle in 1954. They married in 1956 (Schlesinger Library, Radcliffe Institute, Harvard University).

the Canadian border, with 345,000 acres and 9,000 head of cattle, as well as ranches in four other counties. As Wellington monitored these properties from his office in Helena, he faced frequent accusations of mistreating his stock and failing to develop his land. Viewing himself as a modern investor, Wellington rarely visited his extensive holdings. With his profits, he also purchased the Placer Hotel and the Weiss Café/Mint Bar in Helena, an office building in Helena, the Montana Ready-Mix Company in Missoula, and mineral rights and oil leases on other properties, their value increasing along with drilling in the state. He hired managers to oversee these investments as he did his ranches. While property provided a daily rhythm and purpose for John Rankin, it would not for his son.

This legal success and property acquisition didn't help Wellington in politics; in fact his fierceness in the courtroom and business acumen may have hurt him. When he ran for the U.S. Senate in 1948, state senator Dan Maddox spoke about Wellington's commitment to Montana: he would be the first senator born there and the first college graduate; his speeches and analyses were always "logical, alert and forceful." Maddox argued further that Montanans criticized Wellington for being too aggressive, but they went to him when they were in serious trouble—and with a Cold War developing, the nation was in such trouble.[18] But the state's voters did not elect him. His opposition repeatedly stressed his large fees as an attorney, his overgrazed and unmonitored ranches, his practice of having men from the penitentiary paroled to him to work as hired hands, and his overuse of water as the state's largest landowner. In 1948, Chinook attorney Harry L. Burns wrote to Wellington concerning his continuing quest for political power that "you were ready to sell your soul for this honor and never considered defeat nor prepared yourself for it," but defeat was Wellington's primary electoral experience.[19] By the time he ran in 1948, Wellington was long ago a progressive crusader. In comparison to him, James E. Murray, who had been in the Senate since 1934, appeared as "a champion of small business and labour against big business monopoly," including the multiple concerns of the Anaconda Company.[20]

When Wellington died in 1966, from complications after elective hernia surgery at the Mayo Clinic in Rochester, Minnesota, a time in which he decided not to trust in Christian Science practitioners, his widow inherited his large holdings. A bequest of $75,000 went to Jeannette in Watkinsville, Georgia, with similar sums left to his other sisters. In the post-war era, he had built his estate by viewing land and city buildings as investments, oil as a marketable resource to sell to national companies, cattle as an industry, and law as a business that could profitably connect all of the others.

Jeannette and a Response to the Cold War

Given her vote against the declaration of war in December 1941, Jeannette did not run for reelection to Congress. While Wellington in the post-war era developed his various businesses, creating a land and legal empire, Jeannette continued her analysis of war and peace, focusing on the Cold War.

Jeannette felt that the presence of possible new enemies in the late 1940s was expanding American commitment to the war method. As she told an interviewer from the *Chicago Tribune* in January 1947, the country was "going straight to war unless we change our course … as soon as we get another crop of men ready." As she said further during the onset of a tense period, "We've got to change our course. We've got to decide to get rid of the war methods—settling disputes by war and violence."[21]

During the Korean War, Jeannette repeatedly told interviewers that all Americans needed to take an active role, to understand how we had gotten involved in this conflict that had nothing to do with national defense.[22] She argued that Americans had escalated a civil war to a much more dangerous level. At the war's end, after nearly five million people died, more than half of them civilians along with forty thousand American soldiers, Jeannette claimed that this tragic total served no rational purpose.

While Jeannette voiced her opposition to the Cold War and to the

Eight. The Risks and Judgments of the Postwar World 157

military buildup under Truman, Eisenhower, and Kennedy, she became a leader of anti-war activists during the Vietnam War. After her vote concerning World War I, when Jeannette met Wellington in the hallway of the Capitol, she told him that all she cared about was "what they will say fifty years from now."[23] And fifty years later she took another public stand against war, with more public approval than for her World War I vote and certainly her World War II vote. As American war deaths went from 1,863 in 1965, to 6,143 in 1966, and to 11,153 in 1967, Jeannette argued repeatedly that Johnson had led Americans into an escalating war in which they had no actual stake.[24] She completely dismissed the domino theory, of communist governments expanding their territory and ultimately coming across the Pacific to California. She believed that the Vietnamese could engage in a civil war, resolving issues left over from French colonialism, without American involvement. In a tense time, she maintained, it could not be the right answer for citizens to "drop out" or avoid civic engagement: "When we belittle our representative government and fail to support and direct it, we are headed toward a dictator," she declared in a radio address. "No one can let up in this effort to bring about peace."[25] In frequent talks, she reviewed her own voting history concerning war and attempts made to silence her, but she argued that each person taking action, not cowed by authority, could help to decide the fate of civilization, ending the worst of nationalistic and barbaric trends.[26]

As the Vietnam War grew in scope and in casualties, Jeannette decided to use her organizing skills, her connections in the peace and women's movements, and her own access to Congress to engage American women in public protest. In 1967, she lent her name to the "Jeannette Rankin Brigade," women who planned to protest the war by demonstrating in Washington, D.C. In making this decision, she continued her essentialist arguments from the First World War. "You cannot have war without women," she repeatedly claimed in the 1960s as she had through the decades. As she indicated further, "I register the protest of women," who had the ability and right to protect children and the country and to fight against the war system with "woman power."[27]

As Jeannette began to plan a large demonstration, she constructed her women's parade as a response to a counterculture march that had very publicly gone wrong. Abbie Hoffman had promised that "we will dye the Potomac red, burn the cherry trees, panhandle embassies, attack with water pistols, marbles, bubble gum wrappers, bazookas, girls will run naked and piss on the Pentagon walls, sorcerers, swamis, witches, voodoo, warlocks, medicine men and speed freaks will hurl their magic at the faded brown walls." On October 21, 1967, Hoffman's band of protesters gathered at the Lincoln Memorial and marched to the Pentagon. There a full-scale riot erupted, as they encountered three hundred U.S. marshals and five thousand Army troops. The altercation ended with 682 people arrested and forty-seven injured—demonstrators, soldiers, and marshals.[28] What Rankin promised was something quite different, a dignified march of women, of mothers. "There is no reason why old ladies shouldn't be allowed to go into the Capitol," she said as she defended the plans made by her own group for January 1968.[29]

As in the suffrage campaign, Jeannette organized women in every state, asking them to call their congressional representatives and meet with local reporters. She told the press that representatives from each state would submit a resolution to Congress calling for American troops to immediately come home. When she was asked how the government would get out of this war, instead of suggesting a staged plan of withdrawal, she replied, "take the boys home the same way we took them over—on airplanes and ships," an end being simple to achieve in an undeclared war that lacked long-range goals.[30] Jeannette claimed repeatedly that Americans, "outraged by the ruthless slaughter," were ready for that choice, to end a "unilateral war."[31] As she planned a national protest, she told reporters that she might seek a House seat in 1968, again from the western district of Montana, to give further voice to war opposition.[32] After she began to secure publicity for her brigade and the antiwar movement gained ground, she stopped referring to this plan.

Throughout 1967 groups across the country sought publicity as they organized for the Jeannette Rankin Brigade. From Kentucky, for example, well-publicized participants included members of the Appalachian Volunteers, a community-organizing network that initiated summer programs for students and fought against strip mining. Groups quite publicly joined together to head to Washington. In California, the Marin group formed a car caravan to meet up with marchers from San Francisco. In Massachusetts, groups planned to leave from Weston, Wellesley, and Newton, to join with Bostonians on the train to Union Station. Participation by activist leaders led to increased publicity. In Atlanta at a press conference, Coretta Scott King said that she would lead the march, which the Southern Christian Leadership Conference supported as did her husband. King reiterated that women, the "instillers of value in the family," could change American values. Other sponsors and speakers, as announced across the country, included activist Jane Cheney Spock; author Jessica Mitford; actress and activist Ruby Dee; dancer and costume designer Julie Robinson Belafonte; and anti-nuclear protestor Dagmar Wilson, who called on President Kennedy to "end the arms-race—not the human race." From Washington, well-publicized organizers included Judith Morse Easton, daughter of a senator. When asked whether men could march with them, Jeannette

Eight. The Risks and Judgments of the Postwar World   159

replied that "men can stand on the sidelines and encourage us."[33] As plans for the Washington march progressed, the group also decided on parades for adherents who could not make the journey, with events scheduled from San Francisco to Boston.

For January 15, 1968, these activists' plan was to march from Union Station to the Capitol and then to enter the grounds and go in to deliver their petition, all dressed in black to mourn the unnecessary involvement in war and death. As Jeannette and other participants told reporters, the group brought with them a petition that asked for immediate withdrawal from Vietnam as well as help with healing a sick society at home, a reorganization of priorities toward social services and education that could occur after denying the "insatiable demands of the military-industrial complex."[34]

Just a few days before the big day, after a year of planning, the police denied the group the right to march onto Capitol grounds, using the authority of an 1882 law. Jeannette went to the Court of Appeals and then to the Supreme Court without avail. She was told that her group could march to the grounds and from there she would be able to go inside the Capitol and meet with legislators, as a former member of the House, and perhaps bring a small group with her, but no more.

On the opening day of the legislature, a crowd of thousands of marchers, led by what the newspapers labeled as the "dowager queen of the peaceniks," as well as Coretta Scott King, marched along with a trail of reporters, from Union Station. They came six abreast, to the beginning of the Capitol grounds, with ten women in front, reflecting their petition in a huge banner reading "End the War in Vietnam and Social Crisis at Home."[35] Swedish actress Viveca Lindfors read the petition and then asked for a moment of silence for those who had already died and for troops then fighting. Next a delegation of fifteen went with Jeannette to meet with Mike Mansfield, a Montana senator, and John W. McCormack, Speaker of the House.[36] Outside, the talks continued, given by Belafonte and Spock, with Judy Collins speaking and then singing. Along with the march, the event also featured several days of meetings, with workshops to learn about how to plan further antiwar demonstrations and to oppose politicians that supported the war.

Jeannette's Vietnam War activism secured not just press but FBI attention. Much of Jeannette's 1183-page FBI file, ordered in 2000 and finally received nine years later by James Lopach, one of her biographers, concerns accusations that the Brigade was a communist effort. The FBI had authorized Jeannette's inclusion in *The Red Network,* in 1934, listing her as one of 1300 leaders of organizations controlled by communists. But most of the investigations in this file concerned her activities during the Korean and especially the Vietnam wars. These reports portray her as more dupe

The Jeanette Rankin Brigade protesting the Vietnam War in Washington, on their march to the Capitol. Jeannette Rankin, wearing eyeglasses, stands holding the banner at the center, January 15, 1968 (Bettmann/Getty Images).

than traitor: communists had "surreptitiously seized control" of her antiwar activities.[37]

As she opposed the Vietnam War, Jeannette spoke in Congress against the electoral college and for the direct election of the president, just as her brother had advocated for the direct election of senators to extend the power of the citizenry. As she claimed in a 1971 article, "there are military contracts in every Congressman's district" and the "gigantic military establishment" could exercise control over the body of electors, detracting from democracy. Jeannette believed that human beings could choose better methods of choosing lawmakers, dispensing justice and resolving conflicts, and she made that point by referring to her family's history: "When my father first came to Montana from Canada in 1869," she said, "the gun was law and the strongest ruled by force." Western towns had become more civilized, settling disputes through legal means, and the nation and world could follow.[38]

In 1972, Jeannette again considered mounting a third House campaign to voice her opposition to the Vietnam War. Her activism was behind her choice that year as the first inductee in the National Organization for Women's Susan B. Anthony Hall of Fame, the presentation naming her as "the world's outstanding living feminist."[39] Although her legacy rests almost entirely on her pacifism, Jeannette told the Montana Constitutional

Eight. The Risks and Judgments of the Postwar World 161

Convention in 1972 that she would have preferred otherwise. "If I am remembered for no other act," she said, "I want to be remembered as the only woman who ever voted to give women the right to vote." Shortly before her death in 1973, a reporter asked Jeannette whether she would do anything differently if she could relive her life. She replied that she would not, with one exception: "I would have been nastier." When she died, in Carmel where she was staying with Edna, she bequeathed her estate, including the property in Georgia, to help "mature, unemployed women workers" to secure a better education. The Jeannette Rankin Women's Scholarship Fund offers college scholarships to low-income women, age thirty-five and older. With added support from many donors, the fund has awarded more than three million dollars in scholarships.[40]

Jeannette Rankin Hall, University of Montana. The building was named for her in 1983 (Stan Healy Photographs, MSS 430, Archives & Special Collections, Mansfield Library, University of Montana).

In 1983, a neoclassical building erected in 1908, on the main oval at the University of Montana, was named the Jeannette Rankin Hall. It has housed the library, law school, and the psychology and philosophy departments and now the environmental studies department.[41] In 1985, a statue of Jeannette by Terry Mimnaugh, inscribed "I Cannot Vote for War," was placed in the Capitol Statuary Hall in Washington. At its dedication, historian Joan Hoff Wilson called Rankin "one of the most controversial and unique women in Montana and American political history." A replica of the statue stands in Montana's capitol building in Helena.[42] As of 2021, Rankin remains the only woman elected to the U.S. House or Senate from Montana.

In later wars, other strong voices that opposed American involvement quoted Jeannette. Concerning Desert Storm, for example, social critic Jeanne F. Cook commented that "winning is worth little as compared with the cost of war." She quoted Jeannette as she argued that financial gain, in this case from oil, was a chief motivator, what Jeannette would have voted against. As she continued,

Statue of Jeannette Rankin in the U.S. Capitol, located in the Statuary Hall, one of the two chosen to represent the state of Montana. The other one chosen to represent the state is of artist Charles Russell (Architect of the Capitol, Washington, D.C., Library of Congress).

"war is economically and politically profitable for some, damages much and solves little, and sometimes in hindsight makes a bad situation worse."[43]

In the two terms that Jeannette served in Congress, she was constructed in many ways: as an important first in politics, as a representative of American women, as a sign of the west's growth and vitality, as a loyal American, as a hippie or communist—and as a traitor. As she voted against and protested through four wars, she developed and altered her thinking about warfare. Jeannette was not completely a pacifist or an isolationist though critics have labeled her as one or the other or both. She was an independent thinker and voter, willing to take the risks and accept the consequences of her principled choices.

Edna and the Cold War Requirements of Women

While Edna worked in Chicago, she traveled to birth control conferences, funded by Clarence Gamble. In December 1952, they went together to an international conference on planned parenthood in Bombay. With this beginning, Edna involved herself in the international campaign for women's rights and birth control, complicated by Clarence Gamble's drive for a surer means of control: to insure lesser numbers of what he judged to be lesser people. During the Cold War, with the United States depicting itself as a first world, fear over large populations coming under the influence of the Soviet Union led to international birth control efforts. Activists aimed at both helping local citizens and controlling their numbers, complex goals that Edna Rankin McKinnon tried to navigate as she began to conduct her work on the world stage.

By the 1950s, Gamble was concentrating on countries with colonial pasts, in Africa, Latin America, Oceania and Asia, which he designated as the "periphery." Gamble described an unfortunate consequence of western army expansion in the developing world: wartime efforts to maintain the health of the armed forces in tropical areas had led to local adoption of initiatives that reduced the incidence of disease and early death. For Gamble, these western health measures had heightened the need to control the size of these populations, certainly lesser beings than Harvard graduates.[44]

While Gamble tried to convince leaders in India and other countries to move beyond birth control clinics and volunteer choices to control their populations, he also employed these places to further the testing of various contraceptive methods, as he had also done in North Carolina, West Virginia, and Puerto Rico, often without the women's knowledge or consent. In these countries, Gamble often infuriated population-control advocates, who considered his methods and language to be racist and imperialist.[45]

Beginning in her visits to India, Edna witnessed the often intense reaction to Gamble's goals. At his urging and with his funding, in 1951 India adopted a family planning program, not sterilization but birth control, but even with family planning in twenty years the population grew from 356 million to 548 million. In 1971, after decades of pressure and offers of funding, the country began to support voluntary sterilization; India did not endorse a compulsory bill until 1976 but never enforced it, given negative public response.[46]

Although Edna had stopped traveling for Gamble in the United States and she never participated in his eugenics programs, for a new and important challenge, she decided to join the staff that he sent abroad.

Edna Rankin McKinnon boarding an airplane, en route to a Planned Parenthood conference in Bombay, 1952 (Schlesinger Library, Radcliffe Institute, Harvard University).

At first traveling with her daughter Dorothy, she launched what became a first around-the-world trip, with Gamble funding her visits to the Philippines, Malaya, Singapore, Vietnam, Indonesia, Fiji, Tonga, Turkey, Iran, Saudi Arabia, Kuwait, Jordan, and through western Africa, beginning in Lagos and on to Liberia and Sierra Leone, places where she worked to initiate clinics and to which she regularly returned to expand on her efforts.

In many countries to which she traveled, new post-colonial leaders viewed a birth control program as part of establishing rule and prosperity. After World War II, Fiji began to take its first steps towards self-government. An expanded Legislative Council brought native Fijians into the official political structure and fostered a modern political culture, with enfranchisement occurring in 1963. At the beginning of the 1960s, the country faced a population that would double in twenty years, with a dire lack of the food, shelter, and resources to supply for such growth. A new

Edna Rankin McKinnon with Abebi Ibrahim, a Nigerian health nurse, Lagos, 1964 (Schlesinger Library, Radcliffe Institute, Harvard University).

leader with problems to solve and quickly, Kamisese Mara was willing to cooperate with Edna as she laid out plans for clinics. By 1966 government officials in Fiji reported widely that family planning efforts had been integral to providing a new level of health services. Using the Lippes Loop, an IUD, as reports noted, women had been able to space their pregnancies, the country thus growing richer with a larger number of healthy children and a lower number of infant and maternal deaths.[47] This control over the population, bringing greater choices for women, came from voluntary family planning, not the more extreme Gamble choice of involuntary sterilization, which the government rejected.

In many changing countries, both political upheaval and the terrain made for challenging work. Indonesia had gained freedom from the Dutch in 1949. In the early 1960s, the new country was buying arms from the Soviet Union and turning down any connection with the British, Americans, or Dutch. Though President Sukarno sought weapons from the Soviets, he also feared their influence. From 1964 to 1966, a violent anti-communist purge led to the killing of approximately 500,000 Indonesians. In this volatile environment, Edna met with new executives and ministers of health as well as Muslim leaders and local organizations. Between 1961 and 1968, she went repeatedly to Indonesia, traveling by small pack

Edna Rankin McKinnon handing out information to Indonesian women at a lecture on birth control and family planning, 1963 (Schlesinger Library, Radcliffe Institute, Harvard University).

Eight. The Risks and Judgments of the Postwar World

Edna Rankin McKinnon in a garden in Singapore, outside of Singapore Regional Planning, ca. 1960–1963 (Schlesinger Library, Radcliffe Institute, Harvard University).

boat and horseback to more of the 17,000 islands than many residents had visited. There was one small family planning clinic when Edna first went there, but fifty-six when she left and 165 by the time she went back to visit in 1968. Edna claimed in an article that birth control availability in these countries was allowing women to emerge, to take their rightful place and thrive both as mothers and as citizens of the nation.[48]

In Malaysia, a country that gained its independence in 1959, Edna encountered difficulties with government structures. As she stated in an article in June 1961, starting family planning units there had been "uphill work all the way" but was going well. Government officials, with so much to achieve, began by denying her any help, claiming that assistance would have to come from the health office or from rural services, each one sending her repeatedly to the other. She began setting up clinics, in eleven states of Malaysia, by relying on volunteers and then registered nurses who were given additional training, which she finally convinced a new administration to provide. The number of centers in Penang, in the northwest, went from one to thirteen, with additional clinics in the least developed areas. From Melaka midway down the peninsula to Johor on the southern tip, Edna brought help where there had been none. By the time she finished, not a single state on the peninsula lacked a new, reorganized, or strengthened family planning organization. In June 1961, an article in the *Malay Mail* lauded this success, labeling Edna as an "American expert" that was bringing a better status to women and families.[49]

In 1963, venturing on with Gamble's funding, Edna went to Iran in a year of upheaval that created some opportunity for her. There the birth rate was higher than in any other country she had visited, and more than half of babies died before they reached school age.[50] She spoke with women who had been pregnant twelve or fourteen times and had multiple abortions: they desperately needed contraceptives that the country had been reticent to provide. In that year, the Shah was implementing "The White Revolution," an aggressive campaign of social and economic Westernization that met with intense opposition. But it created an opening for Edna to meet with government officials, religious leaders, health-care providers, and school administrators. After these visits, she helped create eight clinics in Teheran and then went out into the country, to small towns and farms, to interact with women there. In a changing but conservative country, where she was often not invited to planning meetings, she allowed local leaders to use her ideas without overt acknowledgment of the impact of an outsider, a Christian Scientist, and a woman.[51]

After working in Iran, Edna went to Ethiopia in May 1964, another site where connections made with leaders enabled her to prevail. There she received help from Lady Emebet Seble Desta, a granddaughter of Haile

Eight. The Risks and Judgments of the Postwar World 169

Selassie. Accompanied by Desta, she met with ministers of health in a place where many doctors had never seen an IUD. Again success involved stressing the long-term health of women and children and not Gamble's preferred method of population control. By 1970 in Ethiopia, where Edna had returned several times, fifty-five hospitals and family planning clinics handled 6000 family planning visits monthly.[52]

Edna went from Ethiopia to Jordan, Syria, Lebanon, and Turkey. But she did not encounter success in every location. When Clarence Gamble asked her to go to Saudi Arabia, she started at Aramco, a national petroleum and natural gas company, where officials introduced her to leading doctors and health educators. She sent out educational materials and supplies, but felt that she was making little progress though visiting with government and Aramco officials allowed her to "breach a few barriers, open a few windows, break a long silence."[53]

As a fieldworker in each locale, Edna adapted written materials and tailored social interactions to the local culture. Wherever she went, she met with small groups that helped her to understand local traditions and foster "the sort of personal-impersonal occasion Edna enjoyed utilizing to the fullest."[54] In Sri Lanka, since a woman did not walk the streets alone, two or three field workers went together to visit patients in their homes. In Indonesia, Edna recognized that a small charge was necessary for women to value what they were being given and that medical services had to be offered through clinics. In Bali, with no words in Balinese for birth control, programs began at a health association, a non-controversial choice, leading to three dispensary centers with the publicly stated emphasis on family security and health.

Edna's enthusiasm and thoughtful personal connections extended these efforts. On the porch of the governor's house in Bali, with a group of influential Balinese, she formed a Planned Parenthood branch on the spot as she discussed family size and a prosperous future. After hearing Edna speak about the role of individual women in the health of the nation, the governor's wife told her husband, "We should be her first patients." As Edna knew, the couple had been married six years and had nine children, including three sets of twins.[55] As her colleague Bernadine Zukosky wrote in a letter to Clarence Gamble, about her well-planned meetings, "Edna McKinnon continues to work like one possessed and to have the success that seems to come only to the possessed."[56]

In June 1966, after Edna had traveled to Kenya and Uganda, she returned to Ethiopia. In Addis Ababa, she received word that Wellington had died. Then in July Clarence Gamble died, and in September, Margaret Sanger. By that fall Edna was living in Missoula and then she retired to Carmel, California. In 1973, she was "gratified" by the Supreme Court opinion

Eight. The Risks and Judgments of the Postwar World

on abortion in *Roe v. Wade* "because everyone can get a good safe abortion instead of the hideous ones women used to have." Though she believed that "the only way to prevent abortion is to do a much better job of educating people about birth control," she supported the legal right as necessary to the health of women and families. At the 1974 commencement at the University of Montana, she received an honorary degree, as a doctor of law.[57]

During the post-war period, the Rankin siblings dealt with their own aging as well as the many changes and risks of the era. Olive and Harriet, as widows, dealt with the difficulty of finding their own place and purpose. Through these changes, women like Grace and Mary still took on traditional roles in families, with a new sense of inferiority and awareness of what they were giving up as they did so. The post-war era brought the business expansion that Wellington sought, as he moved further away from his progressive roots. These decades brought the Cold War and the seeming world division into two super powers and a large but lesser third world. In this environment, Jeannette continued to oppose war, becoming a hero of many Americans, the reaction to opposition changing with the war. In this complex time, Edna worked for Clarence Gamble, attempting to bring services to women in the third world without acquiescing to the worst of his judgments concerning them. The post-war decades created so much change, in the size and power of American business, in American dominance around the world, in women's involvement in fighting injustice and war, and these siblings took on the risks of it all.

Opposite: **Edna Rankin McKinnon dressed in academic robes for the University of Montana graduation at which she was given an honorary degree, 1974 (Schlesinger Library, Radcliffe Institute, Harvard University).**

Conclusion

Missoulian Helen Bonner, who knew the Rankin children, said of these siblings, "once you take on one of the Rankins, you have to whip the whole bunch. And they are formidable."[1] Along with their parents, they were certainly formidable in their impact on American history. They participated, through the decades, in the risks required to build and change the United States.

This family engaged in different frontiers of American life starting with the immigration of John and Duncan as young people, from Canada to the west, drawn by gold mining as so many men were. Women like Olive also took this pioneering risk to establish their own careers, often to become teachers, but also to find adventure and marriage. Ultimately these young people established towns and a western version of eastern social life. In adulthood, their children would participate in and lead the eras and movements of a modern nation.

The Rankin daughters moved beyond the choices of their parents into risky new choices, in repeated patterns of independent decision-making. Jeannette as a young woman sought to get beyond housekeeping and work for the right of women to vote—and to decide how to vote. She saw women as essentially important to politics, in their concern for the town and neighborhood and for rational policies that would keep the nation safe. Her sisters Harriet and Edna also worked to extend the role of women, through access to education, birth control, and the political arena. Certainly these women believed in the individual rights of women as citizens—both to oppose war and to serve the soldiers who waged it. They worked to make a place for women, in colleges, in the voting booth, in the legislature, and in the administrative roles essential to the nation. And through these years Wellington built a legal and ranching empire, taking advantage of what each era offered, as a progressive crusader at the beginning of his career and as a powerful investor towards the end of it, in the postwar era. Through the complexities of the frontier, the Victorian era, progressivism, the Depression, two world wars and beyond, these Americans took risks and found various means of influencing their state and nation, demonstrating the power of the individual and the family. Throughout their lives, these parents and children repeatedly went through a process of independent and risky choice, in decades that presented different challenges and opportunities. They made many controversial decisions as they demonstrated the continuing power of aspiration and resolve.

Chapter Notes

Introduction

1. Quotation from Edna Rankin McKinnon in Wilma Dykeman, *Too Many People, Too Little Love: Edna Rankin McKinnon, Pioneer for Birth Control* (New York: Holt, Rinehart and Winston, 1974), 276.

2. Given how many of my subjects have the last name of Rankin, I will often be using first names in this text—no disrespect intended.

3. Elizabeth Jameson, "Women as Workers, Women as Civilizers: True Womanhood in the American West," *Frontiers* 7 (1984): 1–9.

4. Current work about risk in modern culture includes Stephen Lyng, "Edgework: A Social Psychological Analysis of Voluntary Risk Taking," *American Journal of Sociology* 95, no. 4 (1990): 851–886, as well as Ulrich Beck, *Risk Society: Towards a New Modernity*, trans. Mark Ritter (Newbury Park, CA: Sage Publications, 1992); Stephen Lyng and Rick Matthews, "Risk, Edgework, and Masculinities," in *Gendered Risks*, ed. Kelly Hannah-Moffat and Pat O'Malley (New York: Routledge-Cavendish, 2007), 75–97; Stephen Lyng, *Edgework. The Sociology of Risk-taking* (New York: Routledge, 2005).

5. Works specifically focused on gender and risk include Susan A. Batchelor, "'Getting Mad wi' It': Risk Seeking by Young Women," in *Gendered Risks*, ed. Kelly Hannah-Moffat and Pat O'Malley (London: Routledge-Cavendish, 2007), 205–228; Alex Campbell, "Keeping the 'Lady' Safe: The Regulation of Femininity through Crime Prevention," *Critical Criminology* 13 (2005): 119–140; Per E. Gustafson, "Gender Difference in Risk Perception: Theoretical and Methodological Perspectives," *Risk Analysis* 18, no. 6 (1998): 805–811; Jason Laurendeau, "Gendered Risk Regimes. A Theoretical Consideration of Edgework and Gender," *Sociology of Sport Journal* 25 (2008): 293–309; Jo Little, Ruth Panelli, and Anna Kraack, "Women's Fear of Crime: A Rural Perspective," *Journal of Rural Studies* 21 (2005): 151–163; Staci Newmahr, "Chaos, Order, and Collaboration: Toward a Feminist Conceptualization of Edgework," *Journal of Contemporary Ethnography* 40, no. 6 (2011): 682–712.

One

1. Glenda Riley, *Women and Indians on the Frontier, 1825–1915* (Albuquerque: University of New Mexico Press, 1984), 2.

2. John O'Sullivan, "Annexation," *United States Magazine and Democratic Review* 17 (1845): 5–6, 9–10; Anders Stephanson, *Manifest Destiny: American Expansion and the Empire of the Right* (New York: Hill and Wang, 1995), xi–xiii.

3. Frederick Jackson Turner, "The Significance of the Frontier in American History," in *Rereading Frederick Jackson Turner*, ed. John Mack Faragher (New York: Henry Holt, 1994), 31.

4. Thomas Jefferson, *Notes on the State of Virginia* (London: John Stockdale, 1787), 50–60.

5. Richard Slotkin, *The Fatal Environment: The Myth of the Frontier in the Age of Industrialization, 1800–1890* (New York: Atheneum, 1985), 15–16; Richard Hofstadter, *The Age of Reform: From Bryan to F.D.R.* (New York: Alfred Knopf, 1963), 24–25; Heike Paul, *The Myths that Made America: An Introduction to American Studies*

(Bielefeld, Germany: Transcript-Verlag, 2014), 317; Carroll Smith-Rosenberg, *This Violent Empire: The Birth of an American National Identity* (Chapel Hill: University of North Carolina Press, 2010).

6. Frederick Jackson Turner, "The Significance of the Frontier in American History," 33; Glenda Riley, *Women and Indians on the Frontier, 1825–1915*, 1.

7. Theodore Roosevelt, "The Strenuous Life," in *Selected Speeches and Writings of Theodore Roosevelt*, ed. Gordon Hutner (New York: Vintage Books, 2014), 12–22; Theodore Roosevelt, "What We Can Expect of the American Boy," *St. Nicholas Magazine* (May 1900): 571–574.

8. Charles Manfred Thompson and Fred Mitchell Jones, *Economic Development of the United States: A First Course* (New York: Macmillan, 1939), 269; Susan Armitage, "Through Women's Eyes: A New View of the West," in *The Women's West*, ed. Susan Armitage and Elizabeth Jameson (Norman: University of Oklahoma Press, 1987), 9–18.

9. Annette Kolodny, *The Lay of the Land: Metaphor as Experience and History in American Life and Letters* (Chapel Hill: University of North Carolina Press, 1975).

10. Carroll Smith-Rosenberg, *Disorderly Conduct: Visions of Gender in Victorian America* (New York: Oxford University Press, 1986), 11.

11. Wilfred P. Schoenberg, *Jesuits in Montana: 1840–1960* (Portland: Oregon-Jesuit, 1960), 2–46.

12. "Boom and Bust: The Industries That Settled Montana," DPLA: Digital Public Library of America, accessed November 10, 2020, dp.la/exhibitions.

13. *Challenge to Survive: History of the Salish Tribes of the Flathead Indian Reservation*, vol. 2 (Philadelphia: Franklin Classics Trade Press, 2018).

14. "Silver Wedding," *Butte Daily Post*, January 16, 1901, accessed November 11, 2020, newspapers.com.

15. John Rankin is listed in various sources as being born in 1838, 1839, 1840, 1841 and even 1848. In the 1851 Canadian census, his age is listed as 12, so I am assuming a date of 1839.

16. Marjory Harper, *Adventurers and Exiles: The Great Scottish Exodus* (London: Profile Books, 2003), 3–21; Marjory Harper, "Exiles or Entrepreneurs: Snapshots of the Scots in Canada," in *A Kingdom of the Mind: How the Scots Helped Make Canada*, ed. Peter E. Rider and Heather McNabb (Montreal: McGill-Queen's University Press, 2006), 29.

17. "Scottish Genealogy and Family History," Library and Archives Canada, accessed January 26, 2020, bac-lac.gc.ca.

18. Ian McKay and Robin Bates, *In the Province of History: The Making of the Public Past in Twentieth-Century Nova Scotia* (Montreal: McGill-Queen's University Press, 2010), 262; Marjory Harper, *Adventurers and Exiles*, 16.

19. Marjory Harper, *Adventurers and Exiles*, 282; Marjory Harper, "Some Patterns of Scottish Settlements in Nineteenth-Century Canada," in *Frontiers of European Culture*, ed. Paul Dukes (Lewiston, Wales: Edwin Mellen, 1996), 137–168.

20. Joaquin Miller, *An Illustrated History of the State of Montana* (Chicago: Lewis Publishing, 1894), 565.

21. Richard E. Taylor, *Houghton County, 1870–1920* (Charleston, SC: Arcadia Publishing, 2006), 7, 16.

22. Lillian Schlissel, "Family on the Western Frontier," in *Western Women: Their Land, Their Lives*, ed. Lillian Schlissel, Vicki L. Ruiz, and Janice Monk (Albuquerque: University of New Mexico Press, 1988), 85.

23. Louis M. Hartwick, *Oceana County Pioneers and Business Men of To-day: History, Biography, Statistics and Humorous Incidents* (Pentwater, MI: Pentwater News Steam Print, 1890), 134–144.

24. "The Hudson's Bay Question and Ministerial Policy," *Gazette of Montreal*, February 12, 1857, accessed January 7, 2020, newspapers.com.

25. "News Brevities," *Detroit Free Press*, February 29, 1868, accessed September 9, 2020, newspapers.com.

26. Volney Steele, *Bleed, Blister, and Purge: A History of Medicine on the American Frontier* (Missoula, MT: Mountain Press, 2005), 79.

27. Ferdinand Vandeveer Hayden, *The Great West: Its Attractions and Resources* (Washington, D.C.: C.R. Brodix, 1880), 219.

28. Volney Steele, *Wellington Rankin: His Family, Life and Times: Montana Attorney, Politician, Cattleman, Land Baron* (Bozeman, MT: Bridger Creek Historical Press, 2002), 12–15.

29. Paul Andrew Hutton, *Phil Sheridan*

and His Army (Lincoln: University of Nebraska Press, 1985), 181–200.
30. Wellington Rankin, Interview by Volney Steele, General Oral History Collection, OH 1665, Montana Historical Society Research Center, Archives, 29–31.
31. Volney Steele, *Wellington Rankin: His Family, Life and Times*, 15.
32. Wellington Rankin, Interview by Volney Steele, 29.
33. Joaquin Miller, *An Illustrated History of the State of Montana*, 565.
34. Wellington Rankin, Interview by Volney Steele, 29–31.
35. "Missoula Items," *Helena Weekly Herald*, March 22, 1877, accessed August 8, 2020, newspapers.com; Kim Briggeman, "100 Missoula Icons: Grant Creek Retains Rural Nature," *Missoulian*, September 18, 2014, accessed March 14, 2020, missoulian.com.
36. Jerome Greene, Chapter Five, in *Nez Perce Summer 1877: The U.S. Army and the Nee-Me-Poo Crisis* (Helena, MT: Montana Historical Society Press, 2000), accessed April 22, 2020, nps.gov.
37. Michael A. Bellesiles, *1877: America's Year of Living Violently* (New York: New Press, 2010).
38. "Western Montana News," *Helena Weekly Herald*, July 5, 1877, accessed January 17, 2020, newspapers.com.
39. Glenda Riley, *Women and Indians on the Frontier, 1825–1915*, 3; Sandra Myres, "Victoria's Daughters: English-Speaking Women on Nineteenth Century Frontiers," in *Western Women: Their Land, Their Lives*, ed. Lillian Schlissel, Vicki L. Ruiz, and Janice Monk (Albuquerque: University of New Mexico Press, 1988), 261–282.
40. Robert I. Griswold, "Anglo Women and Domestic Ideology in the American West in the Nineteenth and Early Twentieth Centuries," in *Western Women: Their Land, Their Lives*, ed. Lillian Schlissel, Vicki L. Ruiz, and Janice Monk (Albuquerque: University of New Mexico Press, 1988), 15–17.
41. Glenda Riley, *Women on the American Frontier* (St. Louis: Forum Press, 1977), 15.
42. "Olive Pickering Rankin," in *Mothers of Achievement in American History, 1776–1976* (Rutland, VT: Charles E. Tuttle Company, 1976), 320–321; Jere R. Daniell, *Colonial New Hampshire: A History* (Millwood, NY: KTO Press, 1981), 59–60.

43. Robert I. Vexler and William F. Swindler, *Chronology and Documentary Handbook of the State of New Hampshire* (New York: Oceana Publications, 1978), 25, 40; "Olive Pickering Rankin."
44. Nancy Coffey Heffernan and Ann Page Stecker, *New Hampshire: Crosscurrents in Its Development*, 3rd ed. (Hanover: University Press of New England, 2004), 79–94.
45. Mary Austin Holley, *Texas* (Baltimore: Armstrong and Plaskitt, 1833); Eliza Farnham, *Life in Prairie Land* (New York: Harpers, 1846); Alice Cary, *Clovernook* (New York: Redfield, 1852); Caroline Soule, *Little Alice; Or, the Pet of the Settlement* (Boston: A. Tompkins, 1860); Margaret Fuller, *Summer on the Lakes* (Boston: Charles C. Little and James Brown, 1843), 117; Caroline Kirkland (as Mary Clavers), *A New Home—Who'll Follow?* (New York: Charles S. Francis, 1841), 108–109.
46. Jeannette Rankin, Letter to Edna Rankin McKinnon, Edna Rankin McKinnon Papers, Series 1, Schlesinger Library, Radcliffe Institute, Harvard University.
47. "Charles William Berry," Document Center, City of Missoula Website, accessed January 11, 2020, ci.missoula.mt.us; Michael Moore, "Sheriffs' Lives, Stories, Revealed in Grave Tour," *Missoulian*, June 21, 2008, accessed February 22, 2020, missoulian.com; Joaquin Miller, *An Illustrated History of the State of Montana*, 197–198; Jeremy Agnew, *Crime, Justice and Retribution in the American West, 1850–1900* (Jefferson, NC: McFarland, 2017), 1; Sherry Hodges, "A History of Hatred and Discrimination," *Missoulian*, June 17, 1980, accessed January 4, 2020, newspapers.com.
48. "Civil War Facts," The Civil War, PBS, accessed August 12, 2020, pbs.org/kenburns/civil-war.
49. Norma Smith, *Jeannette Rankin: America's Conscience* (Helena, MT: Montana Historical Society Press, 2002), 30; Glenda Riley, *Women and Indians on the Frontier, 1825–1915*, 121.
50. Wellington Rankin, Interview by Volney Steele, 30.
51. Ronald W. Lackmann, *Women of the Western Frontier in Fact, Fiction, and Film* (Jefferson, NC: McFarland, 1997), 105–117; Kathleen Weiler, "Women's History and the History of Women Teachers," *Journal of Education* 171, no. 3 (1989): 9–30.
52. "Lyman Beecher," *Appleton's*

Cyclopædia of American Biography, vol. 1, ed. James Grant Wilson and John Fiske (New York: D. Appleton, 1888), 216–217.

53. Thomas Woody, *A History of Women's Education in the United States* (Lancaster, PA: Science Press, 1929), 483.

54. Polly Welts Kaufman, *Women Teachers of the Frontier* (New Haven: Yale University Press, 1984), xviii.

55. Wellington Rankin, Interview by Volney Steele, 30.

56. Ellen M. Plante, *Women at Home in Victorian America: A Social History* (New York: Facts on File, 1997), 92.

57. Chris Enss, *Frontier Teachers: Stories of Heroic Women of the Old West* (Helena, MT: TwoDot Press, 2008), 27, 59–68.

58. Chris Enss, *Frontier Teachers*, xi–xii; William Holmes McGuffey, "The Three Boys and the Three Cakes," in *McGuffey's New First Eclectic Reader: For Little Children* (Cincinnati: Sargent, Wilson, Hinkle, 1857), 29–31.

59. Phyllis Rose, *Parallel Lives: Five Victorian Marriages* (New York: Knopf, 1983), 19.

60. James J. Lopach and Jean A. Luckowski, *Jeannette Rankin: A Political Woman* (Boulder: University Press of Colorado, 2005), 17.

61. I want to thank Lynn Thee for showing me around the property.

62. Hannah Josephson, *Jeannette Rankin: First Lady in Congress, A Biography* (Indianapolis: Bobbs-Merrill Company, 1974), 11; Richard K. Hines, "Wellington Duncan Rankin: The Man behind the Myth" (Master's thesis, Washington State University, 1996), 13.

63. Ellen M. Plante, *Women at Home in Victorian America: A Social History*, 75; Helen Bonner, Interview by Winfield Page, July 9, 1980, OH 104, Archives & Special Collections, Mansfield Library, University of Montana.

64. Cathy Luchetti, *Children of the West: Family Life on the Frontier* (New York: Norton, 2001), 60–61.

65. Judith Walzer Leavitt, *Brought to Bed: Child-Bearing in America, 1750–1950* (New York: Oxford University Press, 1986), 25; Ellen M. Plante, *Women at Home in Victorian America*, 75; Mary Melcher, "'Women's Matters': Birth Control, Prenatal Care, and Childbirth in Rural Montana, 1910–1940," in *Montana Legacy: Essays on History, People, and Place*, ed. Harry W. Fritz, Mary Murphy, and Robert R. Swartout, Jr. (Helena, MT: Montana Historical Society, 2002), 139–140.

66. Elizabeth H. Emerson, *Glimpses of a Life* (Burlington, NC: J.S. Sargent, 1960), 4–5; Judith Walzer Leavitt, *Brought to Bed*, 14; Elizabeth Jameson, "Women as Workers, Women as Civilizers: True Womanhood in the American West," *Frontiers* 7 (1984): 1–9.

67. Glenda Riley, *A Place to Grow: Women in the American West* (Arlington Heights, IL: Harlan Davidson, 1992), 152–153; Vera Norwood, "Women's Place: Continuity and Change in Response to Western Landscapes," in *Western Women: Their Land, Their Lives*, ed. Lillian Schlissel, Vicki L. Ruiz, and Janice Monk (Albuquerque: University of New Mexico Press, 1988), 155–182; Wilma Dykeman, *Too Many People, Too Little Love: Edna Rankin McKinnon, Pioneer for Birth Control* (New York: Holt, Rinehart and Winston, 1974), 19; Glenda Riley, *The Female Frontier: A Comparative View of Women on the Prairie and Plains* (Lawrence, KS: University Press of Kansas, 1988), 197.

Two

1. James L. Roark et al., *The American Promise, since 1865: A History of the United States*, vol. 2 (New York: Macmillan, 2012), 605.

2. C. Robert Haywood, *Victorian West: Class and Culture in Kansas Cattle Towns* (Lawrence: University Press of Kansas, 1991), 5–45.

3. Mark Wahlgren Summers, *The Era of Good Stealings* (New York: Oxford University Press, 1993), 4, 303.

4. Robert I. Griswold, "Anglo Women and Domestic Ideology in the American West in the Nineteenth and Early Twentieth Centuries," in *Western Women: Their Land, Their Lives*, ed. Lillian Schlissel, Vicki L. Ruiz, and Janice Monk (Albuquerque: University of New Mexico Press, 1988), 17.

5. Louise Smith Clappe, *California in 1851: The Shirley Letters from California Mines in 1851–52* (San Francisco: T.C. Russell Press, 1922), 72, 100–103.

6. Linda Peavy and Ursula Smith, *Pioneer Women: The Lives of Women on the Frontier* (New York: Smithmark, 1996), 83.

7. Sarah Josepha Hale, *Manners; or, Happy Homes and Good Society All the Year Round* (Boston: J.E. Tilton), 1868.
8. *The Manners That Win* (Minneapolis: Buckeye Publishing 1880), 28.
9. "Missoula, Montana," World Population Review, accessed July 12, 2020, worldpopulationreview.com.
10. H.G. Merriam, *The University of Montana: A History* (Missoula: University of Montana Press, 1970), 5–60.
11. George Dennison, *Montana's Pioneer Naturalist: Morton J. Elrod* (Norman: University of Oklahoma Press, 2016), 3–4.
12. Hannah Josephson, *Jeannette Rankin: First Lady in Congress, A Biography* (Indianapolis: Bobbs-Merrill, 1974), 8.
13. Ellen M. Plante, *Women at Home in Victorian America: A Social History* (New York: Facts on File, 1997), 53–65; Thomas J. Schlereth, *Victorian America: Transformations in Everyday Life, 1876-1915* (New York: HarperCollins, 1991), 117–124.
14. Wilma Dykeman, *Too Many People, Too Little Love: Edna Rankin McKinnon, Pioneer for Birth Control* (New York: Holt, Rinehart and Winston, 1974), 19–20; Hannah Josephson, *Jeannette Rankin*, 8.
15. Sean Dennis Cashman, *America in the Gilded Age: From the Death of Lincoln to the Rise of Theodore Roosevelt*. 2nd ed. (New York: New York University Press, 1984), 265–289.
16. "From Missoula," *New North-West* (Deer Lodge, MT), June 1, 1883, accessed January 14, 2020, newspapers.com; Hannah Josephson, *Jeannette Rankin*, 9.
17. "Pasture," *Missoulian*, April 24, 1897; "Pasture," *Misssoulian*, May 28, 1897; "Excellent Oat Crop," *Anaconda Standard*, August 26, 1901, accessed June 14, 2020, newspapers.com.
18. "From Missoula."
19. Hannah Josephson, *Jeannette Rankin*, 16; Joaquin Miller, *An Illustrated History of the State of Montana* (Chicago: Lewis Publishing, 1894), 565–566; "Brief News Notes," *Anaconda Standard*, October 23, 1895, accessed June 11, 2020, newspapers.com.
20. "Missoula in General," *Missoulian*, September 15, 1894, accessed June 11, 2020, newspapers.com.
21. "Good Men and True," *Anaconda Standard*, March 30, 1891, accessed May 12, 2020, newspapers.com; "Official Election Results for Missoula County," *Missoulian*, November 18, 1894, accessed February 17, 2020, newspapers.com.
22. John Rankin, Account Books, Rankin Family Papers, MSS 280, Series 1.4, Archives & Special Collections, Mansfield Library, University of Montana.
23. John Rankin, Letter to Jessie Rankin Wilson, May 14, 1893, Edna Rankin McKinnon Papers, Series 1, Schlesinger Library, Radcliffe Institute, Harvard University.
24. Glenda Riley, *The Female Frontier: A Comparative View of Women on the Prairie and Plains* (Lawrence, KS: University Press of Kansas, 1988), 196–199; Sara Hayden, "Negotiating Femininity and Power in the Early Twentieth Century West: Domestic Ideology and Feminine Style in Jeannette Rankin's Suffrage Rhetoric," *Communication Studies* 50, no. 2 (Summer 1999), 87.
25. Hannah Josephson, *Jeannette Rankin*, 15.
26. *120 Years of American Education: A Statistical Portrait*, National Center for Educational Statistics (Washington, D.C.: U.S. Department of Education, 1993), 55, 82.
27. Edna Rankin McKinnon, Job Application, Edna Rankin McKinnon Papers, Series 1, Schlesinger Library, Radcliffe Institute, Harvard University.
28. Cathy Luchetti, *Children of the West: Family Life on the Frontier* (New York: Norton, 2001), 55.
29. Hannah Josephson, *Jeannette Rankin*, 17; Kevin S. Giles, *One Woman against War: The Jeannette Rankin Story* (St. Petersburg, FL: BookLocker.com, 2016), 28.
30. Jack O'Connor, *Jack O'Connor, Horse and Buggy West* (New York: Knopf, 1969), 116.
31. Wilma Dykeman, *Too Many People, Too Little Love*, 18.
32. "Purely Local," *Missoulian*, February 9, 1901, accessed June 15, 2019, newspapers.com.
33. "Briefs and Personals," *Anaconda Standard*, January 15, 1897, accessed May 12, 2019, newspapers.com.
34. "Concert," *Missoulian*, December 15, 1896, accessed May 9, 2019, newspapers.com.
35. "Missoula Public Schools," *Missoulian*, May 28, 1897, accessed May 6, 2019, newspapers.com.
36. "Commencement Exercises,"

Missoulian, June 4, 1898, accessed May 7, 2020, newspapers.com.

37. "The Doings of a Week," *Anaconda Standard*, February 9, 1890; "Missoula Society News," *Anaconda Standard*, August 30, 1903, accessed May 2, 2020, newspapers.com.

38. "A Forest Guessing Party," *Missoulian*, July 5, 1903; "Society Notes," *Anaconda Standard*, March 23, 1902; "In Missoula," *Anaconda Standard*, January 5, 1902, accessed April 12, 2020, newspapers.com.

39. "Quanoozeh Club Entertains," *Anaconda Standard*, January 4, 1903, accessed April 13, 2020, newspapers.com.

40. "At the State University," *Anaconda Standard*, November 24, 1902; "Hughes Not Guilty," *Missoulian*, November 30, 1902; "At the State University," *Anaconda Standard*, December 5, 1902; "University Resumes after Vacation," *Anaconda Standard*, January 5, 1903; "Wellington Rankin," *Missoulian*, June 10, 1903, accessed January 29, 2020, newspapers.com.

41. Kevin S. Giles, *One Woman against War*, 23–27; Wellington Rankin, Interview by Volney Steele, General Oral History Collection, OH 1665, Montana Historical Society Research Center, Archives, 18–19.

42. Marion Harland, *Breakfast, Luncheon, and Tea* (New York: Scribners, 1875), 5–15.

43. "Missoula Notes," *Butte Miner*, September 13, 1903; "City in Brief," *Missoulian*, April 13, 1904, accessed February 12, 2020, newspapers.com.

44. W.C. Rucker, "Rocky Mountain Spotted Fever," *Public Health Reports* 36 (September 6, 1912): 1465–1482.

45. "John Rankin Ends Notable Life," *Missoulian*, May 4, 1904, accessed February 14, 2020, newspapers.com; James J. Lopach and Jean A. Luckowski, *Jeannette Rankin: A Political Woman*, 18; Hannah Josephson, *Jeannette Rankin*, 21.

46. James J. Lopach and Jean A. Luckowski, *Jeannette Rankin: A Political Woman* (Boulder: University Press of Colorado, 2005), 18.

47. Hannah Josephson, *Jeannette Rankin*, 17–20; Kevin S. Giles, *One Woman against War*, 33.

48. Kevin S. Giles, *One Woman against War*, 21; Norma Smith, "Fighting Pacifist: Jeannette Rankin and Her Times," Norma Smith Papers, Collection 2329, Montana State University Library; Hannah Josephson, *Jeannette Rankin*, 12.

Three

1. Carol R. Byerly, "War Losses (USA)," *International Encyclopedia of the First World War*, accessed February 12, 2020, encyclopedia.1914-1918-online.net.

2. "U.S. Annual Death Rates per 1,000 Population, 1900–2005," Department of Health and Human Services, 54, no. 20 (August 21, 2007).

3. Volney Steele, *Bleed, Blister, and Purge: A History of Medicine on the American Frontier* (Missoula, MT: Mountain Press, 2005), 89.

4. Robert Kessler, "Outbreak: Pandemic Strikes," accessed February 2, 2020, ecohealthalliance.org; Eric Durr, "Worldwide Flu Outbreak Killed 45,000 American Soldiers during World War I," U.S. Army, August 31, 2018, accessed February 2, 2020, army.mil.

5. Pierce C. Mullen and Michael L. Nelson, "Montanans and 'The Most Peculiar Disease': The Influenza Epidemic and Public Health, 1918–1919," *Montana: The Magazine of Western History* 37, no. 2 (Spring 1987): 50–52.

6. "Doctor of Medicine Profession," Medline Plus, U.S. National Library of Medicine, accessed January 4, 2020, medlineplus.gov; Abraham Flexner, *Medical Education in the United States and Canada: A Report to the Carnegie Foundation for the Advancement of Teaching* (New York: Carnegie Foundation for the Advancement of Teaching, 1910), 12; John S. Haller, *American Medicine in Transition, 1840–1910* (Urbana: University of Illinois Press, 1981), 192–233.

7. Volney Steele, *Bleed, Blister, and Purge: A History of Medicine on the American Frontier* (Missoula, MT: Mountain Press, 2005), 152.

8. Robert F. Karolevitz, *Doctors of the Old West: A Pictorial History of Medicine on the Frontier* (Seattle: Superior Publishing, 1967), 55.

9. Norbert Hirschhorn, R.G. Feldman, and I.A. Greaves, "Abraham Lincoln's Blue Pills: Did Our 16th President Suffer from Mercury Poisoning?" *Perspectives in Biology and Medicine* 44, no. 3 (2001): 315–322.

10. Volney Steele, *Bleed, Blister, and*

Purge: A History of Medicine on the American Frontier, 80–83.

11. Stewart Holbrook, "The Lady of Lynn, Mrs. Pinkham," in *The Golden Age of Quackery* (New York: Collier Books, 1959), 63–70.

12. Margaret M. McGuinness, *Called to Serve: A History of Nuns in America* (New York: New York University Press, 2015), 102.

13. Alexander V. Hamilton, *The Household Cyclopaedia of Practical Receipts and Daily Wants* (Springfield: W.J. Holland & Co., 1873), 362; Glenda Riley, *A Place to Grow: Women in the American West* (Arlington Heights, IL: Harlan Davidson, 1992), 152–153; Vera Norwood, "Women's Place: Continuity and Change in Response to Western Landscapes," in *Western Women: Their Land, Their Lives*, ed. Lillian Schlissel, Vicki L. Ruiz, and Janice Monk (Albuquerque: University of New Mexico Press, 1988), 155–182; Wilma Dykeman, *Too Many People, Too Little Love: Edna Rankin McKinnon, Pioneer for Birth Control* (New York, Holt, Rinehart and Winston, 1974), 19; Glenda Riley, *The Female Frontier*, 197; Cathy Luchetti, *Children of the West: Family Life on the Frontier* (New York: Norton, 2001), 50.

14. Volney Steele, *Bleed, Blister, and Purge*, 138–140; "Missoula Notes," *Butte Miner*, October 16, 1902, accessed March 11, 2020, newspapers.com.

15. "A Sad Bereavement," *Missoula Weekly Gazette*, December 3, 1890, accessed January 30, 2020, newspapers.com; Kevin S. Giles, *One Woman against War*, 25.

16. "John Rankin Ends Notable Life," *Missoulian*, May 4, 1904, accessed January 4, 2020, newspapers.com.

17. Volney Steele, *Wellington Rankin*, 42–44; "Missoula Gossip," *Anaconda Standard*, March 9, 1895; "Missoula in General," *Missoulian*, March 14, 1895, accessed March 12, 2020, newspapers.com.

18. "Montana Matters," *Independent Record* (Helena), September 5, 1883, accessed January 5, 2020, newspapers.com.

19. "Fatal Accident," *Butte Weekly Miner*, April 4, 1885, accessed January 6, 2020, newspapers.com.

20. Volney Steele, *Bleed, Blister, and Purge*, 268–273.

21. Volney Steele, *Wellington Rankin: His Family, Life and Times* (Bozeman, MT: Bridger Creek Historical Press, 2002), 46–50.

22. John T. Bethell, *Harvard Observed: An Illustrated History of the University in the Twentieth Century* (Boston: Harvard University Press, 1998), 24; "Doom of the Gold Coast," *Harvard Alumni Bulletin* 22 (1919): 561.

23. "Memorial Proceedings on the Death of Hon. Oscar A. Sedman," *Helena Weekly Herald*, February 17, 1881, accessed January 31, 2020, newspapers.com.

24. Nellie Bly, *Ten Days in a Mad House* (New York: Ian L. Munro, 1887).

25. Mary de Young, *Madness: An American History of Mental Illness and Its Treatment* (Jefferson, NC: McFarland, 2010), 197.

26. Jeffrey A. Lieberman, *Shrinks: The Untold Story of Psychiatry* (New York: Little, Brown, 2015), 54.

27. Marta Trzebiatowska and Steve Bruce, *Why Are Women More Religious Than Men?* (New York: Oxford University Press, 2012), 51.

28. Several books contain more information about this faith: Ruth Brandon, *The Spiritualists: The Passion for the Occult in the Nineteenth and Twentieth Centuries* (New York: Alfred A. Knopf, 1983); Ann Braude, *Radical Spirits: Spiritualism and Women's Rights in Nineteenth-Century America*, 2nd ed. (Urbana: Indiana University Press, 2001); Bret E. Carroll, *Spiritualism in Antebellum America* (Bloomington: Indiana University Press, 1997); and Amy Lehman, *Victorian Women and the Theatre of Trance: Mediums, Spiritualists and Mesmerists in Performance* (Jefferson, NC: McFarland, 2009).

29. Mary Gabriel, *Notorious Victoria: The Life of Victoria Woodhull, Uncensored* (Chapel Hill, NC: Algonquin Books, 1998), 9–12; Myra MacPherson, *The Scarlet Sisters: Sex, Suffrage, and Scandal in the Gilded Age* (New York: Twelve, 2014), 15; "Their Ugly Past: Reviving the Record of the Claflins," *San Francisco Chronicle*, May 8, 1890, accessed March 31, 2020, newspapers.com; Katherine H. Adams, *Claiming Her Place in Congress: Women from American Political Families as Legislators* (Jefferson, NC: McFarland, 2019), 11–21.

30. Dee Morris, *Boston in the Golden Age of Spiritualism: Séances, Mediums and Immortality* (Charleston, SC: Arcadia Publishing, 2014), 96–103.

31. Stuart Vyse, "William James and the Psychics," *Skeptical Inquirer*, accessed July 12, 2020, csicop.org.

32. Wellington Rankin, Letters to Ellis Sedman, Wellington D. Rankin Papers, MC 288, Personal Subgroup, Series 2.12, Montana Historical Society Research Center, Archives.

33. Mary Baker Eddy, *Science and Health* (Boston: Christian Science Publishing, 1875); Jeremy Rapport, "The Nature of Reality: Christian Science and Spiritualism," in *Handbook of Spiritualism and Channeling*, ed. Cathy Guttierez (Boston: Brill, 2015), 199–218.

34. Bryan R. Wilson, *Sects and Society: A Sociological Study of the Elim Tabernacle, Christian Science, and Christadelphians* (Berkeley: University of California Press, 1961), 121–218; Caryl Emra Farkas, "Destination: Health and Wholeness," *Christian Science Sentinel*, May 13, 2013, accessed February 3, 2020, sentinel.christianscience.com.

35. John M. Tutt, "The Role of the Practitioner," *Christian Science Sentinel*, June 12, 1965, accessed February 4, 2020, sentinel.christianscience.com.

36. Rodney Stark, "The Rise and Fall of Christian Science," *Journal of Contemporary Religion* 13, no. 2 (1998): 190–191; Raymond J. Cunningham, "The Impact of Christian Science on the American Churches, 1880–1910," *American Historical Review* 72, no. 3 (April 1967): 890; Rennie B. Schoepflin, *Christian Science on Trial: Religious Healing in America* (Baltimore: Johns Hopkins University Press, 2003), 221.

37. Raymond J. Cunningham, "The Impact of Christian Science on the American Churches, 1880–1910," *American Historical Review* 72, no. 3 (April 1967), 892.

38. Stephen Gottschalk, *The Emergence of Christian Science in American Religious Life* (Berkeley: University of California Press, 2018), 202–206.

39. Mark Twain, *Mary Baker Eddy* (New York: Harper & Bros., 1907), 208–209.

40. Claire F. Gartrell-Mills, *Christian Science: An American Religion in Britain, 1895–1940* (PhD diss., Oxford University, 1991), 68.

41. Maria Soubier, "The Divine Affluence," *Christian Science Sentinel*, June 1952, accessed January 11, 2020, Christian Science JSH-Online.

42. "Juvenile Society Event," *Missoulian*, August 2, 1908, accessed January 20, 2020, newspapers.com.

43. James J. Lopach and Jean A. Luckowski, *Jeannette Rankin*, 20.

44. Wellington Rankin, Interview by John Board, March 23, 1964, Wellington D. Rankin Papers, Archives West, accessed December 8, 2019, archiveswest.orbiscascade.org.

45. "A Woman Who Made a Difference," *Christian Science Journal*, February 2003, accessed February 1, 2020, journal.christianscience.com.

46. Edna Rankin McKinnon, Letter to Wellington Rankin, June 16, 1959, Wellington D. Rankin Papers, MC 288, Personal Subgroup, Series 2.1, Montana Historical Society Research Center, Archives.

47. Edna Rankin McKinnon, Letter to Wilma Dykeman, March 20, 1973, Edna Rankin McKinnon Papers, Series 1, Schlesinger Library, Radcliffe Institute, Harvard University; Edna Rankin McKinnon, Letter to Mary Rankin Bragg, September 3, 1963, Edna Rankin McKinnon Papers, Series 1, Schlesinger Library, Radcliffe Institute, Harvard University; Dorothy McKinnon Brown, Letter to Jeannette Rankin, December 17, 1968, Jeannette Rankin Papers, Box 3, Montana Historical Society Research Center; Edna Rankin McKinnon, Letter to Dorothy McKinnon Brown, October 2, 1972, Edna Rankin McKinnon Papers, Series 1, Schlesinger Library, Radcliffe Institute, Harvard University.

48. "Trigeminal Neuralgia (Tic Douloureux)," Harvard Health Publishing, accessed June 1, 2020, health.harvard.edu.

49. Alethe A. Hayter, "The Laudanum Bottle Loomed Large': Opium in the English Literary World in the Nineteenth Century," *Ariel: A Review of International English Literature* 11, no. 4 (1980): 46; Caroline Jean Acker, *Creating the American Junkie: Addiction Research in the Classic Era of Narcotic Control* (Baltimore: Johns Hopkins University Press, 2002), 33–37.

50. Jeannette Rankin, Letters to Dr. Sample, 1917, Jeannette Rankin Papers, MC 147, Series 7.2, Montana Historical Society Research Center, Helena.

51. David Margolick, "In Child Deaths, a Test for Christian Science," *New York Times*, August 6, 1990, accessed May 4, 2020,

nytimes.com; Rodney Stark, "The Rise and Fall of Christian Science," *Journal of Contemporary Religion* 13, no. 2 (1998): 191; Timothy D. Callahan, *UFOs, Chemtrails, and Aliens: What Science Says* (Bloomington: Indiana University Press, 2017), 165.

Four

1. Alonzo L. Hamby, "Progressivism: A Century of Change and Rebirth," in *Progressivism and the New Democracy,* ed. Sidney M. Milkis and Jerome M. Mileur (Amherst: University of Massachusetts Press, 1999), 42.
2. Arthur Stanley Link, *Progressivism* (New York: Wiley-Blackwell, 1983), 11–20.
3. Roger Munns, "University Honors Suffragette Despite Racism Charge," *Los Angeles Times,* May 5, 1996, accessed January 14, 2020, newspapers.com.
4. Michael McGerr, *A Fierce Discontent: The Rise and Fall of the Progressive Movement in America* (New York: Simon and Schuster, 2010), 182–218.
5. Wellington Rankin, Interview by Volney Steele, General Oral History Collection, OH 1665, Montana Historical Society Research Center, Archives, 32–33.
6. Volney Steele, *Wellington Rankin: His Family, Life and Times: Montana Attorney, Politician, Cattleman, Land Baron* (Bozeman, Mt: Bridger Creek Historical Press, 2002), 50.
7. Opposition Press Release, 1948 Senate Campaign, Rankin Family Papers, Series II, 4.4, Archives & Special Collections, Mansfield Library, University of Montana.
8. Kevin Giles, *One Woman against War: The Jeannette Rankin Story* (St. Petersburg, FL: BookLocker.com, 2016), 31; James J. Lopach and Jean A. Luckowski, *Jeannette Rankin: A Political Woman* (Boulder: University Press of Colorado, 2005), 50.
9. Howard A. Husock, "Bringing Back the Settlement House," *Public Welfare* 51, no. 4 (1993): 16–25.
10. Norma Smith, *Jeannette Rankin: America's Conscience* (Helena, MT: Montana Historical Society Press, 2002), 46.
11. Jeannette Rankin, Interview by John C. Board, August 29 and 30, 1963, General Oral History Collection, OH1046, Montana Historical Society Research Center, Archives.
12. James J. Lopach and Jean A. Luckowski, *Jeannette Rankin,* 79.
13. "Helena's Society Queen Marries Young Lawyer," *Butte Miner,* March 3, 1910, accessed March 7, 2020, newspapers.com.
14. Elizabeth Wallace Rankin, Letter to Wellington Rankin, August 16, 1913, Wellington D. Rankin Papers, MC 288, Personal Subgroup, Box 2, Montana Historical Society Research Center, Archives; James J. Lopach and Jean A. Luckowski, *Jeannette Rankin,* 26–27.
15. Richard K. Hines, "Wellington Duncan Rankin: The Man behind the Myth" (Master's thesis, Washington State University, 1996), 108–109; Volney Steele, *Wellington Rankin,* 10.
16. Mark Aldrich, "History of Workplace Safety in the United States, 1880–1970," Economic History Association, accessed December 3, 2019, eh.net.
17. Carlos A. Schwantes, *The Pacific Northwest: An Interpretive History* (Lincoln: University of Nebraska Press, 1996), 173.
18. David Mark Chalmers, *Neither Socialism nor Monopoly: Theodore Roosevelt and the Decision to Regulate the Railroads* (Philadelphia: Lippincott, 1976), 2.
19. "Chilly Experience Described in Suit," *Butte Miner,* September 25, 1912, accessed March 20, 2020, newspapers.com; Volney Steele, *Wellington Rankin,* 84.
20. "Arraignment of Rankin Pending," *Independent-Record* (Helena), September 20, 1917; "Helena Lawyer Has Fracas at Inquest," *Butte Miner,* September 20, 1917, accessed December 10, 2019, newspapers.com.
21. Volney Steele, *Wellington Rankin,* 8.
22. "Miss Rankin's Famous Interview Misrepresenting Her State," *Independent-Record* (Helena), August 19, 1917, accessed April 7, 2020, newspapers.com; Maria Braden, *Women Politicians and the Media,* 25–26; Norma Smith, *Jeannette Rankin,* 131.
23. Patrick F. Morris, *Anaconda, Montana: Copper Smelting Boom Town on the Western Frontier* (Bethesda, MD: Swann Publishing, 1997), 125–133, 148–162; Dennis L. Swibold, *Copper Chorus: Mining, Politics, and the Montana Press, 1889–1959* (Helena, MT: Montana Historical Society Press, 2006), 63–92.
24. "Asks $65,000 for Damages," *Helena Independent,* February 23, 1912, accessed December 15, 2019, newspapers.com.

25. Census Reports, 12th Census, 1900, vol. 1 (Washington, D.C.: GPO, 1901), civ.
26. Volney Steele, *Wellington Rankin*, 82–83.
27. Velma H. Riggs v. Lew Webb, Montana Supreme Court, Rankin Family Papers, Series II, 4.1, Archives & Special Collections, Mansfield Library, University of Montana.
28. "Apologies Are Tendered," *Independent-Record* (Helena, MT), December 3, 1912, accessed January 14, 2020, newspapers.com.
29. Theodore Roosevelt, *An Autobiography* (New York: Scribner's, 1913), 578.
30. Wellington Rankin, Interview by Volney Steele, 11.
31. "Wellington Rankin Lets Loose at Amalgamated," *Missoulian*, October 29, 1914, accessed December 20, 2019, newspapers.com.
32. "Rankins Leave Legacy in Politics and More," *Billings Gazette*, June 15, 2003, accessed February 7, 2020, newspapers.com; Michael P. Malone, Richard B. Roeder, and William L. Lang, *Montana: A History of Two Centuries*, rev. ed. (Seattle: University of Washington Press, 1976), 367–368.
33. "Called the Bluff," *Missoulian*, October 17, 1914, accessed January 7, 2020, newspapers.com.
34. "Progressives Hold Meeting," *Billings Gazette*, October 11, 1914, accessed January 8, 2020, newspapers.com.
35. "Unofficial Returns," *Missoulian*, November 4, 1914, accessed February 14, 2020, newspapers.com.
36. Michael P. Malone, Richard B. Roeder, and William L. Lang, *Montana: A History of Two Centuries*, 262–264.
37. Jeannette Rankin, Interview by John C. Board, 3–4.
38. Volney Steele, *Wellington Rankin*, 68.
39. James J. Lopach and Jean A. Luckowski, *Jeannette Rankin*, 81.
40. Jeannette Rankin, Interview by John C. Board, 5.
41. Ronald Schaffer, "The Montana Woman Suffrage Campaign, 1911–14," *Pacific Northwest Quarterly* 55, no. 1 (January 1964): 9–15.
42. "The Congressional Union for Woman Suffrage," *Suffragist*, November 15, 1913: 2; Caroline Katzenstein, *Lifting the Curtain: The State and National Woman Suffrage Campaigns in Pennsylvania as I Saw Them* (Philadelphia: Dorrance, 1955), 175–176; "5000 Women March, Beset by Crowds," *New York Times*, March 4, 1913, accessed February 15, 2020, newspapers.com.
43. Norma Smith, *Jeannette Rankin, America's Conscience*, 69.
44. "From Missoula to Washington, D.C., to Aid Cause of Equal Suffrage," *Missoulian*, August 10, 1913, accessed February 17, 2020, newspapers.com.
45. Doris Faber, *Petticoat Politics: How American Women Won the Right to Vote* (New York: LothroPress, Lee and Shepard, 1967), 130.
46. "Miss Rankin Gains Good Support in North," *Missoulian*, March 23, 1914, accessed January 12, 2020, newspapers.com.
47. Sara Hayden, "Negotiating Femininity and Power in the Early Twentieth Century West: Domestic Ideology and Feminine Style in Jeannette Rankin's Suffrage Rhetoric," *Communication Studies* 50, no. 2 (Summer 1999): 83–103.
48. "Miss Rankin Gains Good Support in North," *Missoulian*, March 23, 1914; "Two Suffragists Will Begin Tour," *Missoulian*, August 10, 1914; "Attendance at Fair Is Twenty Thousand," *Anaconda Standard*, September 26, 1914; "Montana Suffrage Parade Great Success," *Suffrage Daily News*, September 26, 1914, accessed January 12, 2020, newspapers.com; Ronald Schaffer, "The Montana Woman Suffrage Campaign, 1911–14"; Anna Howard Shaw, *The Story of a Pioneer* (New York: Harper and Bros., 1915).
49. Ronald Schaffer, "The Montana Woman Suffrage Campaign, 1911–14"; Katrina Rebecca Cheek, "The Rhetoric and Revolt of Jeannette Rankin" (Master's thesis, University of Georgia, 1969), 58–60.
50. Mary O'Neill, Letter to Jeannette Rankin, Jeannette Rankin Papers, MC 147, Series 7.2, Montana Historical Society Research Center, Archives.
51. Alice Paul, "Interview by Amelia R. Fry: Conversations with Alice Paul, Woman Suffrage and the Equal Rights Amendment," Suffragists Oral History Project, University of California at Berkeley, accessed June 26, 2020, lib.berkeley.edu; Burton Benedict, *The Anthropology of World's Fairs: San Francisco Panama Pacific International Exposition of 1915* (London: Lowie Museum of Anthropology, 1983), 23–31.

52. Donna Ewald and Peter Clute, *San Francisco Invites the World: The Panama-Pacific International Exposition of 1915* (San Francisco: Chronicle Books, 1991), 72.

53. "Advertise Suffrage," *West Virginian*, May 6, 1915, accessed February 29, 2020, newspapers.com.

54. "Chronology of the New Zealand Health System 1840 to 2017," accessed February 3, 2020, health.govt.nz; Rob Lundie and Joy McCann, "Commonwealth Parliament from 1901 to World War I," May 2015, accessed July 3, 2020, newspapers.com.

55. Mary Stewart, Letter to Jeannette Rankin and Potential Supporters, April 1916, Jeannette Rankin Papers, MC 147, Series 7.2, Montana Historical Society Research Center, Archives.

56. Jeannette Rankin, Interview by John C. Board, 12.

57. Jeannette Rankin, Interview by John C. Board, 13.

58. Joan Hoff Wilson, "Remarks," in *Acceptance and Dedication of the Statue of Jeannette Rankin* (Washington, D.C.: U.S. Government Printing Office, 1987), 17–27.

59. Anna Howard Shaw, Letter to Jeannette Rankin, March 1917, Jeannette Rankin Papers, MC 147, Series 7.2, Montana Historical Society Research Center, Archives.

60. Hannah Josephson, *Jeannette Rankin: First Lady in Congress, A Biography* (Indianapolis: Bobbs-Merrill Company, 1974), 51.

61. Richard K. Hines, "Wellington Duncan Rankin," 28 Rankin.

62. Norma Smith, *Jeannette Rankin: America's Conscience*, 98–106.

63. Kathryn Anderson, introduction to *Jeannette Rankin: America's Conscience*, by Norma Smith (Helena, MT: Montana Historical Society Press, 2002), 13; Wellington Rankin, Interview by Volney Steele, 1.

64. Jeannette Rankin, Interview by John C. Board, 13; Norma Smith, *Jeannette Rankin: America's Conscience*, 58.

65. Norma Smith, *Jeannette Rankin: America's Conscience*, 102.

66. Jeannette Rankin, Interview by John C. Board, 16.

67. James J. Lopach and Jean A. Luckowski, *Jeannette Rankin*, 6.

68. "Equal Pay for Women," *New York Times*, November 12, 1916, accessed April 2, 2018, *New York Times* Historical Database.

69. Wellington Rankin, Interview by Volney Steele, 3- 5.

70. Norma Smith, *Jeannette Rankin: America's Conscience*, 99.

71. James J. Lopach and Jean A. Luckowski, *Jeannette Rankin*, 124.

72. Jeannette Rankin, Interview by Malca Chall and Hannah Josephson, Suffragists Oral History Project, University of California at Berkeley, accessed June 26, 2020, lib.berkeley.edu.

73. Wellington Rankin, Interview by Volney Steele, 9.

74. Jeannette Rankin, Interview by John C. Board, 18–23; "Election News at a Glance," *Harrisburg Telegraph*, December 2, 1916, accessed January 15, 2018, newspapers.com.

75. Jeannette Rankin, "Woman and the New Democracy," Proceedings, Wisconsin Teachers' Association 65 (1918): 107.

76. Quoted in Lily Rothman, "How the First Woman Was Elected to U.S. National Office, Exactly 100 Years Ago," *Time*, November 7, 2016, accessed April 12, 2020, time.com.

77. Kevin S. Giles, *Flight of the Dove: The Story of Jeannette Rankin* (Beaverton, OR: Touchstone Press, 1980), 70, 90.

78. Volney Steele, *Wellington Rankin*, 8.

79. Hannah Josephson, *Jeannette Rankin: First Lady in Congress*, 52.

80. Norma Smith, *Jeannette Rankin: America's Conscience*, 193.

81. Wellington Rankin, Interview by Volney Steele, 2–3.

82. Norma Smith, *Jeannette Rankin: America's Conscience*, 193–194.

83. Bert Lennon, "Jeannette Rankin Is Well Qualified to Serve in Congress," *Oregon Daily Journal*, December 3, 1916, accessed August 7, 2019, newspapers.com.

84. Jeannette Rankin, Interview by John C. Board, 18–20.

85. Jeannette Rankin, Interview by John C. Board, 34.

86. Jeannette Rankin, Telegram to Wellington Rankin, June 1917, Jeannette Rankin Papers, MC 147, Series 7.2, Montana Historical Society Research Center, Archives.

87. Jeannette Rankin, Letters concerning the Bureau of Printing and Engraving,

Jeannette Rankin Papers, MC 147, Series 7.2, Montana Historical Society Research Center, Archives.

88. Candace Lewis Bredbenner, *A Nationality of Her Own: Women, Marriage, and the Law of Citizenship* (Berkeley: University of California Press, 1998), 70.

89. Jeannette Rankin, Speech in the U.S. House for Suffrage, January 10, 1918, Rankin Family Papers, Box 4.4, Archives & Special Collections, Mansfield Library, University of Montana.

90. Alice Paul, Interview by Amelia R. Fry.

91. Norma Smith, *Jeannette Rankin: America's Conscience*, 127.

92. Jane Little Botkin, *Frank Little and the IWW: The Blood That Stained an American Family* (Norman: University of Oklahoma Press, 2017), 4–5.

93. Arnon Gutfeld, *Montana's Agony: Years of War and Hysteria, 1917–21* (Gainesville: University Press of Florida, 1979), 28.

94. Jeannette Rankin, Letter to Dear Friend, June 23, 1917, Jeannette Rankin Papers, MC 147, Series 7.2, Montana Historical Society Research Center, Archives.

95. Jeannette Rankin, Letter to Helena Stellway, June 20, 1917, Jeannette Rankin Papers, MC 147, Series 7.2, Montana Historical Society Research Center, Archives.

96. Wellington Rankin, Interview by Volney Steele, 25.

97. Wellington Rankin, Interview by Volney Steele, 22; Hannah Josephson, *Jeannette Rankin*, 92.

98. "Recognition of Independence of Ireland Is to Be Demanded," *Irish Standard* (Minneapolis), January 12, 1918, accessed January 16, 2020, newspapers.com.

99. Mick Gidley, *Edward S. Curtis and the North American Indian, Incorporated* (New York: Cambridge University Press, 2000), 35–36; Jeannette Rankin, Letter to Helen Gray, August 22, 1917, Jeannette Rankin Papers, MC 147, Series 7.2, Montana Historical Society Research Center, Archives.

100. George M. Dennison, *Montana's Pioneer Naturalist: Morton J. Elrod* (Norman, OK: University of Oklahoma Press, 2016), 5; Jeannette Rankin, Letter to Franklin K. Lane, September 10, 1917, Jeannette Rankin Papers, MC 147, Series 7.2, Montana Historical Society Research Center, Archives.

101. *Congressional Record: Proceedings and Debates of the Second Session of the Sixty-Fifth Congress*, vol. 56, part 2, January 22, 1918 (Washington, D.C.: U.S. Government Printing Office, 1918), 1147.

Five

1. William Penn, *A Collection of the Works of William Penn*, vol. 1 (London: Sowle, 1726), 122.

2. Charles Goodell, *Political Prisoners in America* (New York: Random, 1973), 19.

3. Peter Brock, *Pacifism in the United States: From the Colonial Era to the First World War* (Princeton: Princeton University Press, 1968), 691; Valarie H. Ziegler, *The Advocates of Peace in Antebellum America* (Macon, GA: Mercer University Press, 2001), 158.

4. "Minorities during the Gold Rush," California Secretary of State, accessed June 17, 2020, sos.ca.gov; Edward D. Castillo, "California Indian History," California Native American Heritage Commission, accessed June 26, 2020, nahc.ca.gov.

5. Paul Andrew Hutton, *Phil Sheridan and His Army* (Lincoln: University of Nebraska Press, 1985), 181–200.

6. "With the Great Spirit," *Helena Independent*, December 20, 1890; "Hanged by the Neck," *Butte Daily Post*, December 19, 1890, accessed March 23, 2020, newspapers.com.

7. Jeannette Rankin, Interview by Malca Chall and Hannah Josephson, Suffragists Oral History Project, University of California at Berkeley, accessed June 26, 2020, lib.berkeley.edu.

8. Jeannette Rankin, "Two Votes against War: 1917, 1941," *Liberation* 3 (March 1958): 4; Wilma Dykeman, *Too Many People, Too Little Love: Edna Rankin McKinnon, Pioneer for Birth Control* (New York, Holt, Rinehart and Winston 1974), 22.

9. Robert Herrick, "Two Sorts of Pacifists," *Chicago Tribune*, June 4, 1916; "Stories of the Vigilantes in the Days When the Big West Was a Country in the Raw," *San Francisco Chronicle*, March 31, 1912, accessed July 25, 2020, newspapers.com.

10. Louis D. Brandeis, *Other People's Money and How the Bankers Use It* (New York: Frederick A. Stokes, 1914).

11. A.N. Wilson, *Tolstoy* (New York:

Norton, 1988), 408–411; Peter Brock, *Freedom from War: Nonsectarian Pacifism, 1814-1914* (Toronto: University of Toronto Press, 1991), 185–87, 299.

12. Leo Tolstoy, *The Kingdom of God Is Within You*, 1894, trans. Constance Garnett (Lincoln: University of Nebraska Press, 1984), 122; Charles DeBenedetti, *Peace Heroes in Twentieth-Century America* (Bloomington: Indiana University Press, 1988), 36.

13. Jane Addams, *Newer Ideals of Peace* (New York: Macmillan, 1906).

14. Harriet Hyman Alonso, "Jeannette Rankin and the Women's Peace Union," Montana: The Magazine of Western History 39, no. 2 (Spring 1989): 34–49.

15. Dustin Ellis Howes, "The Failure of Pacifism and the Success of Nonviolence," *Perspectives on Politics* 11, no. 2 (2013): 427–446.

16. Alice Paul, Interview by Amelia R. Fry.

17. June Purvis, "'Deeds, Not Words': Daily Life in the Women's Social and Political Union in Edwardian Britain," in *Votes for Women*, eds. June Purvis and Sandra Stanley Holton (London: Routledge, 2000), 135–158.

18. Martin Green, *Gandhi: Voice of a New Age Revolution* (New York: Continuum, 1993), 167–191; Stanley Wolpert, *Gandhi's Passion: The Life and Legacy of Mahatma Gandhi* (New York: Oxford, 2001), 74.

19. Mahatma Gandhi, *Satyagraha in South Africa*, trans. Valji Govindji Desai (Ahmedabad, India: Navajivan, 1961), 111.

20. Katherine H. Adams and Michael L. Keene, *Alice Paul and the American Suffrage Campaign* (Urbana: University of Illinois Press, 2008), 25–30.

21. Jeannette Rankin, "Two Votes against War: 1917, 1941," *Liberation* 3 (March 1958): 4.

22. Jeannette Rankin, Interview by John C. Board, 28.

23. "Our Busy Congresswoman," *Literary Digest* 55 (August 11, 1917): 43.

24. Steven A. Seidman, *Posters, Propaganda, and Persuasion in Election Campaigns around the World and through History* (New York: Peter Lang, 2008), 54.

25. "Woodrow Wilson War Message," accessed June 18, 2020, mtholyoke.edu.

26. Hannah Josephson, *Jeannette Rankin*, 74; Norma Smith, *Jeannette Rankin: America's Conscience*, 106; Wellington Rankin, Interview by John Board, March 23, 1964, Wellington D. Rankin Papers, Archives West, accessed December 8, 2019, archiveswest.orbiscascade.org.

27. Wellington Rankin, Interview by Volney Steele, 33.

28. Kevin S. Giles, *Flight of the Dove*, 70.

29. Hannah Josephson, *Jeannette Rankin*, 73.

30. Jeannette Rankin, Interview with John Board, 29–30.

31. Wellington Rankin, Interview by Volney Steele, 13–14, 35–37; William R. Nester, *Theodore Roosevelt and the Art of American Power: An American for All Time* (New York: Rowman & Littlefield, 2019), 202–203.

32. Jeannette Rankin, Interview by John C. Board, 32.

33. Norma Smith, *Jeannette Rankin: America's Conscience*, 107–108.

34. Jeannette Rankin, Interview by John C. Board, 29–30.

35. Wellington Rankin, Interview by Volney Steele, 16.

36. Wellington Rankin, Interview with Volney Steele, 16.

37. Jeannette Rankin, Interview with John C. Board, 31.

38. Wellington Rankin, Interview by Volney Steele, 31–33.

39. Alice Paul, "Interview by Amelia R. Fry: Conversations with Alice Paul, Woman Suffrage and the Equal Rights Amendment," Suffragists Oral History Project, University of California at Berkeley, accessed June 26, 2020, lib.berkeley.edu; Mary Walton, *A Woman's Crusade: Alice Paul and the Battle for the Ballot* (New York: Palgrave Macmillan, 2010), 162–163.

40. Norma Smith, *Jeannette Rankin: America's Conscience*, 113; "Seek to Explain Miss Rankin's 'No,'" *New York Times*, April 7, 1917, accessed April 15, 2019, *New York Times* Historical Database; Dave Walter, "Rebel with a Cause," *Montana* 110 (November-December 1991): 66–67.

41. Wellington Rankin, Interview by Volney Steele, 33.

42. Jeannette Rankin, Interview by John C. Board, 32.

43. Ronald Bayly and Nancy Landgren, *Jeannette Rankin: The Woman Who Voted No* (Alexandria, VA : PBS Video, 1984), DVD.

44. Jeannette Rankin, Interview by John C. Board, 30–31.

45. Wellington Rankin, Interview with John C. Board; Norma Smith, *Jeannette Rankin: America's Conscience*, 112; Ted Carlton Harris, *Jeannette Rankin: Suffragist, First Woman Elected to Congress, and Pacifist* (New York: Arno Press. 1982), 119; John Board, "The Lady from Montana: Jeannette Rankin" (Master's thesis, University of Wyoming, 1964), 133.

46. Gayle Shirley, *More Than Petticoats: Remarkable Montana Women* (New York: Rowman & Littlefield, 2010), 100.

47. "Seek to Explain Miss Rankin's 'No.'"

48. Hannah Josephson, *Jeannette Rankin*, 76; Jeannette Rankin, Interview by John C. Board, 32–33.

49. Mary Murphy, "Jeannette Rankin: Suffragist, Congresswoman, Pacifist," in *Beyond Schoolmarms and Madams: Montana Women's Stories*, ed. Martha Kohl (Helena: Montana Historical Society Press, 2016), 235–236.

50. Mary Murphy, "When Jeannette Said No: Montana Women's Response to World War I," *Montana: The Magazine of Western History* 65, no. 1 (Spring 2015): 9–14.

51. "Nebraska Opinions," *Lincoln Star*, April 24, 1917, accessed May 8, 2020, newspapers.com.

52. Nina Swinnerton, Letter to Jeannette Rankin, April 5, 1917, Jeannette Rankin Papers, MC 147, Series 7.1, Montana Historical Society Research Center, Archives; James J. Lopach and Jean A. Luckowski, *Jeannette Rankin: A Political Woman* (Boulder: University Press of Colorado, 2005), 149.

53. Jeannette Rankin, Letter to Nina Swinnerton, May 22, 1917, Jeannette Rankin Papers, MC 147, Series 7.1, Montana Historical Society Research Center, Archives; Nina Swinnerton, Letter to Jeannette Rankin, April 2, 1917, Jeannette Rankin Papers, MC 147, Series 7.1, Montana Historical Society Research Center, Archives; Helena Stellway, Letter to Jeannette Rankin, December 25, 1917, Jeannette Rankin Papers, MC 147, Series 7.1, Montana Historical Society Research Center, Archives; Will Englund, *March 1917: On the Brink of War and Revolution* (New York: Norton, 2017), 252.

54. "Strong Pressure, Failed to Influence Congresswoman's Vote on War," *Cincinnati Enquirer*, April 7, 1917, accessed February 23, 2018, newspapers.com.

55. Richard K. Hines, "Wellington Duncan Rankin: The Man behind the Myth" (Master's thesis, Washington State University, 1996), 36.

56. "Jeannette Rankin Explains Peace Pacts to Outlaw War," *Havre* (MT) *Daily News*, September 4, 1928, accessed July 19, 2019, newspapers.com.

57. Krys Holmes, Susan C. Dailey, and David Walter, *Montana: Stories of the Land* (Helena, MT: Montana Historical Society, 2008), 310–314.

58. Jeannette Rankin, Interview by John C. Board, 38; Jeannette Rankin, Interview by Malca Chall and Hannah Josephson, Suffragists Oral History Project, University of California at Berkeley, accessed June 26, 2020, lib.berkeley.edu.

59. Norma Smith, *Jeannette Rankin: America's Conscience*, 137.

60. C.B. Nolan, Letter to Thomas Walsh, August 30, 1918, Thomas James Walsh Papers, Series 1, File A, Library of Congress.

61. A.E. Spriggs, Letter to Thomas Walsh, September 2, 1918, Thomas James Walsh Papers, Series 1, File A, Library of Congress; Kevin S. Giles, *Flight of the Dove*, 118; Ronald Schaffer, "Jeannette Rankin, Progressive-Isolationist" (PhD diss., Princeton, 1959), 141.

62. Jeannette Rankin, Interview by John C. Board, 40.

63. "Miss Rankin to Run," *Boyden* (IA) *Reporter*, September 5, 1918, accessed January 14, 2018, newspapers.com.

64. Joan Holt Wilson, "'Peace Is a Woman's Job': Jeannette Rankin and American Foreign Policy: The Origins of Her Pacifism," in *History of Women in the United States, Women and War*, ed. Nancy F. Cott (Munich: K.G. Saur, 1993), 263.

65. Karl Weiss, Letter to Jeannette Rankin, January 24, 1918; L.C. Butterfield, Letter to Jeannette Rankin, May 10, 1918; Mary Dean, Letter to Jeannette Rankin, July 22, 1918, Jeannette Rankin Papers, MC 147, Box 2.1, Montana Historical Society Research Center, Archives.

66. Joan Holt Wilson, "'Peace Is a Woman's Job': Jeannette Rankin and American Foreign Policy: The Origins of Her Pacifism," 262; "Official Abstract of Votes Cast at the General Election Held in Montana,"

November 5, 1918, Montana Secretary of State, accessed December 19, 2019, sos.mt.gov; James Leonard Bates, *Senator Thomas J. Walsh of Montana: Law and Public Affairs, from TR to FDR* (Urbana: University of Illinois Press, 1999), 166.

67. Joan Hoff Wilson, "'Peace Is a Woman's Job': Jeannette Rankin and American Foreign Policy: Her Lifework as a Pacifist," in *History of Women in the United States*, 15, *Women and War*, ed. Nancy F. Cott (Munich: K.G. Saur, 1993), 277–280.

68. Jeannette Rankin, House Foreign Affairs Committee Testimony, 1933, Jeannette Rankin Papers, MC 147, Series 7.2, Montana Historical Society Research Center, Archives; "Public Must Outlaw War, Says Speaker," *Albany Democrat-Herald*, November 24, 1933, accessed May 22, 2020, newspapers.com.

69. Jeannette Rankin, Interview by John C. Board, 33.

70. Jeannette Rankin, "Democracy and Women," January 16, 1940, Rankin Family Papers, Series II, 4.4, Archives & Special Collections, Mansfield Library, University of Montana; Carol R. Byerly, "War Losses (USA)," *International Encyclopedia of the First World War*, accessed February 12, 2020, encyclopedia.1914-1918-online.net.

71. John Kirkley, "An Afternoon with Jeannette Rankin," Jeannette Rankin: Activist for World Peace, Women's Rights, and Democratic Government, 149–152, University of California at Berkeley Suffragists Oral History Project, accessed June 18, 2020, lib.berkeley.edu; Joan Hoff Wilson, "'Peace Is a Woman's Job': Jeannette Rankin and American Foreign Policy: Her Lifework as a Pacifist," 281.

72. George Washington, "Farewell Address," September 17, 1796, accessed February 17, 2020, mtholyoke.edu.

73. David A. Lake, *Entangling Relations: American Foreign Policy in Its Century* (Princeton, NJ: Princeton University Press, 1999), 3.

74. James Monroe, "Monroe Doctrine," Digital History, accessed February 7, 2020, digitalhistory.uh.edu.

75. Ronald Bayly and Nancy Landgren, *Jeannette Rankin: The Woman Who Voted No*; Joan Hoff Wilson, "Remarks," in *Acceptance and Dedication of the Statue of Jeannette Rankin* (Washington, D.C.: U.S. Government Printing Office, 1987), 17–27.

76. Ronald E. Powaski, *Toward an Entangling Alliance: American Isolationism, Internationalism, and Europe, 1901-1950* (Westport: Greenwood, 1991), 72.

77. Joseph Kinsey Howard, *Montana: High, Wide, and Handsome* (New Haven: Yale University Press, 1959), 202–203.

78. Jeannette Rankin, Interview by John C. Board, 43.

79. Jeannette Rankin, Interview by John C. Board, 47.

80. "Democracy's Mental Dissolution Pictured as Nazi Goal in U.S.," *Christian Science Monitor* (July 20, 1940), 15.

81. "An Election Special—A Voter's Guide," 1948, Rankin Family Papers, Box 4.4, Archives & Special Collections, Mansfield Library, University of Montana.

82. Jeannette Rankin, Interview by John C. Board, 51.

83. Wellington Rankin, Interview by Volney Steele, 17.

84. "U.S. Now at War with Germany and Italy," *New York Times*, December 11, 1941, accessed December 15, 2019, newspapers.com.

85. "Asks Miss Rankin Recant; Montana Republican Leader Says State Deplores Anti-War Vote," *New York Times*, December 9, 1941, accessed December 5, 2017, *New York Times* Historical Database.

86. "Miss Rankin, War Opponent in 1917, Hasn't Changed Mind," *Washington Post*, December 9, 1941, accessed May 16, 2018, newspapers.com; Karen Foerstel and Herbert N. Foerstel, *Climbing the Hill: Gender Conflict in Congress* (Westport, CT: Praeger, 1996), 5; Dave Walter, "Rebel with a Cause," *Montana* 110 (November-December 1991): 68–70.

87. Henry McLemore, "Perfect Montana Congressman Would Make a Perfect 'Enemy' Wife for Any American Male," *Pittsburgh Press*, December 12, 1941, accessed January 29, 2020, newspapers.com.

88. Karen Foerstel and Herbert N. Foerstel, *Climbing the Hill: Gender Conflict in Congress* (Westport, CT: Praeger, 1996), 5.

89. R.J. Bowers, Letter to Jeannette Rankin, December 14, 1941; Harry C. Armin, Letter to Jeannette Rankin, December 9, 1941, Jeannette Rankin Papers, MC 147, Series 7.4, Montana Historical Society Research Center, Archives.

90. "The Complicated Lead Up to Pearl

Harbor," December 7, 2016, accessed March 1, 2020, airandspace.si.edu.

91. "U.S. Expected Japs' Attack, Jeannette Rankin Declares," *News Journal* (Wilmington, DE), December 23, 1942; "Miss Rankin Asks Facts of Pearl Harbor," *Deseret News* (Salt Lake City), December 23, 1942, accessed June 20, 2020, newspapers.com; "Japan's Imports Cut 75% by War," *New York Times*, December 2, 1941, accessed February 20, 2020, *New York Times* Historical Database; "Miss Rankin, War Opponent in 1917, Hasn't Changed Mind," *Washington Post*, December 9, 1941, accessed May 16, 2018, newspapers.com; Jeannette Rankin, Interview by John C. Board, 53.

92. Jeannette Rankin, Interview by John C. Board, 53; Jeannette Rankin, Letters to Correspondents concerning War, Jeannette Rankin Papers, MC 147, Series 7.4, Montana Historical Society Research Center, Archives.

93. Joan Hoff Wilson, "Remarks," in *Acceptance and Dedication of the Statue of Jeannette Rankin* (Washington, D.C.: U.S. Government Printing Office, 1987), 17–27.

94. Ruth Montgomery, "Jeannette Rankin on Trail Again," *Pensacola News Journal*, December 30, 1967, accessed February 21, 2020, newspapers.com.

Six

1. "A Forest Guessing Party," *Missoulian*, July 5, 1903; "Society Notes," *Anaconda Standard*, March 23, 1902; "In Missoula," *Anaconda Standard*, January 5, 1902, accessed April 12, 2020, newspapers.com.

2. "Harriet Rankin," *Missoulian*, June 7, 1903, accessed April 14, 2020, newspapers.com.

3. Lulu Haskell Holmes, *A History of the Position of Dean of Women in a Selected Group of Co-educational Colleges and Universities in the United States* (New York: Teachers College, Columbia University, 1939), 11.

4. Louise G. Kraft, "A History of the Certification of Montana Teachers" (Master's thesis, University of Montana, 1936), 24–25; Mildred Dufresne, *Grant Creek and Its One-Room School* (Missoula: Delta Kappa Gamma, 1981), 11–16.

5. Irene Harwarth, Mindi Maline, and Elizabeth DeBra, *Women's Colleges in the United States* (Washington, D.C.: U.S. Department of Education, 1997), 6–11.

6. Sara Hayden, "Negotiating Femininity and Power in the Early Twentieth Century West: Domestic Ideology and Feminine Style in Jeannette Rankin's Suffrage Rhetoric," *Communication Studies* 50, no. 2 (Summer 1999): 88.

7. Edward Clarke, *Sex and Education: Or, A Fair Chance for Girls* (New York: J.R. Osgood, 1873), 17–18.

8. Henry Adams, *Selected Letters*, ed. Ernest Samuels (Boston: Belknap Press, 1992), 138.

9. Lillian Faderman, *Odd Girls and Twilight Lovers: A History of Lesbian Life in Twentieth-Century America* (New York: Columbia University Press, 1991), 14.

10. Albert Barrere and Charles G. Leland, *Dictionary of Slang, Jargon and Cant*, vol. 1 (London: Ballantyne, 1889), 372.

11. Sarah Pruitt, "How Flappers Redefined Womanhood (Hint: It Involved Jazz, Liquor and Sex)," September 17, 2018, accessed January 14, 2020, history.com; Lynn Dumenil, *The Second Line of Defense: American Women and World War I* (Chapel Hill: University of North Carolina Press, 2017), 255–275.

12. Burt G. Wilder, *What Young People Should Know: The Reproductive Function* (Boston: Estes and Lauriat, 1875); Marion Harland, *Eve's Daughters* (New York: Scribner's, 1881), 80–83; Clelia Duel Mosher, *The Mosher Survey: Sexual Attitudes of 45 Victorian Women*, ed. James MaHood and Kristine Wenburg (New York: Arno Press, 1980), 207.

13. Lulu Haskell Holmes, *A History of the Position of Dean of Women in a Selected Group of Co-educational Colleges and Universities in the United States*, 6.

14. *Oberlin Catalogue and Second Annual Report* (Oberlin, OH: The College, 1869), Appendix, 24; Lulu Haskell Holmes, *A History of the Position of Dean of Women in a Selected Group of Co-educational Colleges and Universities in the United States*, 7.

15. Jana Nidiffer, "Advocates on Campus: Deans of Women Create a New Profession," in *Women Administrators in Higher Education: Historical and Contemporary Perspectives*, ed. Jana Nidiffer and Carolyn Terry Bashaw (Albany: State University of New York Press, 2001), 138.

16. *The Lyre of Alpha Chi Omega*, 1922, vol. 26 (Charleston, SC: Nabu Press, 2012), 397.

17. Una Herrick, "Twenty Years at Montana State College," Merrill G. Burlingame Research Files on MSU History, Series 4, Montana State University Library.

18. H.G. Merriam, "The Clapp Years, 1921–1935," Old Missoula, accessed May 20, 2020, oldmissoula.com.

19. Harriet Rankin Sedman, "The New College Girl," Mary Elrod Ferguson Papers, MSS 205, Series 3, Box 1.11, Archives & Special Collections, Mansfield Library, University of Montana..

20. Michele Gouveia, "Running Wild: College Students in the 1920s, by Mrs. Parker," 2004, accessed March 17, 2020, sarahbaker.org.

21. Harriet Rankin Sedman, "The Dean of Women at Work," Mary Elrod Ferguson Papers, MSS 205, Series 3, Box 1.11, Archives & Special Collections, Mansfield Library, University of Montana.

22. Harriet Rankin Sedman, "Women in the University," January 1926, Mary Elrod Ferguson Papers, MSS 205, Series 3, Box 1.11, Archives & Special Collections, Mansfield Library, University of Montana; Harriet Rankin Sedman, "The Life of the Women Students at the State University of Montana," Mary Elrod Ferguson Papers, MSS 205, Series 3, Box 1.11, Archives & Special Collections, Mansfield Library, University of Montana.

23. Mary Rankin Bragg, Letter to Kappa Kappa Gamma, May 1959, Mary Elrod Ferguson Papers, MSS 205, Series 8, Box 4.3, Archives & Special Collections, Mansfield Library, University of Montana.

24. Report on Student Employment Possibilities, October 23, 1924; Report on Women Students' Employment, November 18, 1922, Mary Elrod Ferguson Papers, MSS 205, Series 3, Box 1.11, Archives & Special Collections, Mansfield Library, University of Montana.

25. Campus Newspaper Clippings, January 4, 1928 and November 7, 1928, Mary Elrod Ferguson Papers, MSS 205, Series 3, Box 1.11, Archives & Special Collections, Mansfield Library, University of Montana; "Mrs. Ingersoll Loses Case in High Court," *Independent-Record* (Helena), May 15, 1928, accessed July 11, 2020, newspapers.com.

26. Harriet Rankin Sedman, "The Dean of Women and Campus Life," Mary Elrod Ferguson Papers, MSS 205, Box 1, Archives & Special Collections, Mansfield Library, University of Montana.

27. Jon Krakauer, *Missoula: Rape and the Justice System in a College Town* (New York: Doubleday, 2015).

28. Harriet Rankin Sedman, "Our Services for Students," April 4, 1924, Mary Elrod Ferguson Papers, MSS 205, Box 1, Archives & Special Collections, Mansfield Library, University of Montana.

29. Lois Mathews, *The Dean of Women* (Boston: Houghton Mifflin, 1915); Michael S. Hevel, "Toward a History of Student Affairs: A Synthesis of Research, 1996–2015," *Journal of College Student Development* 57, no. 7 (October 2016): 852–854.

30. "American Women in World War II," February 28, 2020, accessed April 19, 2020, history.com.

31. George Korson, *At His Side: The Story of the American Red Cross Overseas in World War II* (New York: Coward-McCann, 1945), 259.

32. Emily Yellin, *Our Mothers' War: American Women at Home and at the Front during World War II* (New York: Free Press, 2004), 175–182.

33. *The American Red Cross with the Armed Forces*, 43, World War Regimental Histories, accessed May 15, 2020, digicom.bpl.lib.me.us.

34. Mary Thomas Sargent, *Runway towards Orion: The True Adventures of a Red Cross Girl on a B-29 Air Base in World War II India* (Grand Rapids, MI: Triumph Press, 1984), 19; Julia A. Ramsey, "'Girls' in Name Only: A Study of American Red Cross Volunteers on the Frontlines of World War II" (Master's thesis, Auburn University, 2011), 57–75.

35. George Korson, *At His Side*, 260.

36. Edna Rankin McKinnon, Letter to Wellington Rankin, June 7, 1942, Edna Rankin McKinnon Papers, Series 2, Schlesinger Library, Radcliffe Institute, Harvard University.

37. James H. Madison, *Slinging Doughnuts for the Boys: An American Woman in World War II* (Bloomington: Indiana University Press, 2007), 22–24; *The American Red Cross with the Armed Forces*, 41–43, World War Regimental Histories, accessed May 15, 2020, digicom.bpl.lib.me.us.

38. "World War II and the American Red Cross," accessed June 30, 2020, redcross.org.
39. George Korson, *At His Side*, 261–270; Helen Airy, *Doughnut Dollies: American Red Cross Girls during World War II* (Santa Fe, NM: Sunstone Press, 1995), 52–72; Harriet Rankin McGregor, Letter to Wellington Rankin, April 2, 1944, Wellington D. Rankin Papers, MC 288, Personal Subgroup, Series 2.1, Montana Historical Society, Helena.
40. William H. Chafe, *The American Woman: Her Changing Social, Economic, and Political Roles, 1920–1970* (New York: Oxford University Press, 1972), 136.

Seven

1. Quotation from Edna Rankin McKinnon in Wilma Dykeman, *Too Many People, Too Little Love: Edna Rankin McKinnon, Pioneer for Birth Control* (New York, Holt, Rinehart and Winston, 1974), 276.
2. Kevin Giles, *One Woman against War: The Jeannette Rankin Story*. (St. Petersburg, FL: BookLocker.com, 2016), 29.
3. Wilma Dykeman, *Too Many People, Too Little Love: Edna Rankin McKinnon, Pioneer for Birth Control* (New York: Holt, Rinehart and Winston, 1974), 93, 105.
4. "Seniors Given High School Diplomas," *Missoulian*, June 3, 1911, accessed January 19, 2020, newspapers.com.
5. Edna Rankin McKinnon, Job Application, Edna Rankin McKinnon Papers, Series 1, Arthur and Elizabeth Schlesinger Library, Harvard University.
6. Wilma Dykeman, *Too Many People, Too Little Love*, 273.
7. Edna Rankin McKinnon, Travel Journal, Edna Rankin McKinnon Papers, Series 1, Arthur and Elizabeth Schlesinger Library, Harvard University.
8. Wilma Dykeman, *Too Many People, Too Little Love*, 24; Richard K. Hines, "Wellington Duncan Rankin: The Man behind the Myth" (Master's thesis, Washington State University, 1996), 18.
9. "Jury Finds Frank Hall Guilty," *Missoulian*, March 13, 1917, accessed May 14, 2020, newspapers.com.
10. Wellington Rankin, Interview by John Board, March 23, 1964, Wellington D. Rankin Papers, Archives West, accessed December 8, 2019, archiveswest.orbiscascade.org.
11. James J. Lopach and Jean A. Luckowski, *Jeannette Rankin: A Political Woman* (Boulder: University Press of Colorado, 2005), 24–25.
12. Wilma Dykeman, *Too Many People, Too Little Love*, 26.
13. Judy Flander, "Birth Control Champion at 81," *Washington Star News*, March 28, 1974, accessed January 18, 2020, judyflander.org.
14. Wilma Dykeman, *Too Many People, Too Little Love*, 25.
15. Wilma Dykeman, *Too Many People, Too Little Love*, 271, 276.
16. "Private Life: Limiting Births in the Early Republic," Digital History, accessed January 19, 2020, digitalhistory.uh.edu.
17. Cathy Luchetti, *Children of the West: Family Life on the Frontier* (New York: Norton, 2001), 60–61.
18. Melody Rose, *Abortion: A Documentary and Reference Guide* (Santa Barbara, CA: ABC-CLIO, 2008), 31.
19. Peter Engleman, *A History of the Birth Control Movement in America* (Santa Barbara, CA: Praeger, 2011), 18–19.
20. Jean H. Baker, *Margaret Sanger: A Life of Passion* (New York: Hill and Wang, 2011), 134.
21. William J. Robinson, *Birth Control or the Limitation of Offspring* (New York: Critic and Guide Co., 1916), 113; Margaret Sanger, *Woman and the New Race* (New York: Brentano's, 1920), 59–60.
22. Theodore Roosevelt, "Birth Control—From the Positive Side," *Metropolitan Magazine*, October 1917, repr. in *The Pivot of Civilization in Historical Perspective: The Birth Control Classic by Margaret Sanger*, ed. Michael W. Perry (Seattle: Inkling Books, 2003), 237–241; Margaret Sanger, "Birth Control: Margaret Sanger's Reply to Theodore Roosevelt," *Metropolitan Magazine* (December 1917): 66–67.
23. Margaret Sanger, *The Pivot of Civilization*, 1922 (New York: Humanity Press, 2003), 173–188.
24. Margaret Sanger, *The Pivot of Civilization*, 113.
25. Margaret Sanger, "My Way to Peace," January 17, 1932, Public Writing and Speeches of Margaret Sanger, accessed January 20, 2020, nyu.edu/projects/sanger.
26. Linda Gordon, *The Moral Property of*

Women: A History of Birth Control Politics in America (Urbana: University of Illinois Press, 2002), 235; Margaret Sanger, Letter to Clarence Gamble, October 19, 1939, Margaret Sanger Papers, Smith Libraries Exhibits, accessed June 18, 2020, libex.smith.edu.

27. Edwin Black, *War against the Weak: Eugenics and America's Campaign to Create a Master Race* (Washington, D.C.: Dialog Press, 2012), 127.

28. James S. Lantzer, "The Indiana Way of Eugenics: Sterilization Laws, 1907–1974," in *A Century of Eugenics in America: From the Indiana Experiment to the Human Genome Era*, ed. Paul A. Lombardo (Bloomington: Indiana University Press, 2011), 26–41.

29. Johanna Schoen, *Choice and Coercion: Birth Control, Sterilization, and Abortion in Public Health and Welfare* (Chapel Hill: University of North Carolina Press, 2005), 82–109.

30. Angela Franks, *Margaret Sanger's Eugenic Legacy: The Control of Female Fertility* (Jefferson, NC: McFarland, 2014), 117.

31. Doone Williams, *Every Child a Wanted Child: Clarence James Gamble and His Work in the Birth Control Movement* (Cambridge: Harvard University Press, 1979), 100.

32. Johanna Schoen, *Choice and Coercion*, 8.

33. Clarence Gamble, "Trends in State Programs for the Sterilization of the Mentally Deficient," *American Journal of Mental Deficiency* 53, no. 4 (April 1949): 538–541; Clarence Gamble, "Eugenic Sterilization in the United States," *Eugenical News* 34, no. 1–2 (March–June 1949): 1.

34. Emily Taft Douglas, *Margaret Sanger: Pioneer of the Future* (New York: Holt, Rinehart, and Winston, 1969), 47; Wilma Dykeman, *Too Many People, Too Little Love*, 35.

35. Carole M. McCann, *Birth Control Politics in the United States* (Ithaca: Cornell University Press, 1994), 75–76.

36. Wilma Dykeman, *Too Many People, Too Little Love*, 47.

37. Wilma Dykeman, *Too Many People, Too Little Love*, 47–49, 87, 267.

38. Julius Paul, "'Three Generations of Imbeciles Are Enough': State Eugenic Sterilization Laws in American Thought and Practice," unpublished manuscript, Washington, D.C.: Walter Reed Army Institute of Research, 1965, 404–406; *Buck v Bell Documents*, Paper 95, 1965, 404–406, accessed April 2, 2020, readingroom.law.gsu.edu.

39. Volney Steele, *Bleed, Blister, and Purge: A History of Medicine on the American Frontier* (Missoula, MT: Mountain Press, 2005), 229.

40. "Montana Eugenics," accessed April 26, 2020, uvm.edu; Tona Roth, "Eugenic Sterilization in Montana from 1900 to 1999," research paper, Carroll College, 1999, 6.

41. "Outrage on Mrs. Kelly Permitted," *Independent-Record* (Helena), October 28, 1924; "Patients Mistreated and Mutilated by Illegal Operations at Insane Asylum," *Independent-Record* (Helena), October 5, 1924; "Butchery of Helpless is Officially Reported." *Independent-Record* (Helena), October 5, 1924, accessed April 2, 2020, newspapers.com; Paul A. Lombardo, *Three Generations, No Imbeciles: Eugenics, the Supreme Court, and Buck V. Bell* (Baltimore: Johns Hopkins University Press, 2008), 75.

42. Kayla Blackman, "The Right to Procreate: The Montana State Board of Eugenics and Body Politics," in *Beyond Schoolmarms and Madams: Montana Women's Stories*, ed. by Martha Kohl (Helena: Montana Historical Society Press, 2016), 238.

43. Clarence J. Gamble, "The Sterilization of Psychotic Patients under State Laws," *American Journal of Psychiatry*, 105, no. 1 (July 1948): 60–62; Julius Paul, "Three Generations of Imbeciles Are Enough': State Eugenic Sterilization in American Thought and Practice," 404–406; *Buck v Bell Documents*, Paper 95, 1965, accessed April 2, 2020, readingroom.law.gsu.edu.

44. James J. Lopach and Jean A. Luckowski, *Jeannette Rankin: A Political Woman* (Boulder: University Press of Colorado, 2005), 20; Edna Rankin McKinnon, Letter to Wilma Dykeman, March 20, 1973, Edna Rankin McKinnon Papers, Series 2, Arthur and Elizabeth Schlesinger Library, Harvard University.

45. Newspaper Clippings, *Knoxville News Sentinel*, Edna Rankin McKinnon Papers, Series 1, Arthur and Elizabeth Schlesinger Library, Harvard University.

46. Wilma Dykeman, *Too Many People, Too Little Love*, 207.

47. Wilma Dykeman, *Too Many People, Too Little Love*, 86.
48. Judy Flander, "Birth Control Champion at 81," *Washington Star News*, March 28, 1974, accessed January 18, 2020, judyflander.org.
49. Edna Rankin McKinnon, Letter to Mother and Family, April 12, 1942, Jeannette Rankin Papers, MC 147, Series 7.1, Montana Historical Society Research Center, Archives.
50. "A Vet at Fighting for a Cause," Newspaper Clipping, Edna Rankin McKinnon Papers, Series 1, Arthur and Elizabeth Schlesinger Library, Harvard University.
51. Patrick A. Curtis, "Eugenic Reformers, Cultural Perceptions of Dependent Populations, and the Care of the Feebleminded in Illinois, 1909–1920" (PhD diss., University of Illinois at Chicago, 1983), 4–64, 154; Harry H. Laughlin, *Eugenical Sterilization in the United States* (Chicago: Psychopathic Laboratory of the Municipal Court of Chicago, 1922), 354–355.
52. Wilma Dykeman, *Too Many People, Too Little Love*, 274–275.

Eight

1. Ronald H. Spector, "Vietnam War: 1954–1975," *Encyclopaedia Britannica*, accessed May 17, 2020, britannica.com.
2. Elaine Tyler May, *Homeward Bound: American Families in the Cold War Era* (New York: Basic Books, 2008), 9,12.
3. Ruth Schwartz Cowan, *More Work for Mother: The Ironies of Household Technology from the Open Hearth to the Microwave* (New York: Basic Books, 1985), 203; Mitra Toossi, "A Century of Change: The U.S. Labor Force, 1950–2050," accessed May 17, 2020, bls.gov.
4. "The Postwar Economy: 1945–1960," accessed May 20, 2020, countrystudies.us.
5. Matt Phillips, "American Labor-Union Strikes Are Almost Completely Extinct," February 11, 2015, accessed July 19, 2020, quartz.com.
6. Mark V. Siegler, *An Economic History of the United States: Connecting the Present with the Past* (New York: Springer, 2016), 2; "Life Expectancy in the USA, 1900–98," accessed April 5, 2020, u.demog.berkeley.edu; Ellen M. Plante, *Women at Home in Victorian America: A Social History* (New York: Facts on File, 1997), 2.
7. "Pioneer's Home Wrecked for New Bridge," *Missoulian*, October 1, 1958, accessed April 5, 2020, newspapers.com.
8. John Board, "The Lady from Montana: Jeannette Rankin" (Master's thesis, University of Wyoming, 1964), 6.
9. Wellington Rankin, Interview by Volney Steele, 28.
10. "Local Society," *Missoulian*, August 28, 1913, accessed June 11, 2020, newspapers.com.
11. Wellington Rankin, Interview with Volney Steele, 28.
12. Jeannette Rankin, Letter to Grace and Tom Kinney, April 24, Jeannette Rankin Papers, MC 147, Series 7.1, Montana Historical Society Research Center, Archives.
13. Jeannette Rankin, Letter to Olive Rankin, April 11, 1942, Jeannette Rankin Papers, MC 147, Series 7.1, Montana Historical Society Research Center, Archives; Grace Rankin McKinney. Letter to Jeannette Rankin, May 14, 1942, Jeannette Rankin Papers, MC 147, Series 7.1, Montana Historical Society Research Center, Archives; Grace Rankin McKinney, Letter to Edna McKinnon, January 9, 1946 and August 18, 1946, Edna Rankin McKinnon Papers, Series 1, Arthur and Elizabeth Schlesinger Library, Harvard University.
14. "Missoula Society," *Butte Miner*, August 6, 1916, accessed June 11, 2020, newspapers.com.
15. Wellington Rankin, Interview by John Board, 18.
16. Mary Rankin Bragg, Letter to Jeannette Rankin, July 22, 1942, Jeannette Rankin Papers, MC 147, Series 7.1, Montana Historical Society Research Center, Archives.
17. Mary Rankin Bragg, Letter to Wellington Rankin, November 17, 1933, Wellington D. Rankin Papers, MC 288, Personal Subgroup, Series 2.1, Montana Historical Society Research Center, Archives; James J. Lopach and Jean A. Luckowski, *Jeannette Rankin: A Political Woman* (Boulder: University Press of Colorado, 2005), 24.
18. Dan Maddox, Endorsements of Wellington Rankin, 1948, Rankin Family Papers, Box 4.2 and 4.3, Archives & Special Collections, Mansfield Library, University of Montana.

19. Harry L. Burns, Letter to Wellington Rankin, August 11, 1948, Wellington D. Rankin Papers, MC 288, Personal Subgroup, Series 2.1, Montana Historical Society Research Center, Archives; Richard K. Hines, "Wellington Duncan Rankin," 46.

20. Thomas E. Hachey, "American Profiles on Capitol Hill: A Confidential Study for the British Foreign Office in 1943," *Wisconsin Magazine of History* 57, no. 2 (Winter 1973–1974): 146–147.

21. "Miss Rankin Says War's in Offing," *Fort Worth Star Telegram*, January 24, 1947, accessed April 25, 2020, newspapers.com.

22. "Jeannette Rankin Arrives Here to Spend Summer," *Independent-Record* (Helena), June 3, 1951, accessed April 29, 2020, newspapers.com.

23. Wellington Rankin, Interview with John Board; Norma Smith, *Jeannette Rankin: America's Conscience*, 112; Ted Carlton Harris, *Jeannette Rankin: Suffragist, First Woman Elected to Congress, and Pacifist* (New York: Arno Press. 1982), 119; John Board, "The Lady from Montana: Jeannette Rankin" (Master's thesis, University of Wyoming, 1964), 133.

24. "Vietnam War U.S. Military Fatal Casualty Statistics," National Archives, accessed March 11, 2020, archives.gov.

25. Jeannette Rankin, Radio Address, 1967, Jeannette Rankin Papers, MC 147, Series 7.3, Montana Historical Society Research Center, Archives.

26. "Excerpts from Senate Debate on Tonkin Gulf Resolution," Vassar College, accessed February 25, 2020, vietnam.vassar.edu; Alan Axelrod, *America's Wars* (New York, John Wiley, 2002), 470.

27. "Urges Women's Role in Halting Viet War," *Indiana* (PA) *Gazette*, May 19, 1967, accessed January 3, 2020, newspapers.com.

28. Thomas S. Langston, *The Cold War Presidency: A Documentary History* (Washington, D.C.: CQ Press, 2007), 224; Katie Mettler, "The Day Anti-Vietnam War Protesters Tried to Levitate the Pentagon," *Washington Post*, October 19, 2017, accessed May 11, 2020, newspapers.com.

29. Margaret A. Kilgore, "Protestors Converge on Capital," *Ukiah* (CA) *Daily Journal*, January 15, 1968, accessed January 22, 2020, newspapers.com.

30. "Jeannette Rankin Voices 'Simple' Viet Formula," *Great Falls* (MT) *Tribune*, January 15, 1967, accessed March 30, 2020, newspapers.com.

31. Don Coe, "Jeannette Rankin: Voice against War," *Missoulian*, July 21, 1967, accessed December 31, 2019, newspapers.com.

32. Joan Hoff Wilson, "Remarks," in *Acceptance and Dedication of the Statue of Jeannette Rankin* (Washington, D.C.: U.S. Government Printing Office, 1987), 17–27.

33. "Kentuckians Join Rankin's Brigade," *Courier-Journal* (Lexington), January 16, 1968; "Marin Women to Join Viet Peace March," *Daily Independent Journal* (San Rafael, CA), December 12, 1967; "And Wearing Black," *Boston Globe*, January 9, 1968; Kathryn Johnson, "Jeannette Rankin Recruiting Ladies to Combat Bloodshed," *Selma Times-Journal*, January 5, 1968; "Jeannette Rankin Plans Peace March," *The Record* (Hackensack, NJ), December 15, 1967, accessed December 31, 2019, newspapers.com.

34. "Women's Groups Set War Protest," *Gazette and Daily* (York, PA), December 18, 1967, accessed February 23, 2020, newspapers.com.

35. Margaret A. Kilgore, "Protestors Converge on Capital," *Ukiah* (CA) *Daily Journal*, January 15, 1968, accessed January 22, 2020, newspapers.com.

36. "In Capital March: Women 'Vote' against War," *Springfield* (MO) *News-Leader*, January 16, 1968, accessed December 31, 2019, newspapers.com.

37. Elizabeth Dilling, *The Red Network: A "Who's Who" and Handbook of Radicalism for Patriots* (Chicago: Elizabeth Dilling, 1934); "Jeannette Rankin, FBI File," Jeannette Rankin Papers, MSS 785, Box 1, Archives & Special Collections, Mansfield Library, University of Montana; Walter Winchell, "New York Press Pass," *Lebanon* (PA) *Daily News*, January 24, 1968, accessed December 31, 2019, newspapers.com.

38. Jeannette Rankin, "On War and Nonviolence," in *Ten Fighters for Peace*, ed. Don Lawson (New York: Lothrop, Lee, & Shepard, 1971), 85–86.

39. Kate Walbert, "Has Anything Changed for Female Politicians? Familiar Echoes in the Candidacy of Jeannette Rankin, the First Woman Elected to Congress," *New Yorker*, August 16, 2016, accessed January 24, 2020, newyorker.com.

40. Jeannette Rankin Women's

Scholarship Fund, accessed July 11, 2020, rankinfoundation.org.

41. Allan James Mathews, *A Guide to Historic Missoula* (Helena: Montana Historical Society Press, 2002), 148–150.

42. Libby Morris, "Inspiration and Action: Life and Legacy of Jeannette Rankin," *Innovative Higher Education* 34, no. 5 (2009): 283–284.

43. Jeanne F. Cook, "Winning Isn't Everything: Jeannette Rankin's Views on War," *Affilia: Journal of Women & Social Work* 6, no. 4 (1991): 92.

44. Randy Engel, "The International Population-Control Machine and the Pathfinder Fund," accessed July 20, 2020, uscl.info.

45. Johanna Schoen, *Choice and Coercion: Birth Control, Sterilization, and Abortion in Public Health and Welfare* (Chapel Hill: University of North Carolina Press, 2005), 198.

46. Rosanna Ledbetter, "Thirty Years of Family Planning in India," *Asian Survey* 24, no. 7 (July 1984): 736–758.

47. Newspaper Clippings, *Fiji Times*, Edna Rankin McKinnon Papers, Series 1, Arthur and Elizabeth Schlesinger Library, Harvard University; Philip R. Reilly, *The Surgical Solution: A History of Involuntary Sterilization in the United States* (Baltimore: Johns Hopkins University Press, 1991), 2.

48. Donald P. Warwick, "The Indonesian Family Planning Program: Government Influence and Client Choice," *Population and Development Review* 12, no. 3 (September 1986): 453–490; Newspaper Clippings, *Fiji Times*, Edna Rankin McKinnon Papers, Series 1, Arthur and Elizabeth Schlesinger Library, Harvard University.

49. Newspaper Clippings, *Fiji Times* and *Malay Mail*, October 1960 and June 1961, Edna Rankin McKinnon Papers, Series 1, Arthur and Elizabeth Schlesinger Library, Harvard University.

50. Max Roser, Hannah Ritchie, and Bernadeta Dadonaite, "Child and Infant Mortality," accessed April 3, 2020, ourworldindata.org.

51. Wilma Dykeman, *Too Many People, Too Little Love*, 221–222.

52. Wilma Dykeman, *Too Many People, Too Little Love*, 236, 269–270.

53. Wilma Dykeman, *Too Many People, Too Little Love*, 236.

54. Wilma Dykeman, *Too Many People, Too Little Love*, 120.

55. Judy Flander, "Birth Control Champion at 81," *Washington Star News*, March 28, 1974, accessed January 18, 2020, judyflander.org.

56. Wilma Dykeman, *Too Many People, Too Little Love*, 83.

57. Judy Flander, "Birth Control Champion at 81."

Conclusion

1. Helen Bonner, Interview by Winfield Page, July 9, 1980, OH 104, Archives & Special Collections, Mansfield Library, University of Montana.

Bibliography

Acker, Caroline Jean. *Creating the American Junkie: Addiction Research in the Classic Era of Narcotic Control.* Baltimore: Johns Hopkins University Press, 2002.
Adams, Henry. *Selected Letters.* Edited by Ernest Samuels. Boston: Belknap Press, 1992.
Adams, Katherine H. *Claiming Her Place in Congress: Women from American Political Families as Legislators.* Jefferson, NC: McFarland, 2019.
Adams, Katherine H., and Michael L. Keene. *Alice Paul and the American Suffrage Campaign.* Urbana: University of Illinois Press, 2008.
Addams, Jane. *Newer Ideals of Peace.* New York: Macmillan, 1906.
"Advertise Suffrage." *West Virginian.* May 6, 1915. Accessed February 29, 2020, newspapers.com.
Agnew, Jeremy. *Crime, Justice and Retribution in the American West, 1850–1900.* Jefferson, NC: McFarland, 2017.
Airy, Helen. *Doughnut Dollies: American Red Cross Girls during World War II.* Santa Fe, NM: Sunstone Press, 1995.
Aldrich, Mark. "History of Workplace Safety in the United States, 1880–1970." Economic History Association. Accessed December 3, 2019, eh.net.
Alonso, Harriet Hyman. "Jeannette Rankin and the Women's Peace Union." *Montana: The Magazine of Western History* 39, no. 2 (Spring 1989): 34–49.
The American Red Cross with the Armed Forces. World War Regimental Histories. Accessed May 15, 2020, digicom.bpl.lib.me.us.
"American Women in World War II." February 28, 2020. Accessed April 19, 2020, history.com.
"And Wearing Black." *Boston Globe.* January 9, 1968. Accessed December 31, 2019, newspapers.com.
"Apologies Are Tendered." *Independent-Record* (Helena, MT). December 3, 1912. Accessed January 14, 2020, newspapers.com.
Armin, Harry C. Letter to Jeannette Rankin, December 9, 1941. Jeannette Rankin Papers. MC 147, Series 7.4. Montana Historical Society Research Center, Archives.
Armitage, Susan. "Through Women's Eyes: A New View of the West." In *The Women's West,* 9–18. Edited by Susan Armitage and Elizabeth Jameson. Norman: University of Oklahoma Press, 1987.
"Arraignment of Rankin Pending." *Independent-Record* (Helena). September 20, 1917. Accessed December 10, 2019, newspapers.com.
"Asks $65,000 for Damages." *Helena Independent.* February 23, 1912. Accessed December 15, 2019, newspapers.com.
"Asks Miss Rankin Recant; Montana Republican Leader Says State Deplores Anti-War Vote." *New York Times.* December 9, 1941. Accessed December 5, 2017, *New York Times* Historical Database.
"At the State University." *Anaconda Standard.* November 24, 1902. Accessed January 29, 2020, newspapers.com.
———. *Anaconda Standard.* December 5, 1902. Accessed January 29, 2020, newspapers.com.

Bibliography

"Attendance at Fair Is Twenty Thousand." *Anaconda Standard*. September 26, 1914. Accessed January 12, 2020, newspapers.com.
Axelrod, Alan. *America's Wars*. New York: John Wiley, 2002.
Baker, Jean H. *Margaret Sanger: A Life of Passion*. New York: Hill and Wang, 2011.
Barrere, Albert, and Charles G. Leland. *Dictionary of Slang, Jargon and Cant*. Vol. 1. London: Ballantyne, 1889.
Batchelor, Susan A. "'Getting Mad wi' It': Risk Seeking by Young Women." In *Gendered Risks*, 205–228. Edited by Kelly Hannah-Moffat and Pat O'Malley. London: Routledge-Cavendish, 2007.
Bates, James Leonard. *Senator Thomas J. Walsh of Montana: Law and Public Affairs, from TR to FDR*. Urbana: University of Illinois Press, 1999.
Bayly, Ronald, and Nancy Landgren. *Jeannette Rankin: The Woman Who Voted No*. Alexandria, VA: PBS Video, 1984. DVD.
Beck, Ulrich. *Risk Society: Towards a New Modernity*. Translated by Mark Ritter. Newbury Park, CA: Sage Publications, 1992.
Bellesiles, Michael A. *1877: America's Year of Living Violently*. New York: New Press, 2010.
Benedict, Burton. *The Anthropology of World's Fairs: San Francisco Panama Pacific International Exposition of 1915*. London: Lowie Museum of Anthropology, 1983.
Bethell, John T. *Harvard Observed: An Illustrated History of the University in the Twentieth Century*. Boston: Harvard University Press, 1998.
Black, Edwin. *War against the Weak: Eugenics and America's Campaign to Create a Master Race*. Washington, D.C.: Dialog Press, 2012.
Blackman, Kayla. "The Right to Procreate: The Montana State Board of Eugenics and Body Politics." In *Beyond Schoolmarms and Madams: Montana Women's Stories*, 237–240. Edited by Martha Kohl. Helena: Montana Historical Society Press, 2016.
Bly, Nellie. *Ten Days in a Mad House*. New York: Ian L. Munro, 1887.
Board, John. "The Lady from Montana: Jeannette Rankin." Master's thesis, University of Wyoming, 1964.
Bonner, Helen. Interview by Winfield Page, July 9, 1980. OH 104-001. Archives & Special Collections, Mansfield Library, University of Montana.
"Boom and Bust: The Industries That Settled Montana." DPLA: Digital Public Library of America. Accessed November 10, 2020, dp.la/exhibitions.
Botkin, Jane Little. *Frank Little and the IWW: The Blood That Stained an American Family*. Norman: University of Oklahoma Press, 2017.
Bowers, R.J. Letter to Jeannette Rankin, December 14, 1941. Jeannette Rankin Papers, MC 147, Series 7.4, Montana Historical Society Research Center, Archives.
Braden, Maria. *Women Politicians and the Media*. Lexington: University Press of Kentucky, 1996.
Bragg, Mary Rankin. Letter to Jeannette Rankin, July 22, 1942. Jeannette Rankin Papers. MC 147, Series 7.1. Montana Historical Society Research Center, Archives.
_____. Letter to Kappa Kappa Gamma, May 1959. Mary Elrod Ferguson Papers. MSS 205, Series 8, Box 4.3. Archives & Special Collections, Mansfield Library, University of Montana.
Brandeis, Louis D. *Other People's Money and How the Bankers Use It*. New York: Frederick A. Stokes, 1914.
_____. "A Speech on Suffrage Given by Louis D. Brandeis at the Tremont Temple." Louis D. Brandeis School of Law Library. Accessed February 7, 2020, louisville.edu/law/library.
Brandon, Ruth. *The Spiritualists: The Passion for the Occult in the Nineteenth and Twentieth Centuries*. New York: Alfred A. Knopf, 1983.
Braude, Ann. *Radical Spirits: Spiritualism and Women's Rights in Nineteenth-Century America*. 2nd ed. Urbana: Indiana University Press, 2001.
Bredbenner, Candace Lewis. *A Nationality of Her Own: Women, Marriage, and the Law of Citizenship*. Berkeley: University of California Press, 1998.
"Brief News Notes." *Anaconda Standard*. October 23, 1895. Accessed June 11, 2020, newspapers.com.
"Briefs and Personals." *Anaconda Standard*. January 15, 1897. Accessed May 12, 2019, newspapers.com.

Bibliography 199

Briggeman, Kim. "100 Missoula Icons: Grant Creek Retains Rural Nature." *Missoulian*. September 18, 2014. Accessed March 14, 2020, missoulian.com.
Brock, Peter. *Freedom from War: Nonsectarian Pacifism, 1814–1914*. Toronto: University of Toronto Press, 1991.
———. *Pacifism in the United States: From the Colonial Era to the First World War*. Princeton: Princeton University Press, 1968.
Brown, Dorothy McKinnon. Letter to Jeannette Rankin, December 17, 1968. Jeannette Rankin Papers. Box 3. Montana Historical Society Research Center, Archives.
Buck v Bell Documents, Paper 95. 1965. Accessed April 2, 2020, readingroom.law.gsu.edu.
"Butchery of Helpless is Officially Reported." *Independent-Record* (Helena). October 5, 1924. Accessed April 22, 2020, newspapers.com.
Butterfield, L.C. Letter to Jeannette Rankin, May 10, 1918. Jeannette Rankin Papers. MC 147, Box 2.1. Montana Historical Society Research Center, Archives.
Byerly, Carol R. "War Losses (USA)." *International Encyclopedia of the First World War*. Accessed February 12, 2020, encyclopedia.1914-1918-online.net.
Callahan, Timothy D. *UFOs, Chemtrails, and Aliens: What Science Says*. Bloomington: Indiana University Press, 2017.
"Called the Bluff." *Missoulian*. October 17, 1914. Accessed January 7, 2020, newspapers.com.
Campbell, Alex. "Keeping the 'Lady' Safe: The Regulation of Femininity through Crime Prevention." *Critical Criminology* 13 (2005): 119–140.
Campus Newspaper Clippings, January 4, 1928 and November 7, 1928. Mary Elrod Ferguson Papers. MSS 205, Series 3, Box 1.11. Archives & Special Collections, Mansfield Library, University of Montana.
Carroll, Bret E. *Spiritualism in Antebellum America*. Bloomington: Indiana University Press, 1997.
Cary, Alice. *Clovernook*. New York: Redfield, 1852.
Cashman, Sean Dennis. *America in the Gilded Age: From the Death of Lincoln to the Rise of Theodore Roosevelt*. 2nd ed. New York: New York University Press, 1984.
Castillo, Edward D. "California Indian History." California Native American Heritage Commission. Accessed June 26, 2020, nahc.ca.gov.
Census Reports. 12th census, 1900. Vol. 1. Washington, D.C.: GPO, 1901.
Chafe, William H. *The American Woman: Her Changing Social, Economic, and Political Roles, 1920–1970*. New York: Oxford University Press, 1972.
Challenge to Survive: History of the Salish Tribes of the Flathead Indian Reservation. Vol. 2. Philadelphia: Franklin Classics Trade Press, 2018.
Chalmers, David Mark. *Neither Socialism nor Monopoly: Theodore Roosevelt and the Decision to Regulate the Railroads*. Philadelphia: Lippincott, 1976.
"Charles William Berry." Document Center, City of Missoula Website. Accessed January 11, 2020, ci.missoula.mt.us.
Cheek, Katrina Rebecca. "The Rhetoric and Revolt of Jeannette Rankin." Master's thesis, University of Georgia, 1969.
"Chilly Experience Described in Suit." *Butte Miner*. September 25, 1912. Accessed March 20, 2020, newspapers.com.
"Chronology of the New Zealand Health System 1840 to 2017." Accessed February 3, 2020, health.govt.nz.
"City in Brief." *Missoulian*. April 13, 1904. Accessed February 12, 2020, newspapers.com.
"Civil War Facts." The Civil War. PBS. Accessed August 12, 2020, pbs.org/kenburns/civil-war.
Clappe, Louise Smith. *California in 1851: The Shirley Letters from California Mines in 1851–52*. San Francisco: T.C. Russell Press, 1922.
Clarke, Edward. *Sex and Education: Or, A Fair Chance for Girls*. New York: J.R. Osgood, 1873.
"Commencement Exercises." *Missoulian*. June 4, 1898. Accessed May 7, 2020, newspapers.com.
"The Complicated Lead Up to Pearl Harbor." December 7, 2016. Accessed March 1, 2020, airandspace.si.edu.
"Concert." *Missoulian*. December 15, 1896. Accessed May 9, 2019, newspapers.com.
Congressional Record: Proceedings and Debates of the Second Session of the Sixty-Fifth

Bibliography

Congress. Vol. 56. Part 2. January 22, 1918. Washington, D.C.: U.S. Government Printing Office, 1918.
"The Congressional Union for Woman Suffrage." *Suffragist* (November 15, 1913): 2.
"Contraception: Past, Present, and Future." Accessed April 1, 2020, fpa.org.uk.
Cook, Jeanne F. "Winning Isn't Everything: Jeannette Rankin's Views on War." *Affilia: Journal of Women & Social Work* 6, no. 4 (1991): 92–104.
Cunningham, Raymond J. "The Impact of Christian Science on the American Churches, 1880–1910." *American Historical Review* 72, no. 3 (April 1967): 885–905.
Curtis, Patrick A. "Eugenic Reformers, Cultural Perceptions of Dependent Populations, and the Care of the Feebleminded in Illinois, 1909–1920." PhD diss., University of Illinois at Chicago, 1983.
Daniell, Jere R. *Colonial New Hampshire: A History.* Millwood, NY: KTO Press, 1981.
Dean, Mary. Letter to Jeannette Rankin, July 22, 1918. Jeannette Rankin Papers. MC 147, Box 2.1. Montana Historical Society Research Center, Archives.
DeBenedetti, Charles. *Peace Heroes in Twentieth-Century America.* Bloomington: Indiana University Press, 1988.
"Democracy's Mental Dissolution Pictured as Nazi Goal in U.S." *Christian Science Monitor* (July 20, 1940): 15.
Dennison, George M. *Montana's Pioneer Naturalist: Morton J. Elrod.* Norman: University of Oklahoma Press, 2016.
de Young, Mary. *Madness: An American History of Mental Illness and Its Treatment.* Jefferson, NC: McFarland, 2010.
Dilling, Elizabeth. *The Red Network: A "Who's Who" and Handbook of Radicalism for Patriots.* Chicago: Elizabeth Dilling, 1934.
"Doctor of Medicine Profession." Medline Plus. U.S. National Library of Medicine. Accessed January 4, 2020, medlineplus.gov.
"The Doings of a Week." *Anaconda Standard.* February 9, 1890. Accessed May 2, 2020, newspapers.com.
"Doom of the Gold Coast." *Harvard Alumni Bulletin* 22 (1919): 561.
Douglas, Emily Taft. *Margaret Sanger: Pioneer of the Future.* New York: Holt, Rinehart, and Winston, 1969.
Dufresne, Mildred. *Grant Creek and Its One-Room School.* Missoula: Delta Kappa Gamma, 1981.
Dumenil, Lynn. *The Second Line of Defense: American Women and World War I.* Chapel Hill: University of North Carolina Press, 2017.
Durr, Eric. "Worldwide Flu Outbreak Killed 45,000 American Soldiers during World War I." U.S. Army. August 31, 2018. Accessed February 2, 2020, army.mil.
Dykeman, Wilma. *Too Many People, Too Little Love: Edna Rankin McKinnon, Pioneer for Birth Control.* New York: Holt, Rinehart and Winston, 1974.
Eddy, Mary Baker. *Science and Health.* Boston: Christian Science Publishing, 1875.
Edgerton, Keith. "Wellington Rankin: His Family, Life, and Times." *Montana: The Magazine of Western History* 53, no. 2 (June 2003): 86–87.
"An Election Special—A Voter's Guide." 1948. Rankin Family Papers. Box 4.4. Archives & Special Collections, Mansfield Library, University of Montana.
Emerson, Elizabeth H. *Glimpses of a Life.* Burlington, NC: J.S. Sargent, 1960.
Engel, Randy. "The International Population-Control Machine and the Pathfinder Fund." Accessed July 20, 2020, uscl.info.
Engleman, Peter. *A History of the Birth Control Movement in America.* Santa Barbara, CA: Praeger, 2011.
Englund, Will. *March 1917: On the Brink of War and Revolution.* New York: Norton, 2017.
Enss, Chris. *Frontier Teachers: Stories of Heroic Women of the Old West.* Helena, MT: TwoDot, 2008.
"Equal Pay for Women." *New York Times.* November 12, 1916. Accessed April 2, 2018, *New York Times* Historical Database.
Ewald, Donna, and Peter Clute. *San Francisco Invites the World: The Panama-Pacific International Exposition of 1915.* San Francisco: Chronicle Books, 1991.

"Excellent Oat Crop." *Anaconda Standard*. August 26, 1901. Accessed June 14, 2020, newspapers.com.
"Excerpts from Senate Debate on Tonkin Gulf Resolution." Vassar College. Accessed February 25, 2020, vietnam.vassar.edu.
Faber, Doris. *Petticoat Politics: How American Women Won the Right to Vote*. New York: LothroPress, Lee and Shepard, 1967.
Faderman, Lillian. *Odd Girls and Twilight Lovers: A History of Lesbian Life in Twentieth-Century America*. New York: Columbia University Press, 1991.
Farkas, Caryl Emra. "Destination: Health and Wholeness." *Christian Science Sentinel*. May 13, 2013. Accessed February 3, 2020, sentinel.christianscience.com.
Farnham, Eliza. *Life in Prairie Land*. New York: Harpers, 1846.
"Fatal Accident." *Butte Weekly Miner*. April 4, 1885. Accessed January 6, 2020, newspapers.com.
"5000 Women March, Beset by Crowds." *New York Times*. March 4, 1913. Accessed February 15, 2020, newspapers.com.
Flander, Judy. "Birth Control Champion at 81." *Washington Star News*. March 28, 1974. Accessed January 18, 2020, judyflander.org.
Flexner, Abraham. *Medical Education in the United States and Canada: A Report to the Carnegie Foundation for the Advancement of Teaching*. New York: Carnegie Foundation for the Advancement of Teaching, 1910.
Foerstel, Karen, and Herbert N. Foerstel. *Climbing the Hill: Gender Conflict in Congress*. Westport, CT: Praeger, 1996.
"A Forest Guessing Party." *Missoulian*. July 5, 1903. Accessed April 12, 2020, newspapers.com.
Franks, Angela. *Margaret Sanger's Eugenic Legacy: The Control of Female Fertility*. Jefferson, NC: McFarland, 2014.
"From Missoula." *New North-West* (Deer Lodge, MT). June 1, 1883. Accessed January 14, 2020, newspapers.com.
"From Missoula to Washington, D.C., to Aid Cause of Equal Suffrage." *Missoulian*. August 10, 1913. Accessed February 17, 2020, newspapers.com.
Fuller, Margaret. *Summer on the Lakes*. Boston: Charles C. Little and James Brown, 1843.
Gabriel, Mary. *Notorious Victoria: The Life of Victoria Woodhull, Uncensored*. Chapel Hill, NC: Algonquin Books, 1998.
Gamble, Clarence. "Eugenic Sterilization in the United States." *Eugenical News* 34, no. 1–2 (March-June 1949): 1–5.
Gandhi, Mahatma. *Satyagraha in South Africa*. Translated by Valji Govindji Desai. Ahmedabad, India: Navajivan, 1961.
Gartrell-Mills, Claire F. *Christian Science: An American Religion in Britain, 1895–1940*. PhD diss., Oxford University, 1991.
Gidley, Mick. *Edward S. Curtis and the North American Indian, Incorporated*. New York: Cambridge University Press, 2000.
Giles, Kevin S. *Flight of the Dove: The Story of Jeannette Rankin*. Beaverton, OR: Touchstone Press, 1980.
———. *One Woman against War: The Jeannette Rankin Story*. St. Petersburg, FL: BookLocker.com, 2016.
"Good Men and True." *Anaconda Standard*. March 30, 1891. Accessed May 12, 2020, newspapers.com.
Goodell, Charles. *Political Prisoners in America*. New York: Random House, 1973.
Gordon, Linda. *The Moral Property of Women: A History of Birth Control Politics in America*. Urbana: University of Illinois Press, 2002.
Gottschalk, Stephen. *The Emergence of Christian Science in American Religious Life*. Berkeley: University of California Press, 1973.
Gouveia, Michele. "Running Wild: College Students in the 1920s, by Mrs. Parker." 2004. Accessed March 17, 2020, sarahbaker.org.
Green, Martin. *Gandhi: Voice of a New Age Revolution*. New York: Continuum, 1993.
Greene, Jerome. *Nez Perce Summer 1877: The U.S. Army and the Nee-Me-Poo Crisis*. Helena, MT: Montana Historical Society Press, 2000. Accessed April 22, 2020, nps.gov.

Bibliography

Griswold, Robert I. "Anglo Women and Domestic Ideology in the American West in the Nineteenth and Early Twentieth Centuries." In *Western Women: Their Land, Their Lives*, 15–34. Edited by Lillian Schlissel, Vicki L. Ruiz, and Janice Monk. Albuquerque: University of New Mexico Press, 1988.

Gustafson, Per E. "Gender Difference in Risk Perception: Theoretical and Methodological Perspectives." *Risk Analysis* 18, no. 6 (1998): 805–811.

Gutfeld, Arnon. *Montana's Agony: Years of War and Hysteria, 1917–21*. Gainesville: University Press of Florida, 1979.

Hachey, Thomas E. "American Profiles on Capitol Hill: A Confidential Study for the British Foreign Office in 1943." *Wisconsin Magazine of History* 57, no. 2 (Winter 1973–1974): 141–153.

Hale, Sarah Josepha. *Manners; or, Happy Homes and Good Society All the Year Round*. Boston: J.E. Tilton, 1868.

Haller, John S. *American Medicine in Transition, 1840–1910*. Urbana: University of Illinois Press, 1981.

Hamby, Alonzo L. "Progressivism: A Century of Change and Rebirth." In *Progressivism and the New Democracy*, 40–80. Edited by Sidney M. Milkis and Jerome M. Mileur. Amherst: University of Massachusetts Press, 1999.

Hamilton, Alexander V. *The Household Cyclopaedia of Practical Receipts and Daily Wants*. Springfield: W.J. Holland & Co., 1873.

"Hanged by the Neck." *Butte Daily Post*. December 19, 1890. Accessed March 23, 2020, newspapers.com.

Harland, Marion. *Breakfast, Luncheon, and Tea*. New York: Scribners, 1875.

———. *Eve's Daughters*. New York: Scribner's, 1881.

Harper, Marjory. *Adventurers and Exiles: The Great Scottish Exodus*. London: Profile Books, 2003.

———. "Exiles or Entrepreneurs: Snapshots of the Scots in Canada." In *A Kingdom of the Mind: How the Scots Helped Make Canada*, 22–39. Edited by Peter E. Rider and Heather McNabb. Montreal: McGill-Queen's University Press, 2006.

———. "Some Patterns of Scottish Settlements in Nineteenth-Century Canada." In *Frontiers of European Culture*, 137–168. Edited by Paul Dukes. Lewiston, Wales: Edwin Mellen, 1996.

"Harriet Rankin." *Missoulian*. June 7, 1903. Accessed April 14, 2020, newspapers.com.

Harris, Ted Carlton. *Jeannette Rankin: Suffragist, First Woman Elected to Congress, and Pacifist*. New York: Arno Press. 1982.

Hartwick, Louis M. *Oceana County Pioneers and Business Men of To-day: History, Biography, Statistics and Humorous Incidents*. Pentwater, MI: Pentwater News Steam Print, 1890.

Harwarth, Irene, Mindi Maline, and Elizabeth DeBra. *Women's Colleges in the United States*. Washington, D.C.: U.S. Department of Education, 1997.

Hayden, Ferdinand Vandeveer. *The Great West: Its Attractions and Resources*. Washington, D.C.: C.R. Brodix, 1880.

Hayden, Sara. "Negotiating Femininity and Power in the Early Twentieth Century West: Domestic Ideology and Feminine Style in Jeannette Rankin's Suffrage Rhetoric." *Communication Studies* 50, no. 2 (Summer 1999): 83–103.

Hayter, Alethe A. "'The Laudanum Bottle Loomed Large': Opium in the English Literary World in the Nineteenth Century." *Ariel: A Review of International English Literature* 11, no. 4 (1980): 37–51.

Haywood, C. Robert. *Victorian West: Class and Culture in Kansas Cattle Towns*. Lawrence: University Press of Kansas, 1991.

Heffernan, Nancy Coffey, and Ann Page Stecker. *New Hampshire: Crosscurrents in Its Development*. 3rd ed. Hanover: University Press of New England, 2004.

"Helena Lawyer Has Fracas at Inquest." *Butte Miner*. September 20, 1917. Accessed December 10, 2019, newspapers.com.

"Helena's Society Queen Marries Young Lawyer." *Butte Miner*. March 3, 1910. Accessed March 7, 2020, newspapers.com.

Herrick, Robert. "Two Sorts of Pacifists." *Chicago Tribune*. June 4, 1916. Accessed July 25, 2020, newspapers.com.

Herrick, Una. "Twenty Years at Montana State College." Merrill G. Burlingame Research Files on MSU History. Series 4. Montana State University Library.
Hevel, Michael S. "Toward a History of Student Affairs: A Synthesis of Research, 1996–2015." *Journal of College Student Development* 57, no. 7 (October 2016): 844–862.
Hines, Richard K. "Wellington Duncan Rankin: The Man behind the Myth." Master's thesis, Washington State University, 1996.
Hirschhorn, Norbert, R.G. Feldman, and I.A. Greaves. "Abraham Lincoln's Blue Pills: Did Our 16th President Suffer from Mercury Poisoning?" *Perspectives in Biology and Medicine* 44, no. 3 (2001): 315–322.
Hodges, Sherry. "A History of Hatred and Discrimination." *Missoulian*. June 17, 1980. Accessed January 4, 2020, newspapers.com.
Hofstadter, Richard. *The Age of Reform: From Bryan to F.D.R.* New York: Alfred Knopf, 1963.
Holbrook, Stewart. "The Lady of Lynn, Mrs. Pinkham." In *The Golden Age of Quackery*, 63–70. New York: Collier Books, 1959.
Holley, Mary Austin. *Texas*. Baltimore: Armstrong and Plaskitt, 1833.
Holmes, Krys, Susan C. Dailey, and David Walter. *Montana: Stories of the Land*. Helena: Montana Historical Society, 2008.
Holmes, Lulu Haskell. *A History of the Position of Dean of Women in a Selected Group of Co-educational Colleges and Universities in the United States*. New York: Teachers College, Columbia University, 1939.
Howard, Joseph Kinsey. *Montana: High, Wide, and Handsome*. New Haven: Yale University Press, 1959.
Howes, Dustin Ellis. "The Failure of Pacifism and the Success of Nonviolence." *Perspectives on Politics* 11, no. 2 (2013): 427–446.
"The Hudson's Bay Question and Ministerial Policy." *Gazette of Montreal*. February 12, 1857. Accessed January 30, 2020, newspapers. com.
"Hughes Not Guilty." *Missoulian*. November 30, 1902. Accessed January 29, 2020, newspapers.com.
Husock, Howard A. "Bringing Back the Settlement House." *Public Welfare* 51, no. 4 (1993): 16–25.
Hutton, Paul Andrew. *Phil Sheridan and His Army*. Lincoln: University of Nebraska Press, 1985.
"In Capital March: Women 'Vote' against War." *Springfield* (MO) *News-Leader*. January 16, 1968. Accessed December 31, 2019, newspapers.com.
"In Missoula." *Anaconda Standard*. January 5, 1902. Accessed April 12, 2020, newspapers. com.
Jameson, Elizabeth. "Women as Workers, Women as Civilizers: True Womanhood in the American West." *Frontiers* 7 (1984): 1–9.
"Japan's Imports Cut 75% by War." *New York Times*. December 2, 1941. Accessed February 20, 2020, *New York Times* Historical Database.
"Jeannette Rankin Explains Peace Pacts to Outlaw War." *Havre* (MT) *Daily News*. September 4, 1928. Accessed July 19, 2019, newspapers.com.
"Jeannette Rankin, FBI File." Jeannette Rankin Papers. MSS 785, Box 1. Archives & Special Collections, Mansfield Library, University of Montana.
"Jeannette Rankin Plans Peace March." *The Record* (Hackensack, NJ). December 15, 1967. Accessed December 31, 2019, newspapers.com.
"Jeannette Rankin Voices 'Simple' Viet Formula." *Great Falls* (MT) *Tribune*. January 15, 1967. Accessed March 30, 2020, newspapers.com.
Jeannette Rankin Women's Scholarship Fund. Accessed July 11, 2020, rankinfoundation.org.
Jeansonne, Glen. "The Lone Dissenting Voice." *American History* 34, no. 6 (2006): 46–53.
Jefferson, Thomas. *Notes on the State of Virginia*. London: John Stockdale, 1787.
"John Rankin Ends Notable Life." *Missoulian*. May 4, 1904. Accessed February 14, 2020, newspapers.com.
Johnson, Kathryn. "Jeannette Rankin Recruiting Ladies to Combat Bloodshed." *Selma Times-Journal*. January 5, 1968. Accessed December 31, 2019, newspapers.com.
Josephson, Hannah. *Jeannette Rankin: First Lady in Congress, A Biography*. Indianapolis: Bobbs-Merrill, 1974.

"Jury Finds Frank Hall Guilty." *Missoulian*. March 13, 1917. Accessed May 14, 2020, newspapers.com.
"Juvenile Society Event." *Missoulian*. August 2, 1908. Accessed January 20, 2020, newspapers.com.
Karolevitz, Robert F. *Doctors of the Old West: A Pictorial History of Medicine on the Frontier.* Seattle: Superior Publishing, 1967.
Katzenstein, Caroline. *Lifting the Curtain: The State and National Woman Suffrage Campaigns in Pennsylvania as I Saw Them.* Philadelphia: Dorrance, 1955.
Kaufman, Polly Welts. *Women Teachers of the Frontier.* New Haven: Yale University Press, 1984.
"Kentuckians Join Rankin's Brigade." *Courier-Journal* (Lexington). January 16, 1968. Accessed December 31, 2019, newspapers.com.
Kessler, Robert. "Outbreak: Pandemic Strikes." Accessed February 2, 2020, ecohealthalliance.org.
Kilgore, Margaret A. "Protestors Converge on Capital." *Ukiah* (CA) *Daily Journal.* January 15, 1968. Accessed January 22, 2020, newspapers.com.
Kirkland, Caroline (as Mary Clavers). *A New Home—Who'll Follow?* New York: Charles S. Francis, 1841.
Kirkley, John. "An Afternoon with Jeannette Rankin." Jeannette Rankin: Activist for World Peace, Women's Rights, and Democratic Government, 149–152. University of California at Berkeley Suffragists Oral History Project. Accessed June 18, 2020, lib.berkeley.edu.
Kolodny, Annette. *The Lay of the Land: Metaphor as Experience and History in American Life and Letters.* Chapel Hill: University of North Carolina Press, 1975.
Korson, George. *At His Side: The Story of the American Red Cross Overseas in World War II.* New York: Coward-McCann, 1945.
Kraft, Louise G. "A History of the Certification of Montana Teachers." Master's thesis, University of Montana, 1936.
Krakauer, Jon. *Missoula: Rape and the Justice System in a College Town.* New York: Doubleday, 2015.
Lackmann, Ronald W. *Women of the Western Frontier in Fact, Fiction, and Film.* Jefferson, NC: McFarland, 1997.
Lake, David A. *Entangling Relations: American Foreign Policy in Its Century.* Princeton, NJ: Princeton University Press, 1999.
Langston, Thomas S. *The Cold War Presidency: A Documentary History.* Washington, D.C.: CQ Press, 2007.
Lantzer, James S. "The Indiana Way of Eugenics: Sterilization Laws, 1907–1974." In *A Century of Eugenics in America: From the Indiana Experiment to the Human Genome Era,* 26–41. Edited by Paul A. Lombardo. Bloomington: Indiana University Press, 2011.
Laughlin, Harry H. *Eugenical Sterilization in the United States.* Chicago: Psychopathic Laboratory of the Municipal Court of Chicago, 1922.
Laurendeau, Jason. "Gendered Risk Regimes: A Theoretical Consideration of Edgework and Gender." *Sociology of Sport Journal* 25 (2008): 293–309.
Leavitt, Judith Walzer. *Brought to Bed: Child-Bearing in America, 1750–1950.* New York: Oxford University Press, 1986.
Ledbetter, Rosanna. "Thirty Years of Family Planning in India." *Asian Survey* 24, no. 7 (July 1984): 736–758.
Lehman, Amy. *Victorian Women and the Theatre of Trance: Mediums, Spiritualists and Mesmerists in Performance.* Jefferson, NC: McFarland, 2009.
Lennon, Bert. "Jeannette Rankin Is Well Qualified to Serve in Congress." *Oregon Daily Journal.* December 3, 1916. Accessed August 7, 2019, newspapers.com.
Lieberman, Jeffrey A. *Shrinks: The Untold Story of Psychiatry.* New York: Little, Brown, 2015.
"Life Expectancy in the USA, 1900–98." Accessed April 5, 2020, u.demog.berkeley.edu.
Lindley, Susan Hill. *Woman's Profession in the Life and Thought of Catharine Beecher: A Study of Religion and Reform.* Durham: Duke University Press, 1978.
Link, Arthur Stanley. *Progressivism.* New York: Wiley-Blackwell, 1983.
_____. *Wilson: Campaigns for Progressivism and Peace, 1916–1917.* Vol. 5. New Haven: Princeton University Press, 1965.

Little, Jo, Ruth Panelli, and Anna Kraack. "Women's Fear of Crime: A Rural Perspective." *Journal of Rural Studies* 21 (2005): 151–163.
"Local Society." *Missoulian*. August 28, 1913. Accessed June 11, 2020, newspapers.com.
Lombardo, Paul A. *Three Generations, No Imbeciles: Eugenics, the Supreme Court, and Buck v. Bell*. Baltimore: Johns Hopkins University Press, 2008.
Lopach, James J., and Jean A. Luckowski. *Jeannette Rankin: A Political Woman*. Boulder: University Press of Colorado, 2005.
Luchetti, Cathy. *Children of the West: Family Life on the Frontier*. New York: Norton, 2001.
Lundie, Rob, and Joy McCann. "Commonwealth Parliament from 1901 to World War I." May 2015. Accessed July 3, 2020, newspapers.com.
"Lyman Beecher." In *Appleton's Cyclopædia of American Biography*. Vol. 1, 216–217. Edited by James Grant Wilson and John Fiske. New York: D. Appleton, 1888.
Lyng, Stephen. "Edgework: A Social Psychological Analysis of Voluntary Risk Taking." *American Journal of Sociology* 95, no. 4 (1990): 851–886.
Lyng, Stephen, and Rick Matthews. "Risk, Edgework, and Masculinities." In *Gendered Risks*, 75–97. Edited by Kelly Hannah-Moffat and Pat O'Malley. New York: Routledge-Cavendish, 2007.
The Lyre of Alpha Chi Omega. 1922. Vol. 26. Charleston, SC: Nabu Press, 2012.
MacPherson, Myra. *The Scarlet Sisters: Sex, Suffrage, and Scandal in the Gilded Age*. New York: Twelve, 2014.
Madison, James H. *Slinging Doughnuts for the Boys: An American Woman in World War II*. Bloomington: Indiana University Press, 2007.
Malone, Michael P., and Dianne G. Dougherty. "Montana's Political Culture: A Century of Evolution." *Montana: The Magazine of Western History* 31, no. 1 (1981): 44–58.
Malone, Michael P., Richard B. Roeder, and William L. Lang. *Montana: A History of Two Centuries*. Rev. ed. Seattle: University of Washington Press, 1976.
The Manners That Win. Minneapolis: Buckeye Publishing, 1880.
Margolick, David. "In Child Deaths, a Test for Christian Science." *New York Times*. August 6, 1990. Accessed April 30, 2020, nytimes.com.
"Marin Women to Join Viet Peace March." *Daily Independent Journal* (San Rafael, CA). December 12, 1967. Accessed December 31, 2019, newspapers.com.
Mathews, Allan James. *A Guide to Historic Missoula*. Helena: Montana Historical Society Press, 2002.
Mathews, Lois. *The Dean of Women*. Boston: Houghton Mifflin, 1915.
May, Elaine Tyler. *Homeward Bound: American Families in the Cold War Era*. New York: Basic Books, 2008.
McCann, Carole M. *Birth Control Politics in the United States*. Ithaca: Cornell University Press, 1994.
McGerr, Michael. *A Fierce Discontent: The Rise and Fall of the Progressive Movement in America*. New York: Simon & Schuster, 2010.
McGregor, Harriet Rankin. Letter to Wellington Rankin, April 2, 1944. Wellington D. Rankin Papers. MC 288, Personal Subgroup, Series 2.1. Montana Historical Society Research Center, Archives.
McGuffey, William Holmes. "The Three Boys and the Three Cakes." In *McGuffey's New First Eclectic Reader: For Little Children*, 29–31. Cincinnati: Sargent, Wilson, Hinkle, 1857.
McGuinness, Margaret. *Called to Serve: A History of Nuns in America*. New York: New York University Press, 2015.
McKay, Ian, and Robin Bates. *In the Province of History: The Making of the Public Past in Twentieth-Century Nova Scotia*. Montreal: McGill-Queen's University Press, 2010.
McKinney, Grace Rankin. Letter to Edna McKinnon, January 9, 1946. Edna Rankin McKinnon Papers. Series 1. Schlesinger Library, Radcliffe Institute, Harvard University.
———. Letter to Jeannette Rankin, May 14, 1942. Jeannette Rankin Papers. MC 147, Series 7.1. Montana Historical Society Research Center, Archives.
McKinnon, Edna Rankin. Job Application. Edna Rankin McKinnon Papers. Series 1. Schlesinger Library, Radcliffe Institute, Harvard University.

Bibliography

———. Letter to Dorothy McKinnon Brown, October 2, 1972. Edna Rankin McKinnon Papers. Series 1. Schlesinger Library, Radcliffe Institute, Harvard University.

———. Letter to Mary Rankin Bragg, September 3, 1963. Edna Rankin McKinnon Papers. Series 1. Schlesinger Library, Radcliffe Institute, Harvard University.

———. Letter to Mother and Family, April 12, 1942. Jeannette Rankin Papers. MC 147, Series 7.1. Montana Historical Society Research Center, Archives.

———. Letter to Wellington Rankin, June 7, 1942. Edna Rankin McKinnon Papers. Series 2. Schlesinger Library, Radcliffe Institute, Harvard University.

———. Letter to Wellington Rankin, June 16, 1959. Wellington D. Rankin Papers. MC 288, Personal Subgroup, Series 2.1. Montana Historical Society Research Center, Archives.

———. Letter to Wilma Dykeman, March 20, 1973. Edna Rankin McKinnon Papers. Series 2. Schlesinger Library, Radcliffe Institute, Harvard University.

McLemore, Henry. "Perfect Montana Congressman Would Make a Perfect 'Enemy' Wife for Any American Male." *Pittsburgh Press*. December 12, 1941. Accessed January 29, 2020, newspapers.com.

Melcher, Mary. "'Women's Matters': Birth Control, Prenatal Care, and Childbirth in Rural Montana, 1910–1940." In *Montana Legacy: Essays on History, People, and Place*, 132–151. Edited by Harry W. Fritz, Mary Murphy, and Robert R. Swartout, Jr. Helena, MT: Montana Historical Society, 2002.

"Memorial Proceedings on the Death of Hon. Oscar A. Sedman." *Helena Weekly Herald*. February 17, 1881. Accessed January 31, 2020, newspapers.com.

Merriam, H.G. "The Clapp Years, 1921–1935." Old Missoula. Accessed May 20, 2020, oldmissoula.com.

———. *The University of Montana: A History*. Missoula: University of Montana Press, 1970.

Mettler, Katie. "The Day Anti-Vietnam War Protesters Tried to Levitate the Pentagon." *Washington Post*. October 19, 2017. Accessed May 11, 2020, newspapers.com.

Miller, Joaquin. *An Illustrated History of the State of Montana*. Chicago: Lewis Publishing, 1894.

"Minorities During the Gold Rush." California Secretary of State. Accessed June 17, 2020, sos.ca.gov.

"Miss Alice Paul Returns." *Woman's Journal*. January 29, 1910: 19.

"Miss Rankin Asks Facts of Pearl Harbor." *Deseret News* (Salt Lake City). December 23, 1942. Accessed June 20, 2020, newspapers.com

"Miss Rankin Elected: Montana Woman Will Be the First to Sit in Congress." *New York Times*. November 11, 1916. Accessed January 7, 2018, newspapers.com.

"Miss Rankin Gains Good Support in North." *Missoulian*. March 23, 1914. Accessed January 12, 2020, newspapers.com.

"Miss Rankin Says War's in Offing." *Fort Worth Star Telegram*. January 24, 1947. Accessed April 25, 2020, newspapers.com.

"Miss Rankin to Run." *Boyden* (IA) *Reporter*. September 5, 1918. Accessed January 14, 2018, newspapers.com.

"Miss Rankin, War Opponent in 1917, Hasn't Changed Mind." *Washington Post*. December 9, 1941. Accessed May 16, 2018, newspapers.com.

"Miss Rankin's Famous Interview Misrepresenting Her State." *Independent-Record* (Helena). August 19, 1917. Accessed April 7, 2020, newspapers.com.

"Missoula Gossip." *Anaconda Standard*. March 9, 1895. Accessed March 12, 2020, newspapers.com.

"Missoula in General." *Missoulian*. September 15, 1894. Accessed June 11, 2020, newspapers.com.

———. *Missoulian*. March 14, 1895. Accessed March 12, 2020, newspapers.com.

"Missoula Items." *Helena Weekly Herald*. March 22, 1877. Accessed February 8, 2020, newspapers.com.

"Missoula, Montana." World Population Review. Accessed July 12, 2020, worldpopulationreview.com.

"Missoula Notes." *Butte Miner*. October 16, 1902. Accessed March 11, 2020, newspapers.com.

———. *Butte Miner*. September 13, 1903. Accessed February 12, 2020, newspapers.com.

"Missoula Public Schools." *Missoulian*. May 28, 1897. Accessed May 6, 2019, newspapers.com.

"Missoula Society." *Butte Miner*. August 6, 1916. Accessed June 11, 2020, newspapers.com.

"Missoula Society News." *Anaconda Standard*. August 30, 1903. Accessed May 2, 2020, newspapers.com.
Monroe, James. "Monroe Doctrine." Digital History. Accessed February 7, 2020, digitalhistory.uh.edu.
"Montana Eugenics." Accessed April 26, 2020, uvm.edu.
"Montana Matters." *Independent Record* (Helena). September 5, 1883. Accessed January 5, 2020, newspapers.com.
"Montana Suffrage Parade Great Success." *Suffrage Daily News*. September 26, 1914. Accessed January 12, 2020, newspapers.com.
Montgomery, Ruth. "Jeannette Rankin on Trail Again." *Pensacola News Journal*. December 30, 1967. Accessed February 21, 2020, newspapers.com.
Moore, Michael. "Sheriffs' Lives, Stories, Revealed in Grave Tour." *Missoulian*. June 21, 2008. Accessed February 22, 2020, missoulian.com.
Morgenroth, Thekla, Cordelia Fine, Michelle K. Ryan, and Anne E. Genat. "Sex, Drugs, and Reckless Driving: Are Measures Biased toward Identifying Risk-Taking in Men?" *Social Psychological and Personality Science* 9, no. 6 (2018): 744–753.
Morris, Dee. *Boston in the Golden Age of Spiritualism: Séances, Mediums and Immortality*. Charleston, SC: Arcadia Publishing, 2014.
Morris, Libby. "Inspiration and Action: Life and Legacy of Jeannette Rankin." *Innovative Higher Education* 34, no. 5 (2009): 283–284.
Morris, Patrick F. *Anaconda, Montana: Copper Smelting Boom Town on the Western Frontier*. Bethesda, MD: Swann Publishing, 1997.
Mosher, Clelia Duel. *The Mosher Survey: Sexual Attitudes of 45 Victorian Women*. Edited by James MaHood and Kristine Wenburg. New York: Arno Press, 1980.
"Mrs. Ingersoll Loses Case in High Court." *Independent-Record* (Helena). May 15, 1928. Accessed July 11, 2020, newspapers.com.
Mullen, Pierce C., and Michael L. Nelson. "Montanans and 'The Most Peculiar Disease': The Influenza Epidemic and Public Health, 1918–1919." *Montana: The Magazine of Western History* 37, no. 2 (Spring 1987): 50–61.
Munns, Roger. "University Honors Suffragette Despite Racism Charge." *Los Angeles Times*. May 5, 1996. Accessed January 14, 2020, newspapers.com.
Murphy, Mary. "Jeannette Rankin: Suffragist, Congresswoman, Pacifist." In *Beyond Schoolmarms and Madams: Montana Women's Stories*, 234–237. Edited by Martha Kohl. Helena: Montana Historical Society Press, 2016.
———. "When Jeannette Said No: Montana Women's Response to World War I." *Montana: The Magazine of Western History* 65, no. 1 (Spring 2015): 3–23.
Myres, Sandra. "Victoria's Daughters: English-Speaking Women on Nineteenth Century Frontiers." In *Western Women: Their Land, Their Lives*, 261–282. Edited by Lillian Schlissel, Vicki L. Ruiz, and Janice Monk. Albuquerque: University of New Mexico Press, 1988.
"Nebraska Opinions." *Lincoln Star*. April 24, 1917. Accessed May 8, 2020, newspapers.com.
Nester, William R. *Theodore Roosevelt and the Art of American Power: An American for All Time*. New York: Rowman & Littlefield, 2019.
Newmahr, Staci. "Chaos, Order, and Collaboration: Toward a Feminist Conceptualization of Edgework." *Journal of Contemporary Ethnography* 40, no. 6 (2011): 682–712.
"News Brevities." *Detroit Free Press*. February 29, 1868. Accessed September 9, 2020, newspapers.com.
Newspaper Clippings. *Knoxville News Sentinel*. Edna Rankin McKinnon Papers. Series 1. Schlesinger Library, Radcliffe Institute, Harvard University.
Nidiffer, Jana. "Advocates on Campus: Deans of Women Create a New Profession." In *Women Administrators in Higher Education: Historical and Contemporary Perspectives*, 135–156. Edited by Jana Nidiffer and Carolyn Terry Bashaw. Albany: State University of New York Press, 2001.
Nolan, C.B. Letter to Thomas Walsh, August 30, 1918. Thomas James Walsh Papers, Series 1, File A. Library of Congress.
Norwood, Vera. "Women's Place: Continuity and Change in Response to Western Landscapes." In *Western Women: Their Land, Their Lives*, 155–182. Edited by Lillian Schlissel, Vicki L. Ruiz, and Janice Monk. Albuquerque: University of New Mexico Press, 1988.

Bibliography

Oberlin Catalogue and Second Annual Report. Oberlin, OH: The College, 1869.
O'Connor, Jack. *Jack O'Connor, Horse and Buggy West.* New York: Knopf, 1969.
"Official Abstract of Votes Cast at the General Election Held in Montana." November 5, 1918. Montana Secretary of State. Accessed December 19, 2019, sos.mt.gov.
"Official Election Results for Missoula County." *Missoulian.* November 18, 1894. Accessed February 17, 2020, newspapers.com.
"Olive Pickering Rankin." In *Mothers of Achievement in American History, 1776–1976*, 320–321. Rutland, VT: Charles E. Tuttle Company, 1976.
120 Years of American Education: A Statistical Portrait. National Center for Educational Statistics. Washington, D.C.: U.S. Department of Education, 1993.
O'Neill, Mary. Letter to Jeannette Rankin. Jeannette Rankin Papers. MC 147, Series 7.2. Montana Historical Society Research Center, Archives.
Opposition Press Release, 1948 Senate Campaign. Series II, 4.4. Rankin Family Papers. Archives & Special Collections, Mansfield Library, University of Montana.
Ordover, Nancy. *American Eugenics: Race, Queer Anatomy, and the Science of Nationalism.* Minneapolis: University of Minnesota Press, 2003.
O'Sullivan, John. "Annexation." *United States Magazine and Democratic Review* 17 (1845): 5–6, 9–10.
"Our Busy Congresswoman." *Literary Digest* 55 (August 11, 1917): 43.
"Outrage on Mrs. Kelly Permitted." *Independent-Record* (Helena). October 28, 1924. Accessed April 2, 2020, newspapers.com.
"Pasture." *Missoulian.* April 24, 1897. Accessed June 14, 2020, newspapers.com.
———. *Missoulian.* May 28, 1897. Accessed June 14, 2020, newspapers.com.
"Patients Mistreated and Mutilated by Illegal Operations at Insane Asylum." *Independent-Record* (Helena). October 5, 1924. Accessed April 2, 2020, newspapers.com.
Paul, Alice. Interview by Amelia R. Fry: Conversations with Alice Paul, Woman Suffrage and the Equal Rights Amendment. Suffragists Oral History Project, University of California at Berkeley. Accessed June 26, 2020, lib.berkeley.edu.
Paul, Heike. *The Myths That Made America: An Introduction to American Studies.* Bielefeld, Germany: Transcript-Verlag, 2014.
Paul, Julius. "'Three Generations of Imbeciles Are Enough': State Eugenic Sterilization in American Thought and Practice." *Buck v Bell Documents.* Paper 95, 1965. Accessed April 2, 2020, readingroom.law.gsu.edu.
Peavy, Linda, and Ursula Smith. *Pioneer Women: The Lives of Women on the Frontier.* New York: Smithmark, 1996.
Penn, William. *A Collection of the Works of William Penn.* Vol. 1. London: Sowle, 1726.
Phillips, Matt. "American Labor-Union Strikes Are Almost Completely Extinct." February 11, 2015. Accessed July 19, 2020, quartz.com.
"The Pickets at the White House Gates: Have They Helped Suffrage?" *Suffragist* (September 28, 1918): 8.
"Pioneer's Home Wrecked for New Bridge." *Missoulian.* October 1, 1958. Accessed April 5, 2020, newspapers.com.
Plante, Ellen M. *Women at Home in Victorian America: A Social History.* New York: Facts on File, 1997.
"The Postwar Economy: 1945–1960." Accessed May 20, 2020, countrystudies.us.
Powaski, Ronald E. *Toward an Entangling Alliance: American Isolationism, Internationalism, and Europe, 1901–1950.* Westport: Greenwood, 1991.
"Private Life: Limiting Births in the Early Republic." Digital History. Accessed January 19, 2020, digitalhistory.uh.edu.
"Progressives Hold Meeting." *Billings Gazette.* October 11, 1914. Accessed January 8, 2020, newspapers.com.
Pruitt, Sarah. "How Flappers Redefined Womanhood (Hint: It Involved Jazz, Liquor and Sex)." September 17, 2018. Accessed January 14, 2020, history.com.
"Public Must Outlaw War, Says Speaker." *Albany Democrat-Herald.* November 24, 1933. Accessed May 22, 2020, newspapers.com.
"Purely Local." *Missoulian.* February 9, 1901. Accessed June 15, 2019, newspapers.com.

Purvis, June. "'Deeds, Not Words': Daily Life in the Women's Social and Political Union in Edwardian Britain." In *Votes for Women*, 135–158. Edited by June Purvis and Sandra Stanley Holton. London: Routledge, 2000.

"Quanoozeh Club Entertains." *Anaconda Standard*. January 4, 1903. Accessed April 13, 2020, newspapers.com.

Ramsey, Julia. "'Girls' in Name Only: A Study of American Red Cross Volunteers on the Frontlines of World War II." Master's thesis, Auburn University, 2011.

Rankin, Elizabeth Wallace. Letter to Wellington Rankin, August 16, 1913. MC 288, Personal Subgroup, Box 2. Wellington D. Rankin Papers. Montana Historical Society Research Center, Archives.

Rankin, Jeannette. "Democracy and Women," January 16, 1940. Rankin Family Papers. Series II, 4.4. Archives & Special Collections, Mansfield Library, University of Montana.

———. House Foreign Affairs Committee Testimony, 1933. Jeannette Rankin Papers. MC 147, Series 7.2. Montana Historical Society Research Center, Archives.

———. Interview by John C. Board, August 29 and 30, 1963. General Oral History Collection. OH1046. Montana Historical Society Research Center, Archives. With credit also given to Schlesinger Library, Radcliffe Institute, Harvard University.

———. Interview by Malca Chall and Hannah Josephson. Suffragists Oral History Project, University of California at Berkeley. Accessed June 26, 2020, lib.berkeley.edu.

———. Letter to Dear Friend, June 23, 1917. Jeannette Rankin Papers. MC 147, Series 7.2. Montana Historical Society Research Center, Archives.

———. Letter to Franklin K. Lane, September 10, 1917. Jeannette Rankin Papers. MC 147, Series 7.2. Montana Historical Society Research Center, Archives.

———. Letter to Grace and Tom Kinney, April 24. Jeannette Rankin Papers. MC 147, Series 7.2. Montana Historical Society Research Center, Archives.

———. Letter to Helen Gray, August 22, 1917. Jeannette Rankin Papers. MC 147, Series 7.2. Montana Historical Society Research Center, Archives.

———. Letter to Nina Swinnerton, May 22, 1917. Jeannette Rankin Papers. MC 147, Series 7.1. Montana Historical Society Research Center, Archives.

———. Letter to Olive Rankin, April 11, 1942. Jeannette Rankin Papers. MC 147, Series 7.1. Montana Historical Society Research Center, Archives.

———. Letters concerning the Bureau of Printing and Engraving. Jeannette Rankin Papers. MC 147, Series 7.2. Montana Historical Society Research Center, Archives.

———. Letters to Dr. Sample, 1917. Jeannette Rankin Papers. MC 147, Series 7.2. Montana Historical Society Research Center, Archives.

———. "On War and Nonviolence." In *Ten Fighters for Peace*, 82–92. Edited by Don Lawson. New York: Lothrop, Lee, & Shepard, 1971.

———. Speech in the U.S. House for Suffrage, January 1918. Rankin Family Papers. Box 4.4. Archives & Special Collections, Mansfield Library, University of Montana.

———. Telegram to Wellington Rankin, June 1917. Jeannette Rankin Papers. MC 147, Series 7.2. Montana Historical Society Research Center, Archives.

———. "Two Votes against War: 1917, 1941." *Liberation* 3 (March 1958): 4–7.

———. "Woman and the New Democracy." Proceedings, Wisconsin Teachers' Association. 65 (1918): 100–113.

Rankin, John. Account Books. Rankin Family Papers. MSS 280, Series 1.4. Archives & Special Collections, Mansfield Library, University of Montana.

———. Letter to Jessie Rankin Wilson, May 14, 1893. Edna Rankin McKinnon Papers. Series 1. Schlesinger Library, Radcliffe Institute, Harvard University.

Rankin, Wellington. Interview by John Board, March 23, 1964. Wellington D. Rankin Papers. Archives West. Accessed December 8, 2019, archiveswest.orbiscascade.org.

———. Interview by Volney Steele. General Oral History Collection. OH 1665. Montana Historical Society Research Center, Archives.

———. Letters to Ellis Sedman. Wellington D. Rankin Papers. MC 288, Personal Subgroup, Series 2.12. Montana Historical Society Research Center, Archives.

"Rankins Leave Legacy in Politics and More." *Billings Gazette*. June 15, 2003. Accessed February 7, 2020, newspapers.com.

Bibliography

Rapport, Jeremy. "The Nature of Reality: Christian Science and Spiritualism." In *Handbook of Spiritualism and Channeling*, 199–218. Edited by Cathy Guttierez. Boston: Brill, 2015.

"Recognition of Independence of Ireland Is to Be Demanded." *Irish Standard* (Minneapolis). January 12, 1918. Accessed January 16, 2020, newspapers.com.

Reed, James. *The Birth Control Movement and American Society: From Private Vice to Public Virtue*. Princeton, NJ: Princeton University Press, 2014.

Reilly, Philip R. *The Surgical Solution: A History of Involuntary Sterilization in the United States*. Baltimore: Johns Hopkins University Press, 1991.

Report on Student Employment Possibilities, October 23, 1924. Mary Elrod Ferguson Papers. MSS 205, Series 3, Box 1.11. Archives & Special Collections, Mansfield Library, University of Montana.

Report on Women Students' Employment, November 18, 1922. Mary Elrod Ferguson Papers. MSS 205, Series 3, Box 1.11. Archives & Special Collections, Mansfield Library, University of Montana.

Riley, Glenda. *The Female Frontier: A Comparative View of Women on the Prairie and Plains*. Lawrence, KS: University Press of Kansas, 1988.

_____. *A Place to Grow: Women in the American West*. Arlington Heights, IL: Harlan Davidson, 1992.

_____. *Women and Indians on the Frontier, 1825–1915*. Albuquerque: University of New Mexico Press, 1984.

_____. *Women on the American Frontier*. St. Louis: Forum Press, 1977.

Roark, James L., Michael P. Johnson, Patricia Cline Cohen, Sarah Stage, and Susan M. Hartmann. *The American Promise, since 1865: A History of the United States*. Vol. 2. New York: Macmillan, 2012.

Robinson, William J. *Birth Control or the Limitation of Offspring*. New York: Critic and Guide Co., 1916.

Robison, Ken. *Montanans in the Great War: Open Warfare Over There*. Charleston, SC: History Press, 2019.

Roosevelt, Theodore. *An Autobiography*. New York: Scribner's, 1913.

_____. "Birth Control—From the Positive Side." *Metropolitan Magazine*. October 1917. Reprinted in *The Pivot of Civilization in Historical Perspective: The Birth Control Classic by Margaret Sanger*, 237–241. Edited by Michael W. Perry. Seattle: Inkling Books, 2003.

_____. "The Strenuous Life." In *Selected Speeches and Writings of Theodore Roosevelt*, 12–22. Edited by Gordon Hutner. New York: Vintage Books, 2014.

_____. "What We Can Expect of the American Boy." *St. Nicholas Magazine* (May 1900): 571–574.

Rose, Melody. *Abortion: A Documentary and Reference Guide*. Santa Barbara, CA: ABC-CLIO, 2008.

Rose, Phyllis. *Parallel Lives: Five Victorian Marriages*. New York: Knopf, 1983.

Roser, Max, Hannah Ritchie, and Bernadeta Dadonaite. "Child and Infant Mortality." Accessed March 3, 2020, ourworldindata.org.

Roth, Tona. "Eugenic Sterilization in Montana from 1900 to 1999." Research paper. Carroll College, 1999.

Rothman, Lily. "How the First Woman Was Elected to U.S. National Office, Exactly 100 Years Ago." *Time*. November 7, 2016. Accessed April 12, 2020, time.com.

Rucker, W. C. "Rocky Mountain Spotted Fever." *Public Health Reports* 36 (September 6, 1912): 1465–1482.

"A Sad Bereavement." *Missoula Weekly Gazette*. December 3, 1890. Accessed January 30, 2020, newspapers.com.

Sanger, Margaret. "Birth Control: Margaret Sanger's Reply to Theodore Roosevelt." *Metropolitan Magazine* (December 1917): 66–67.

_____. Letter to Clarence Gamble, October 19, 1939. Margaret Sanger Papers, Smith Libraries Exhibits, Accessed June 18, 2020, libex.smith.edu.

_____. "My Way to Peace." January 17, 1932. Public Writing and Speeches of Margaret Sanger. Accessed January 20, 2020, nyu.edu/projects/sanger.

_____. *The Pivot of Civilization*. 1922. New York: Humanity Press, 2003.

Bibliography

———. *Woman and the New Race.* New York: Brentano's, 1920.
Sargent, Mary Thomas. *Runway towards Orion: The True Adventures of a Red Cross Girl on a B-29 Air Base in World War II India.* Grand Rapids, MI: Triumph Press, 1984.
Schaffer, Ronald. "Jeannette Rankin, Progressive-Isolationist." PhD diss., Princeton, 1959.
———. "The Montana Woman Suffrage Campaign, 1911–14." *Pacific Northwest Quarterly* 55, no. 1 (January 1964): 9–15.
Schlereth, Thomas J. *Victorian America: Transformations in Everyday Life, 1876–1915.* New York: HarperCollins, 1991.
Schlissel, Lillian. "Family on the Western Frontier." In *Western Women: Their Land, Their Lives,* 81–91. Edited by Lillian Schlissel, Vicki L. Ruiz, and Janice Monk. Albuquerque: University of New Mexico Press, 1988.
Schoen, Johanna. *Choice and Coercion: Birth Control, Sterilization, and Abortion in Public Health and Welfare.* Chapel Hill: University of North Carolina Press, 2005.
Schoenberg, Wilfred, S.J. *Jesuits in Montana: 1840–1960.* Portland: Oregon-Jesuit, 1960.
Schoepflin, Rennie B. *Christian Science on Trial: Religious Healing in America.* Baltimore: Johns Hopkins University Press, 2003.
Schwantes, Carlos A. *The Pacific Northwest: An Interpretive History.* Lincoln: University of Nebraska Press, 1996.
"Scottish Genealogy and Family History." Library and Archives Canada. Accessed January 26, 2020, bac-lac.gc.ca/eng.
Sedman, Harriet Rankin. "The Dean of Women and Campus Life." Mary Elrod Ferguson Papers. MSS 205, Series 3, Box 1.11. Archives & Special Collections, Mansfield Library, University of Montana.
———. "The Dean of Women at Work." Mary Elrod Ferguson Papers. MSS 205, Series 3, Box 1.11. Archives & Special Collections, Mansfield Library, University of Montana.
———. "The Life of the Women Students at the State University of Montana." Mary Elrod Ferguson Papers. MSS 205, Series 3, Box 1.11. Archives & Special Collections, Mansfield Library, University of Montana.
———. "The New College Girl." Mary Elrod Ferguson Papers, MSS 205, Series 3, Box 1.11, Archives & Special Collections, Mansfield Library, University of Montana.
———. "Our Services for Students," April 4, 1924. Mary Elrod Ferguson Papers. MSS 205, Box 1. Archives & Special Collections, Mansfield Library, University of Montana.
———. "Women in the University," January 1926. Mary Elrod Ferguson Papers. MSS 205, Series 3, Box 1.11. Archives & Special Collections, Mansfield Library, University of Montana.
"Seek to Explain Miss Rankin's 'No.'" *New York Times.* April 7, 1917. Accessed April 15, 2019, *New York Times* Historical Database.
Seidman, Steven A. *Posters, Propaganda, and Persuasion in Election Campaigns around the World and through History.* New York: Peter Lang, 2008.
"Seniors Given High School Diplomas." *Missoulian.* June 3, 1911. Accessed January 19, 2020, newspapers.com.
Shaw, Anna Howard. Letter to Jeannette Rankin, March 1917. Jeannette Rankin Papers. MC 147, Series 7.2. Montana Historical Society Research Center, Archives.
———. *The Story of a Pioneer.* New York: Harper and Bros., 1915.
Shirley, Gayle. *More Than Petticoats: Remarkable Montana Women.* New York: Rowman & Littlefield, 2010.
Siegler, Mark V. *An Economic History of the United States: Connecting the Present with the Past.* New York: Springer, 2016.
"Silver Wedding." *Butte Daily Post.* January 16, 1901. Accessed November 11, 2020, newspapers.com.
Slotkin, Richard. *The Fatal Environment: The Myth of the Frontier in the Age of Industrialization, 1800–1890.* New York: Atheneum, 1985.
Smith, Norma. "Fighting Pacifist: Jeannette Rankin and Her Times." Norma Smith Papers. Collection 2329. Montana State University Library.
———. *Jeannette Rankin: America's Conscience.* Helena: Montana Historical Society Press, 2002.

Smith-Rosenberg, Carroll. *Disorderly Conduct: Visions of Gender in Victorian America.* New York: Oxford University Press, 1986.

———. *This Violent Empire: The Birth of an American National Identity.* Chapel Hill: University of North Carolina Press, 2010.

"Society Notes." *Anaconda Standard.* March 23, 1902. Accessed April 12, 2020, newspapers.com.

Soubier, Maria. "The Divine Affluence." *Christian Science Sentinel.* June 1952. Christian Science JSH-Online. Accessed January 11, 2020, jsh.christianscience.com.

Soule, Caroline. *Little Alice; Or, the Pet of the Settlement.* Boston: A. Tompkins, 1860.

Spector, Ronald H. "Vietnam War: 1954–1975." *Encyclopaedia Britannica.* Accessed May 17, 2020, britannica.com.

Spriggs, A.E. Letter to Thomas Walsh, September 2, 1918. Thomas James Walsh Papers. Series 1, File A. Library of Congress.

Stark, Rodney. "The Rise and Fall of Christian Science." *Journal of Contemporary Religion* 13, no. 2 (1998): 189–214.

Steele, Volney. *Bleed, Blister, and Purge: A History of Medicine on the American Frontier.* Missoula, MT: Mountain Press, 2005.

———. *Wellington Rankin: His Family, Life and Times: Montana Attorney, Politician, Cattleman, Land Baron.* Bozeman, MT: Bridger Creek Historical Press, 2002.

Stellway, Helena. Letter to Jeannette Rankin, December 25, 1917. Jeannette Rankin Papers. MC 147, Series 7.1. Montana Historical Society Research Center, Archives.

Stephanson, Anders. *Manifest Destiny: American Expansion and the Empire of the Right.* New York: Hill and Wang, 1995.

"The Sterilization of Psychotic Patients under State Laws." *American Journal of Psychiatry* 105, no. 1 (July 1948): 60–62.

———. "Trends in State Programs for the Sterilization of the Mentally Deficient." *American Journal of Mental Deficiency* 53, no. 4 (April 1949): 538–541.

Stern, Alexandra Minna. *Eugenic Nation: Faults and Frontiers of Better Breeding in Modern America.* Berkeley: University of California Press, 2005.

Stewart, Mary. Letter to Jeannette Rankin and Potential Supporters, April 1916. Jeannette Rankin Papers. MC 147, Series 7.2. Montana Historical Society Research Center, Archives.

"Stories of the Vigilantes in the Days When the Big West Was a Country in the Raw." *San Francisco Chronicle.* March 31, 1912. Accessed July 25, 2020, newspapers.com.

"Strong Pressure, Failed to Influence Congresswoman's Vote on War." *Cincinnati Enquirer.* April 7, 1917. Accessed February 23, 2018, newspapers.com.

Summers, Mark Wahlgren. *The Era of Good Stealings.* New York: Oxford University Press, 1993.

Swibold, Dennis L. *Copper Chorus: Mining, Politics, and the Montana Press, 1889–1959.* Helena, MT: Montana Historical Society Press, 2006.

Swinnerton, Nina. Letter to Jeannette Rankin, April 2, 1917. Jeannette Rankin Papers. MC 147, Series 7.1. Montana Historical Society Research Center, Archives.

———. Letter to Jeannette Rankin, April 5, 1917. Jeannette Rankin Papers. MC 147, Series 7.1. Montana Historical Society Research Center, Archives.

Taylor, Richard E. *Houghton County, 1870–1920.* Charleston, SC: Arcadia Publishing, 2006.

"Their Ugly Past: Reviving the Record of the Claflins." *San Francisco Chronicle.* May 8, 1890. Accessed March 31, 2020, newspapers.com.

Thompson, Charles Manfred, and Fred Mitchell Jones. *Economic Development of the United States: A First Course.* New York: Macmillan, 1939.

Tolstoy, Leo. *The Kingdom of God Is Within You.* 1894. Translated by Constance Garnett. Lincoln: University of Nebraska Press, 1984.

Toossi, Mitra. "A Century of Change: The U.S. Labor Force, 1950–2050." Accessed May 17, 2020, bls.gov.

"Trigeminal Neuralgia (Tic Douloureux)." Harvard Health Publishing. Accessed June 1, 2020, health.harvard.edu.

Trzebiatowska, Marta, and Steve Bruce. *Why Are Women More Religious Than Men?* New York: Oxford University Press, 2012.

Turner, Frederick Jackson. "The Significance of the Frontier in American History." In *Rereading Frederick Jackson Turner*, 31–60. Edited by John Mack Faragher. New York: Henry Holt, 1994.
Tutt, John M. "The Role of the Practitioner." *Christian Science Sentinel*. June 12, 1965. Accessed February 4, 2020, sentinel.christianscience.com.
Twain, Mark. *Mary Baker Eddy*. New York: Harper & Bros., 1907.
"Two Suffragists Will Begin Tour." *Missoulian*. August 10, 1914. Accessed January 12, 2020, newspapers.com.
"University Resumes after Vacation." *Anaconda Standard*. January 5, 1903. Accessed January 29, 2020, newspapers.com.
"Unofficial Returns." *Missoulian*. November 4, 1914. Accessed February 14, 2020, newspapers.com.
"Urges Women's Role in Halting Viet War." *Indiana (PA) Gazette*. May 19, 1967. Accessed January 3, 2020, newspapers.com.
"U.S. Annual Death Rates per 1,000 Population, 1900–2005." Department of Health and Human Services. 54, no. 20 (August 21, 2007).
"U.S. Expected Japs' Attack, Jeannette Rankin Declares." *News Journal* (Wilmington, DE). December 23, 1942. Accessed June 20, 2020, newspapers.com.
"U.S. Now at War with Germany and Italy." *New York Times*. December 11, 1941. Accessed December 15, 2019, newspapers.com.
Velma H. Riggs v. Lew Webb. Montana Supreme Court. Rankin Family Papers. Series II, 4.1. Archives & Special Collections, Mansfield Library, University of Montana.
"A Vet at Fighting for a Cause." Newspaper Clipping. Edna Rankin McKinnon Papers. Series 1. Schlesinger Library, Radcliffe Institute, Harvard University.
Vexler, Robert I., and William F. Swindler. *Chronology and Documentary Handbook of the State of New Hampshire*. New York: Oceana Publications, 1978.
"Vietnam War U.S. Military Fatal Casualty Statistics." National Archives. Accessed March 11, 2020, archives.gov.
Vyse, Stuart. "William James and the Psychics." *Skeptical Inquirer*. Accessed July 12, 2020, csicop.org.
Walbert, Kate. "Has Anything Changed for Female Politicians? Familiar Echoes in the Candidacy of Jeannette Rankin, the First Woman Elected to Congress." *New Yorker*. August 16, 2016. Accessed January 24, 2020, newyorker.com.
———. "Rebel with a Cause." *Montana* 110 (November-December 1991): 66–67.
Walton, Mary. *A Woman's Crusade: Alice Paul and the Battle for the Ballot*. New York: Palgrave Macmillan, 2010.
Warwick, Donald P. "The Indonesian Family Planning Program: Government Influence and Client Choice." *Population and Development Review* 12, no. 3 (September 1986): 453–490.
Washington, George. "Farewell Address." September 17, 1796. Accessed February 17, 2020, mtholyoke.edu.
Weiler, Kathleen. "Women's History and the History of Women Teachers." *Journal of Education* 171, no. 3 (1989): 9–30.
Weiss, Karl. Letter to Jeannette Rankin, January 24, 1918. Jeannette Rankin Papers. MC 147, Box 2.1. Montana Historical Society Research Center, Archives.
"Wellington Rankin." *Missoulian*. June 10, 1903. Accessed January 29, 2020, newspapers.com.
"Wellington Rankin Lets Loose at Amalgamated." *Missoulian*. October 29, 1914. Accessed December 20, 2019, newspapers.com.
"Western Montana News." *Helena Weekly Herald*. July 5, 1877. Accessed March 12, 2020, newspapers.com.
Wilder, Burt G. *What Young People Should Know: The Reproductive Function*. Boston: Estes and Lauriat, 1875.
Williams, Doone. *Every Child a Wanted Child: Clarence James Gamble and His Work in the Birth Control Movement*. Cambridge: Harvard University Press, 1979.
Wilson, A.N. *Tolstoy*. New York: Norton, 1988.
Wilson, Bryan R. *Sects and Society: A Sociological Study of the Elim Tabernacle, Christian Science, and Christadelphians*. Berkeley: University of California Press, 1961.

Bibliography

Wilson, Joan Hoff. "'Peace Is a Woman's Job': Jeannette Rankin and American Foreign Policy: Her Lifework as a Pacifist." In *History of Women in the United States, Women and War*, 270–306. Edited by Nancy F. Cott. Munich: K.G. Saur, 1993.

———. "'Peace Is a Woman's Job': Jeannette Rankin and American Foreign Policy: The Origins of Her Pacifism." In *History of Women in the United States, Women and War*, 236–269. Edited by Nancy F. Cott. Munich: K.G. Saur, 1993.

———. "Remarks." In *Acceptance and Dedication of the Statue of Jeannette Rankin*, 17–27. Washington, D.C.: U.S. Government Printing Office, 1987.

Winchell, Walter. "New York Press Pass." *Lebanon* (PA) *Daily News*. January 24, 1968. Accessed December 31, 2019, newspapers.com.

"With the Great Spirit." *Helena Independent*. December 20, 1890. Accessed March 23, 2020, newspapers.com.

Wolpert, Stanley. *Gandhi's Passion: The Life and Legacy of Mahatma Gandhi*. New York: Oxford, 2001.

"A Woman Who Made a Difference." *Christian Science Journal*. February 2003. Accessed February 1, 2020, journal.christianscience.com.

"Women Can Be Just as Daring and Risk-taking as Men." *Science Daily*. Accessed January 28, 2020, sciencedaily.com.

"Women's Groups Set War Protest." *Gazette and Daily* (York, PA). December 18, 1967. Accessed February 23, 2020, newspapers.com.

"Woodrow Wilson War Message." Accessed June 18, 2020, mtholyoke.edu.

Woody, Thomas. *A History of Women's Education in the United States*. Lancaster, PA: Science Press, 1929.

"World War II and the American Red Cross." Accessed June 30, 2020, redcross.org.

"World War II." *Encyclopedia of Chicago*. Accessed April 24, 2020, encyclopedia.chicagohistory.org.

Yellin, Emily. *Our Mothers' War: American Women at Home and at the Front during World War II*. New York: Free Press, 2004.

Ziegler, Valarie H. *The Advocates of Peace in Antebellum America*. Macon, GA: Mercer University Press, 2001.

Index

Addams, Jane 55–56, 58, 72, 87–88, 98, 101
American expansionism, nineteenth century 2–6
Anaconda Copper Mining Company 60–66, 74–75, 79–81, 97, 103, 123, 147, 156

Beecher, Catharine 17–18
Berry, Billy (Charles William) 15, 26, 57, 85–86
birth control movement: on the frontier 23, 135; internationally 163–172; in the United States 135–145
Bonner, Helen 23, 172
Bragg, Mary Rankin 33–38, 42–43, 51–52, 69, 74, 110–111, 120, 132, 149–153, 171
Brandeis, Louis 87–88

Catt, Carrie Chapman 56, 73, 91, 95, 98
child bearing: in the west in the nineteenth century 12, 19–20, 23–24
Christian Science 45, 50–54, 156, 168
Claflin, Tennessee (Tennie) 47
Cooper, Gary 60

deans of women 108, 113, 117–122, 126
De Smet, Father Pierre-Jean 5

Eddy, Mary Baker 45, 48–49
edgework and risk 2–3
eugenics and involuntary sterilization 136–138, 141–144, 164

Fligelman, Belle 68, 74, 94, 112, 130
Fort Fizzle 11–12, 85
Fox, Kate 46–47
Fox, Margaret 46–47
frontier, and the American west in myth and reality 1–4, 8, 11–12, 15–19, 23–26, 33, 36–40, 54

Gamble, Clarence 138–145, 163–171
Garfield Agreement of 1872 5–6
gender essentialism and the suffrage movement 88–89, 157, 172
gold mining, in Montana 8–11, 13–15, 19, 23, 39–40, 59, 85–86, 110

Grant Creek ranch 11, 19–20, 29, 33, 37–38, 110, 118, 133–134
Greeley, Horace 7–8

Helena, Montana, development as a mining community 5, 8–10
Hell Gate Treaty 5–6
higher education for women: deans of women helping women students find acceptance 108, 117–122; enrollment numbers through the decades 116, 121–122; and the Morrill Act 115–116; negative responses to women's enrollment 115–116; in residence halls 116–121; at seminaries 108, 114; at state universities 108, 110, 115; at women's colleges 108, 114

illness, treatments in the west in the nineteenth century 37, 41–45, 112
isolationism 35–36, 83–84, 100–101, 163

Jeannette Rankin Brigade 156–161
Johnson-Reed Immigration Act 137–138

Laidlaw, Harriet 92
Lewis and Clark Expedition 4, 9, 69

manifest destiny 3, 9
McGregor, Harriet Rankin Sedman: at the Bureau of War Risk Insurance 113; in the childhood social whirl 20–23, 35, 43–44, 95, 109; as a Christian Scientist 51; as a college student 109–110; as a dean of women 114–122; in Jeannette's congressional office 112–113; marriages and children 51, 109–112, 122–123; with the Red Cross in London 123–126; as a teacher 110
McKinney, Grace Rankin 21, 33, 38, 42–43, 52, 69, 74, 122, 130–132, 149–153, 171
McKinnon, Edna Rankin: in the Chicago birth-control office 144–145; childhood in Missoula 33–34, 42–43, 128–129; as a Christian Scientist 51–53; with Clarence Gamble 138–145, 163–171; in college and law school 129–132; with Margaret Sanger

216 Index

135–136, 140–141; marriage and divorce 132–134; One Package legal case 140; at the Resettlement Administration in Washington 133; as suffrage worker 69, 74, 130–131; traveling for the birth-control movement 141–144, 163–171
medical education and the nineteenth century 41
medical treatment on the frontier 40–44
mental health care in the nineteenth century 23, 45–50
Missoula 5–6
Montana 4–6

Native Americans in Montana: onflicts with white settlers and the American army 4–5, 10–12, 84–85; impact on Jeannette Rankin 81, 84–87; movement to reservations 5–6, 81
Nolan, Colonel C.B. 57–59, 68, 97
Northern Pacific Railroad 27–29, 61–62, 65

O'Neill, Mary 71, 74
O'Sullivan, John 3

pacifism, history of 83–87, 93, 96, 100, 160
Paul, Alice 57–58, 69–70, 88–93, 98
Pickering (Foss), Mandana 14–17
Pickering (Hanson), Philena 16
Pickering, John S. 13
Pickering, Mary J. Berry 13
Pickering (Pinkham), Mary 16
Pickering family history 12–19
Progressive Party, Montana 64–65
Progressivism 55–57, 61, 67, 81–84

Quimby, Phineas 48

Rankin, Angus 7
Rankin, Annie Agnes 7
Rankin, Donald Hugh (D.H.) 8, 11–12
Rankin, Duncan 8–13
Rankin, Elizabeth Floweree Wallace 59–60
Rankin (Galt), Louise Replogle 153–155
Rankin, Hugh (Big Hugh) 6–8
Rankin, Jannet (Jeannette) Stewart 6–7
Rankin, Jeannette: childhood on the ranch and in Missoula 20–22, 35, 43, 108; on Christianity and Christian Science 52–53; and family requirements 33, 38; against the Korean and Vietnam Wars 156–162; at New York School of Philanthropy 57–58; in New Zealand and Australia 72; pacifism and isolationism 84–89, 98–101; running for office 72–78, 96–98, 101–103; at settlement houses in the west 58; in suffrage campaign 67–70, 79; tic douloureux and opiate cures 53–54; votes against World War I and II 89–95, 103–107
Rankin, John: as builder in Missoula 11, 27–36; childhood in Canada 6–8; death from tick fever 37; as father 33–34; at Fort Fizzle 11–12; as miner 8–10; as politician 30–32; as rancher 11, 19–20, 29, 32; and the Rankin House hotel and block 30–32; trip west to Montana 9–11
Rankin, Olive Pickering: childhood 13–14; childrearing 19–24; as Christian Scientist 51; influences to venture west from New Hampshire 15–18; marriage 19–20; responsibility for ill children and adults 37, 42–44; teaching in Missoula 17–19; as widow 148–152
Rankin, Philena 14, 20–23, 42–43
Rankin, Wellington: childhood and early education 20–21, 23, 33–38, 43; death of father 37–38; enlistment during World War I 95–96; at Harvard and Rhodes 50, 57; marriage to Elizabeth Floweree Wallace 59; marriage to Louise Replogle 153–154; mental issues and Christian Science 44–52; pressure on Jeannette concerning war votes 91–95, 102–104; as Progressive young lawyer 57–65, 79–81; ranching business 154–155; reaction to Edna's birth control campaign 141–142; relationship with Jeannette 56, 67–68; running for office 65–66, 155–156; as suffrage supporter 69–73; support for Jeannette's congressional campaigns 73–76, 96–98, 102–103
Rankin home in Missoula, as reflective of Victorian social status 28–35
Red Cross, recruitment and services in England in World War II 123–127
risk, theory of and the frontier 2–5
Rocky Mountain Spotted Tick Fever, in Montana 37, 41, 44, 53
Roosevelt, Theodore: arguments with Jeannette Rankin concerning war 92; and eugenics 136–137; and the meaning of the west 64–65, 90; and the Progressive Party 64–65

Salish Indians 4–6
Sanger, Margaret 134–145, 169
Scottish emigration to North America 6–7, 12
Sedman, Ellis 44–50, 110
Sedman, Oscar 51–53, 110–112, 126
Shaw, Anna Howard 70–73, 91
Spiritualism 46–54
Swinnerton, Cornelia (Nina) 95

teaching, as a western career for women in the nineteenth century 17–19
Thompson, David 4–5
Tolstoy, Leo 87–88, 98
Turner, Frederick Jackson 3–4, 25

University of Montana, beginnings and growth 27, 35, 115–117

Victorianism: in the American west 25–27; in Missoula involving the Rankin family 27–39

Walsh, Thomas J. 57, 59, 97–98

western tales of adventure 9–10, 13–17

Wilson, Woodrow 65, 69, 71, 89–90, 92, 96–98, 106–107, 130

women and marriage, after the Civil War 15–17

www.ingramcontent.com/pod-product-compliance
Lightning Source LLC
Chambersburg PA
CBHW021353300426
44114CB00012B/1215